# MAPREADERS & MULTITASKERS

# MAPREADERS & MULTITASKERS

## MEN, WOMEN, NATURE, NURTURE

Gavin Evans

THISTLE
PUBLISHING

First published in 2016 by:
Thistle Publishing
36 Great Smith Street
London
SW1P 3BU

www.thistlepublishing.co.uk

# CHAPTER ONE

## AN INTRODUCTION IN PINK AND BLUE

I'm a man and therefore I'm genetically programmed to rape, murder unfaithful spouses and brutalise step-children; I'm drawn to the same standard of beauty as all other men, even the same hip-waist ratio; my innate single-mindedness means I am adept at providing but not so hot at nurturing or showing empathy; 'male brains' like mine account for the bulk of the world's geniuses and most of its imbeciles; we're inherently adept at geometry and upside-down map-reading but have a hard-wired resistance to 'retail therapy'; our favourite colour is blue, and, most of all, men like me are pre-programmed to spread our seed as widely as possible.

If you're reading this, I guess there's a better than 50 percent chance you're a woman, in which case you should know that you're a natural at jobs demanding cuddling and caring but you'll struggle with shapes and directions, and competitiveness is just not your thing; your 'female brain' has evolved to 'multi-task'; you're naturally chattier than men like me and better with words; you're also hard-wired to wear lipstick; your favourite colour is pink; you have evolved to go shopping and, most of all, you're genetically programmed to seek out an older, wealthier partner for life, to be faithful to him and to become his little homemaker.

How do we know all this? Because people with a bent towards genetic determinism, calling themselves socio-biologists and evolutionary psychologists, tell us so. And how do they ferret out such conclusions? Well, something like this: they conduct research among their students – on, let's say, whether men are better at map reading than women – and decide their results reflect human universals that evolved through natural selection, so they cast their minds back to consider how such an adaptation could have occurred, way, way back in the Pleistocene era of human evolution. Then comes the 'Aha!' moment: Men were hunters, which meant following game, giving them superior senses of direction, space and ... *voila!*

You might find yourself wondering why womanly foraging – 'where the hell did I bury those pesky cashews last autumn?' – wouldn't equally be likely to prompt spatial awareness. But, if you follow the text, you'll soon put aside such doubting Thomas apostasy and discover that all 'universal' human behaviour (like upside-down map reading in men) is 'adaptive' – in other words, evolved through the natural selection of traits that emerge from random genetic mutations and are advantageous for survival and breeding – and 'hard-wired' into a mental module. Not much space for nurture, societal influence or even psychology here – in fact, for some of the neo-Darwinian frontrunners, almost no room at all. Violence? Rape? Yobbishness? All evolved – nothing to do with parents, peers or environment. We are what we are because evolution made us so. Live with it!

I suppose I could rightly be accused of setting up a strawman caricature of something more nuanced and complex, but it is worth mentioning here that all of the bizarre claims made in the first two paragraphs were seriously advanced in the 21st century by prominent socio-biologists and evolutionary psychologists who were adamant that these behaviours and preferences were evolved, gender-based traits – and, more importantly, they very loudly trumpeted in the media in the United States, Britain and elsewhere.

To row back a bit, my own journey of discovery on this terrain started 26 years ago when my eldest daughter was born. My adoration for my baby was soon combined with exasperation that my role in her life should be confined by conventions presented as intrinsic. The more time I spent with her, and then with her younger sister, the more I felt my potential as a nurturer was no less 'natural' than my potential as a provider – and I became irritated by the array of casual prejudices I encountered in the opposite direction, which had the bi-product of making me more aware of the casual prejudices encountered by women in the working world. But, as I soon discovered, these prejudices went way beyond casual. Through newspaper columns, self-help-type books and television programmes I found myself regularly accosted by biologically-based claims about fathers and mothers and about male and female behaviour more generally that did not come close to fitting my own experience, which was taking me in a direction very different from that lived by my own father. This prompted my journey – what some might call a typically male obsession – that eventually led to this book.

The more I read, the more I realised that the pink brain-blue brain perspectives I was encountering were being backed up by references to a particular slant on evolutionary biology. Up until then, my biological education had not gone far past high school level (except for a sprinkling of neuro-biology when studying psychology as an undergraduate). My PhD was in 'political science', not science, so as a kind of private project I set about remedying this gap in my education, starting out by devouring works of popular science by, for example, Richard Dawkins, Daniel Dennett, David Buss and Stephen Pinker on the one hand, and Steven Jay Gould, Richard Lewontin, Paul Ehrlich and Steven Rose on the other, and eventually graduating to academic journals, to the critiques and the counter-critiques – sometimes having to refer back to biology textbooks and to friends who were biologists, neurologists and psychiatrists to check that I had all my biological ducks in a row. Later still, I went back to the oracle, reading Darwin and his co-founder of the theory of evolution by natural selection, Alfred Russel Wallace.

I found myself trying to keep up with a concerted campaign from people often wrongly described as scientists who were trying to turn the clock back on gender relations by claiming that men and women came from different metaphorical planets. Many of these no doubt well-meaning missionaries were adherents to what was then a relatively new craze in the psychological firmament, known as 'evolutionary psychology', which, in turn, drew some its inspiration from a controversial branch of ethology called 'socio-biology'. This first emerged in full bloom in the late 1960s as an attempt by a few zoologists devoted to studying animal behaviour to apply a version of evolutionary theory to understanding human behaviour, based on the view that, in common with all animals, we are products of our genes and that the workings of our minds are determined by them.

EP is a branch of psychology (or, in its own view, a framework *for* psychology) that explains human behavioural traits in terms of evolutionary adaptations. Like socio-biologists, evolutionary psychologists have the ambition of subsuming the soft 'social sciences' under the biological umbrella, which is one reason why they like to refer to themselves as scientists. They therefore tend to downgrade the significance of culture, seeing it as a by-product of natural selection. Just as biologists explain the origins of body and brain in terms of natural selection, so they explain the human mind (as opposed to the brain). The body has arms, legs, a heart, liver and lungs and so on, each serving a different function; so it is with the 'modules' of the mind.

In common with socio-biologists they believe the specifics of human behaviour are the result of gene-prompted psychological adaptations that occurred when our lot were roaming the African savannah. Our minds evolved to deal with challenges faced by Stone Age people – Stone Age minds for a post-industrial era. To test their theories they look for behaviour patterns they regard as culturally universal, which they then assume to be biologically inbuilt. Part of their focus is on guessing what aspects of Stone Age life might have encouraged these adaptations.

The origins of evolutionary psychology and socio-biology lie in a catholic version of the theory of natural selection first advanced by Darwin and Wallace, which is why they are called neo-Darwinians or ultra-Darwinians. But, as we shall see in later chapters, EP has an additional element: this idea of an instinct-packed modular mind. Because there are few lengths of DNA for supposedly universal behaviours, they use the notion of 'mechanisms' encoded in the genes to ensure that humans are, on average, so inclined. And most go further, by proposing what they call a Swiss army knife model of the mind, equipped by its architecture with a collection of thousands of discreet, genetically-prompted modules and atomised behaviours, each of which evolved separately to allow humans to face the challenges of life in the African savannah[1].

The reason socio-biologists and evolutionary psychologists focus on sex and gender is because, in their view, the evolution of the mind occurs in the same way as evolution of the body: through sexual selection. This, they argue, has led to adaptations that prompt human males to compete for females and to try to spread their genes as far and wide as possible. But human females, with their nine-month pregnancies and responsibility for child care, have adapted to be more picky – to choose high status, high earning, genetically suitable males with care. The result is that the 'male mind' and 'female mind' evolved differently, leading to profoundly different outcomes.

This idea has seeped deep into public consciousness and pops up all over the place. For example, I recently read the autobiography of apartheid South Africa's spy chief, Niel Barnard, who felt compelled to inform his readers: 'It is without doubt a genetic truism: women have far more emotional intelligence than men and they use it in ingenious ways. They pick up waves and tremors of which I am totally unaware.'[2]

Once I began to delve into this terrain by reading the works of the evolutionary psychologists and their critics, I came across an

5

intriguing conundrum. While the Mars and Venus perspectives of the genetic determinists were becoming ubiquitous in the media, they were frequently treated with contempt by real scientists working in evolutionary biology, genetics and neuro-science (including Barnard's baseless claim that women have more innate emotional intelligence than men). In other words, they were getting a far better press than deserved, whereas their critics were underplayed and often ignored. And yet, despite this favourable exposure over the last 25 years, they insist on being seen as intrepid iconoclasts, bravely rowing against the tide of nurture-not-nature orthodoxy, whereas, in fact, their all-nature-no-nurture views have been very much the conventional wisdom for the past generation, at least as far as the media and the self-help and pop psychology shelves are concerned.

I should add that there was another, subsidiary element in all this that concerned me: when I was researching my previous book, *Black Brain, White Brain*, on the insidious revival of scientific racism, I found that several of those pumping out books and papers advancing the thoroughly discredited and deeply racist view that different human populations had evolved different mental machinery from each other, were the same people at the extremes of the Mars and Venus end of the genes and gender debate, including several prominent evolutionary psychologists.

Criticisms of EP and socio-biology, come in six related areas, each of which I amplify in far more detail later in this book. A quick sketch:

First, there's their reductionist understanding of evolution – one that assumes a direct input-output relationship between genes and behaviour. As one of the world's leading evolutionary biologists, Stanford's Paul Ehrlich, put it, a key problem with EP is that 'knowledge of genetics and evolution tends to trail far behind the knowledge of psychology.'[3]

The alternative approach stresses that evolution is by no means restricted to natural selection, and, perhaps more significantly for this debate, that the evolution of the human brain generated a far richer variety of non-adaptive side consequences than EP allows. In other words, the automatic assumption that any common human behaviour was 'hard-wired' through natural selection is unsustainable. Put differently, evolutionary psychologists routinely overstate the impact of genes and understate the impact of culture and environment more generally.

Second, there's their idea of the 'modular mind', a view that has no provable relation to genetics and is at odds with that held by most contemporary neuroscience which stress the complexity, plasticity and integration of the brain, and its perpetual receptiveness to being moulded by the environment, contributing to the flexibility of human nature. Their point is that the brain and its product, the mind, constantly change through experience, particularly during childhood, and that the 'specialisation' comes not through inbuilt mental modules, but through living.

Third, their research methodology is not always up to scratch. Instead of going on quixotic quests to find evidence of genes that might be implicated in specific behaviour patterns, they miss out this step altogether and work backwards, starting with the assumption that the behaviour is innate. They then devise a questionnaire to test whether the majority of their respondents think in this way. When a majority does indeed confirm the hypothesis they assert that this proves that the behaviour is hard-wired, after which they go back to the Stone Age, when it was assumed that males and females faced comparable challenges and therefore evolved comparable minds.

One problem lies in their frequently small and culturally specific sampling (invariably their own students). Another relates to their assumptions about what their results prove. Why does a result showing that a majority of a group of 56 students prefer their cousins on their mothers' sides to those on their fathers' (to mention one University of Texas study[4] co-headed by one of the giants of EP, David Buss) give any hint that this preference is hard-wired? These results would need to be replicated in other far larger studies in other cultures before even the most tentative claims to universality could reasonably be advanced. And even then, they would need to consider whether other factors might have produced these results.

Fourth, they're criticised more specifically for their backward-looking logic – Just-So Story trawls that explain modern behaviour in terms of imagined stone-age parallels. These behaviours are somehow thought to have prompted the genetic mutations that hard-wired our lot to evolve mental modules that, in turn, nudged us to act one way or another. In this way today's habits and prejudices are provided with the timeless and unbreakable seal of Human Nature, and Stone Age man and woman is clothed in the garments of contemporary models.

Part of the problem is that their pre-historical conclusions amount to no more than guesswork because we know very little about our ancestors' behaviour in the Pleistocene, hundreds of thousands of years ago, let alone whether such challenges might have led to selection for gender-specific traits produced by random genetic mutations. We can surmise they lived in small, hunter-gatherer, or fisher-gatherer, groups but we know next to nothing about their kinship relations, their social structures and ways of relating to each other, how far and often they moved, their belief systems, and so on. We don't even have a clear picture of the family tree that led to the arrival of homo sapiens sapiens (modern human beings) 200 000 years ago. And we know little more about most of what followed, which includes well over 95 percent of modern human existence. Specifically, we have no idea when and how various gender-based divisions of labour and life occurred or what form it may have taken in different places and pre-agricultural periods.

Fifth, their notions of evolutionary biology, when combined with their particular methodology, have prompted them to exaggerate the gender divide and to confuse what is environmental and cultural with what is biological. It has led them to assume that any common gender-related behaviour must be genetically-routed and must have evolved through natural selection. And because of their set-in-stone faith that most human behaviour is hard-wired in this way, they discount cultural explanations. With many of their research conclusions it is easy to think of possible independent, non-genetic variables that could have prompted their results. For instance, as we shall see in the cousin preference case, we might consider whether Texan students spent more time with their mums than their dads, and whether that might have influenced their preferences.

To pull these points together it is worth taking a preliminary peak at EP in action through a couple more examples. A small acknowledgement here: these two case studies could, with some justification, be said to be all-too-convenient low hanging fruit. This is true, and later in the book we will consider many more case studies that require a more detailed and nuanced argument, but it is also true that these particular examples received a rather astonishing amount of positive publicity in the media, which is of rather more concern than their academic reception.

In 2007 a team of evolutionary psychologists and neuroscientists from the University of Newcastle-upon-Tyne conducted research based on the hypothesis that men evolved to prefer blue and women, pink. They showed pairs of colours to 208 volunteers aged 20 to 26 – mostly 'British white Caucasians' plus a subgroup of 37 Chinese volunteers, and asked them to select the colour they preferred by clicking a computer mouse. While the most favoured colour was blue, women favoured pinks and lilacs more than men.[5]

Because of the researchers' reflex assumption that this evolved through natural selection, the team put on their thinking caps and devised a retrospective solution. 'The explanation might date back to humans' hunter-gatherer days, when women were the primary gatherers and would have benefited from an ability to home in on ripe, red fruits,' said Dr Anya Hurlbert, who led the team. She did not explain how these red fruits prompted a preference for pink. Referring to the preference for blue she added: 'Going back to our savannah days we would have a natural preference for a blue sky because it signalled good weather. Clear blue also signals a good water source.'[6]

These results, packaged for the media in a university press release[7] were enthusiastically embraced by numerous major newspapers in the UK, USA and several other countries. Time Magazine asserted in their story's intro that 'women may be biologically programmed to prefer the colour pink'.[8] The Times headed theirs with, 'At last, science discovers why blue is for boys but girls really do prefer pink' and their intro left no doubt about their endorsement: 'Now it emerges that parents who dress their boys in blue and girls in pink may not just be following tradition but some deep-seated evolutionary instinct'[9] and the rest of the story lifts the quotes directly from the press release. None of the publications bothered to query the methodology, let alone the conclusions, of this study, with the result that it rapidly began to settle into the realm of conventional wisdom.

In this case, however, the remedy arrived relatively early. A week later, Dr Ben Goldacre ripped it to pieces in his 'Bad Science' column in The Guardian[10] but, as usual, the antidote drew far fewer column lines than the bane. One of his quibbles was that the test was devised to measure preference rather than ability to discriminate between shades of red (which might, possibly, have conferred an advantage in berry picking). But the more damning criticism came from evidence that the female preference for pink was a recent phenomenon – only settling in over the last 75 years or so as a result of advertising campaigns in the United States. In fact, at the start of the first world war, blue was often considered a girly colour while pink was considered masculine. The American Sunday Sentinel advised its readers in 1914: '[U]se pink for a boy and blue for a girl, if you are a follower of convention.'[11] Likewise the British Ladies' Home Journal noted in 1918: '[T]he generally accepted rule is pink for the boy and blue for the girl. The reason is that pink being a more decided and stronger colour is more suitable for the boy, while blue, which is more delicate and dainty, is prettier for the girl.'[12]

What this strongly suggests is that colour preference has nothing to do with genes, and everything to do with culture. And yet, I have to concede, very often it doesn't feel that way. Think for a second about the colour pink, and it's hard to separate it from the idea that it's essentially girly. So how does that happen if it is not innate? What planted this presumption in our minds? The answer relates to the process we all go through from as early as six months old in developing our awareness of ourselves as boys or girls, and what that means in terms of consciousness and behaviour. Right from the start many girl babies are smothered in pink and boys in blue. By the time they're consciously aware of their gender, well before their second birthdays, they associate their femininity with pink (and with the importance of their prettiness, and with dolls and tea sets and so-on). So by the time they grow up, this preference for pink feels natural and is constantly reinforced.

Similar logic has been used for my second strawman case study: the oft-repeated claim that women have a 'shopping gene' making them more inclined to hit the mall. In December 2009, an evolutionary psychologist from the University of Michigan, Daniel Kruger, co-wrote a paper in the *Journal of Social, Evolutionary, & Cultural Psychology* that explained the greater inclination of women students to go shopping in classic EP jargon – using their pet terms and theories to tell us that men evolved in the Pleistocene era to go hunting and women to go foraging, and that the shopping behaviours are therefore 'influenced by sexually divergent adaptations for gathering and hunting'.[13]

The paper goes on to tell us that back in the Pleistocene era most food came from gathering, and most gathering was done by women, who had evolved to be 'more sensitive to pinks, reds, and yellows than men'[14] Again, I'm at a loss to explain which pink things they may have wanted to gather (the African savannah is hardly full of edible pink-skinned fruits), but, never mind – this superior female ability to discern colours (and shapes) led the authors to conclude that shopping ability and potential was 'sex-based' because 'women will exhibit more proficiency at shopping behaviours resembling gathering than men'.[15]

Kruger said he chose this study after a winter holiday trip to Europe where he found that once he and his friends reached Prague all the women wanted to do was shop and the men couldn't understand why. He commented: 'We have evidence that the kind of skills, abilities and behaviours that are important for hunting and gathering in current foraging societies emerge predictably in our modern consumer environment. ... Anytime you come into a new area you want to scope out the landscape and find out where the food patches are.'[16]

I've already dealt with the questionable premises of evolutionary psychology, but the initial problem with this conclusion is the leap of logic it requires. First, it requires a Flintstones version of the Pleistocene era. Second, it assumes that because of foraging, females evolved through natural selection to be more observant and picky and so-on (in other words, that there was selection for traits produced by random genetic mutations, prompting them in this direction). Third, it assumes that the inclination of modern women to go shopping is a result of this evolutionary path. A key flaw is that it fails to consider any other factors along the way – independent variables – that might prompt more women than men to relish shopping.

One rather obvious alternative is that rather than having anything to do with mutations for traits favouring foraging behaviour, it has everything to do with our gendered culture. Women are pulled, pushed and prodded by advertising, parents and peers to worry a great deal about how they look, which in turn prompts them to be more interested in clothes and cosmetics, which means they are bombarded with advertising and other media images in this direction. They also do far more of the household shopping, on average, than men, although as we shall see, this is changing. Their greater inclination to go shopping may be explained entirely by this combination of interest, inducement and habit.

Yet none of the many stories I read on this paper bothered to consider any of these alternative explanations. Instead, they swallowed Kruger's research whole. To take just four of scores of examples, the magazine *Psychology Today* went with 'Shopping Brings Out Our Inner Hunter/Gatherer'[17], *ABC News* opted for 'Why Women Love to Shop, and Men Don't: Blame Evolution,'[18] the Indian newspaper, *The Hindu,* went with 'Genes dictate shopping styles'[19] while the *Toronto Sun* settled on the magnificent 'What else can you expect from a caveman?'[20]

As I show in the chapters that follow, most of the pet hypotheses emerging from the world of evolutionary psychology and sociobiology have met with a similarly decisive (but under-publicised) fate as the pink-and-blue one, but this has not discouraged them. Buss, Pinker and their colleagues fervently defend their methods and fire back at their critics, accusing them of being soft-headed 'blank-slatists' with no concept of human nature. And when it comes to their primary concern, gender, they accuse their critics of believing that there are no essential differences between males and females.

Actually, I don't know any serious critic of genetic determinism who today advocates anything approximating a blank slate approach to human nature. This behaviourist lineage could be said to have started with John Locke in the 17th century, and it continued through Jean Jacques Rousseau in the 18th, Emile Durkheim in the 19th and the American psychologist John B Watson early in the 20th – and it had another spurt after the second world war, reaching its peak in the late 1960s, partly as a reaction to the eugenics of previous generations. But certainly over the last 25 years I struggle to think of any prominent scientist, psychologist, anthropologist or sociologist who has advocated a pure tabula rasa, where we are born utterly malleable, entirely subject to environmental moulding, and few would question the assumption that natural selection has played a vital role in the evolutionary road that led the human brain to grow to its current complexity. But that is hardly the end of the story.

Some time in the last quarter of a million years our brains evolved to their current form and intellectual capacity. The nature of the intelligence that these complex brains exhibited, with its capacity for memory, learning, abstraction, symbolism, empathy and, most of all, its sense of self, encouraged creativity, innovation, imagination and invention – for making it up as we go along.

We're all born with intrinsic drives and capacities: for survival, sexual gratification, for giving and responding to love and companionship, for acquiring language, for reflecting on our own actions and those of others, for analysing and applying this understanding to other situations and for passing this on to others, for imagining things we can't see, for making up stories and absorbing myths. We are also born with the same potential range of emotions – joy, sadness, fear, hate, disgust, anger, delight, grief, anxiety, surprise, sulkiness, disappointment, guilt, remorse, shame, embarrassment and so on. We all can smile, laugh, sigh and cry. We all have moods and attitudes and beliefs, motives and intentions. And we all go through the same developmental stages at more or less the same time, from face recognition to walking and talking and as we grow up we all develop the potential to appreciate music, create art, tell stories, make plans and think about other people's thoughts.

This is some of what we share: the common part of our human nature. But the adaptability, creativity and plasticity of these big, complex, self-conscious brains of ours is immense. Love and hate, selfishness and generosity, friendliness and aloofness, competition and co-operation, war-making and peace-making, slavery and rebellion, genocide and self-sacrifice, fidelity and promiscuity, cruelty and kindness, meanness and compassion, aggression and passivity, narcissism and altruism and on and on, are all part of human nature because they are all within our potential range.

In the search for similes, it's hard to top Tolstoy's idea that people (or 'men' as he preferred) are like rivers: '(T)he water is the same in each, and alike in all but every river is narrow here, more rapid there,

here slower, there broader, now clear, now cold, now dull, now warm. It is the same with men. Every man carries in himself the germs of every human quality, and sometimes one manifests itself, sometimes another, and the man often becomes unlike himself, while still remaining the same man.'[21]

As the decoding of the human genome has affirmed so decisively, we don't have the 'germs' or genes 'for' any particular quality. Rather, the qualities we display are consequences of the kinds of flexible, environmentally-sensitive brains we developed in evolving to become homo sapiens. The late Harvard biologist and palaeontologist Stephen Jay Gould said our brains were 'bursting with spandrels' – a reference to non-adaptive mental properties.

As I argue in more detail in later chapters, the implication is that most human behaviour is not the specific result of genetic impulse. How we emerge as individuals will certainly be influenced by our individual genetic inheritance. But this, alone, is unlikely to make us wife beaters, rapists, child molesters, murderers or miscreants, nor anything positive for that matter. These are mainly products of our experience in the womb and of the way we are raised, particularly in our first few years, and of the values we absorb from parents and peers, our formative experiences, our socio-economic circumstances, and, in the widest sense, the environment we grow up in.

In other words, human nature is a moveable feast. Ehrlich prefers, instead, to speak of 'human natures' because of the impact of culture in moulding our brains and our minds and the way we behave – a process that happens in different forms and at different rates in different cultures. As he puts it: 'Uniquely in our species, changes in culture have been fully as important in producing our natures as have changes in the hereditary information passed on by our ancestors.'[22]

So why is it that these kinds of stories get so little currency in the media, whereas stories stressing intrinsic differences between men and women get all the airplay? The reflex response would simply be to blame hidden media agendas, but as I show in chapter 15, this is off the mark. In so many ways, the media reflects back to people the kinds of things they want to read, see and hear.

The second half of the 20th century saw remarkably rapid changes in gender relations, particularly in the industrialised nations. Previous advances made by women in war time were followed by retreat but since the late 1960s these changes have been continuous and relentless. However, social upheaval invariably comes with fervent resistance. In this case it has involved a concerted attack on the ideas underpinning much of the feminist narrative, most notably the notion that our potential as human beings is not defined by gender.

This backlash is not only the province of out-and-out reactionary elements, fiercely resisting some supposed drive towards androgyny. The narrowing of previous gender gaps – in employment, politics, the household and in male-female companionship – has prompted a thirst for reassurance: that whatever happens at work or at home, we really are very different. The popularity of EP-inspired media stories and self-help books that offer precisely this succour is just one of the many indications of the huge market for this kind of ego-soothing reassurance.

An added reason relates to the priorities of those conducting the research. If you examine a number of studies of the same thing, you're bound to get a few aberrant results – perhaps one in 20. This could be the result of sampling and other aspects of methodology, or simply coincidence. But when looking at whether gender differences can be found in the brain, or in behavioural patterns, those conducting the research are unlikely to report the majority of studies that show no significant difference between males and females. Instead, it is the five out the 100 that do show difference that will published, and later publicised with the aim of media exposure – perhaps with good reason, because if their university press offices were to release the results of studies showing no difference between males and females, the media would be unlikely to report them. They are interested in what seems to be new and different.

But frequently what they publicise is neither new nor different – it is merely dressed up this way. Here's an example: In 2012 several American and British newspapers and news websites prominently ran stories on a University of Manchester research paper entitled 'The Distance Between Mars and Venus: Measuring Global Sex Differences in Personality'. It concluded that the average man and woman shared only 10 percent of personality traits. 'Psychologically, men and women are almost a different species,'[23] said one of its co-authors, Paul Irwing.

The British and American media devoured this line – and made no attempt to look at the possible agendas of the researchers[24] – running stories declaring that the Mars and Venus case had been confirmed. The Daily Mail's version carried the headline, 'Surprise! Men and women really ARE different: Sexes share just 10 per cent of their personality traits. Psychologists reach verdict after probing 10,000 people.'[25] CBS News took a more sober approach: 'Sex and personality differences underestimated: divide between male and female characteristics great, researchers say'[26] while The Telegraph's version, written by their science correspondent, and headed 'Men and Women Have Distinct Personalities', began with this intro: 'Men and women really do have fundamentally different characteristics, according to a study which has confirmed many long-held gender stereotypes.'[27]

None of the newspapers bothered to pry beyond the publicity material they received but if they'd looked further they would have found that the research was really conducted 19 years earlier. The data was based entirely on an American survey completed in 1993, entitled 'Sixteen Personality Factor Questionnaire', which asked questions on traits such as warmth, sensitivity, tension, perfectionism, dominance, vigilance and self-reliance. The obvious point of caution here is that respondents are inclined to rate themselves highly in qualities they admire. Men know that vigilance, dominance and self-reliance are considered masculine so it follows that they might want to rate themselves highly in these areas, whereas women might be more likely to rate themselves highly in 'feminine' zones such as sensitivity and warmth. There have been several studies showing that self-perception is a particularly unreliable measure of people's personality traits. Further, while most media stories on this research, along with the researchers' comments, suggested the differences that emerged in the survey were innate, the data shows nothing of the sort. The most that could be said about it is that it reflects the attitudes of a sample of American men and women about themselves, in the early 1990s.

Which is not to say that all of the differences between men and women are culturally-based, or that biology is irrelevant when it comes to behaviour. It's worth taking a step back here by stressing that my observation about the dubiousness of so much of the Mars and Venus research doesn't imply that the only hardwired differences between males and females relate to size, strength and breeding equipment. As we shall see, the few cases of baby boys who've had their genders 'reclassified' because of damage to their penises, but have ultimately re-emerged as males, offer tentative indication that the basis of masculinity and femininity is more profound than the appearance of genitals[28].

To take just four of the examples that I will expand on later in the book: males produce significantly more testosterone than females, starting with the initial in utero burst that determines their sex, and this has an impact not only on male bodies, but also on male minds – and is one of several factors in explaining why men are, on average, more violent than women; many women experience pre-menstrual tension, and then, when they cease menstruating, go through the menopause, both of which can affect mood and mindset; as far as we know about twice as many males as females are on the autistic spectrum. In addition, a higher proportion of males are colour blind than females, and a higher proportion of females have enhanced perception of certain colours.

Still, we can't simply assume that all of the common behavioural differences between males and females that we observe in day-to-day life are hard-wired or even that they are universal. Which is why there's so much variation between generations and between countries, communities and classes in how people relate, and most particularly, how men and women and boys and girls relate. Compare the way males and females rub along together – or keep far apart – in, say, Saudi Arabia and Sweden, Afghanistan and Ghana, and you'll be struck not so much by how we are all alike, but by how different we are, and how our assumptions about human nature – about what is normal and timeless and natural – fall to dust when we consider a wider sweep of humanity.

But most of us do not walk around with this wider sweep in mind. Put differently, the idea that the biologically-based differences between men and women might be exaggerated can be hard to accept because, wherever we live, we see men and women behaving differently, with different expectations of each other and themselves, and it's often difficult to appreciate that our own experience is not typical of the rest of humanity's, let alone the idea that our own brains have been moulded by our gendered upbringings.

To take one example, in 2013 I attended the *umgidi* of my then-19-year-old nephew in Port Elizabeth, South Africa. This involved his return from a month in the 'bush' after being ritually circumcised – an amaXhosa practice as deeply rooted in their culture as the *bris* is for eight-day old Jewish boys. While in the bush, only males visit these initiates, and it is the men who talk to them and advise them at the celebration after their return, before the women can have their chance. It seemed to me that this warmly affirming community event, and the four weeks that preceded it, was of immense significance to the young men involved. Afterwards, my nephew told me: 'Now I feel like a real man. I feel more grown-up.' There was no equivalent or comparable rite of passage for his sister. This was essentially a male-led event, with the women and girls enthusiastically playing the ululating, cheerleading support role, and I am sure that very few who were there would have thought of questioning this separation or the perception that it reflected real differences in the appropriate societal roles of males and females.

When I returned home to London my reflections on this experience made me wonder whether there were areas in my own life where I unthinkingly accepted different gender roles, regarding them as just a natural and unchanging part of life, so I began looking out for zones in my own milieu where men and women were expected to behave differently, and where these differences were considered timeless.

To take just two of very many examples, the day after my return, I opened my paper and saw a double-page spread on the Academy Awards ceremony. It was full of pictures of actresses on display in their gowns, which were extensively discussed along with their hairstyles, and even their finger nails. The male actors in their identical tuxedos were virtually ignored. Shortly after, two friends of mine got married and opted for the white wedding with all the trappings. The bride had an engagement ring, not the groom; the bride's father 'gave' her away to the groom; the groom made a wedding speech, the bride didn't, she took his surname; he didn't reciprocate, and the next day most of the pictures and comments on Facebook were of the 'gorgeous', 'stunning', 'beautiful' bride in her white gown, not of the groom in his suit, which seemed natural because, of course, it was *her* big day.

It was hard to escape the impression that whatever had changed in the position of women in society, they were still expected to be on display – that their appearance was a major part of their lives in a way that just didn't apply to men, whether film stars or bride grooms or homebodies. I noticed that my own home was not immune from this expectation – a realisation reinforced every morning when I watched, or, more accurately, waited for, the production process as my then-teenaged younger daughter busied herself getting ready for her day. The image she presented as she showed her face to the world was an important part of her sense of self in a way that it was not, and never had been, for me (a subject discussed in chapter 12).

When newspapers and websites reflect on research carried out by evolutionary psychologists to show that, for example, women have evolved to wear lipstick or to shop-shop-shop or that men have evolved to favour a particular hip-waist ratio, or when the Daily Mail tells us that 'men and women really are a different species', even the more sceptical among us might have a subliminal sense that there could be a hint of truth lurking beneath the headlines.

In the chapters that follow I will show that many of the most cherished myths about men and women, boys and girls, mums and dads, promoted by genetic determinists can safely be put to bed – and that most of the obvious differences we observe in everyday life between the way males and females behave are deeply rooted in cultural history rather than in evolutionary biology. In other words, males and females are far more similar than is generally acknowledged. So to wrap up this introductory chapter, a return to the starting point ... .

I'm a man and like most men I have an inbuilt capacity to share, and to nurture my own children and other people's children too; I'm capable of living co-operatively and of preferring fidelity to promiscuity; I can't read a map upside-down or find my way in a maze but I can chat away incessantly and I'm quite good at multitasking, and like most men I'm sexually drawn to differing forms of female beauty. And my friends who are women, well: I've noticed they often prefer men the same age as themselves – or younger; they may well choose to 'sleep around'; they enjoy their orgasms just as much as we men enjoy ours – or more so; a large number are useless at languages and great at maths and science; most have considerably better senses of direction than me and many have no desire to become homemakers and every desire to compete with each other and with men.

# CHAPTER TWO

# DARWINS LATTER DAY PITBULLS

When I was a child I thought as a child, which in my case meant being immersed in evangelical Christianity. I embraced the idea that the Bible was the word of God, with no contradictions, no errors, nothing out-of-date. Certainly, there were fierce disputes on how to interpret God's Word – for example, whether the universe was created in six literal days or whether 'day' meant 'period of time' – but the essential point that the Bible was an instruction manual for life was not in dispute, and its words were sweated over, prayed over and applied to every contemporary issue.

Later in my teen years I became immersed in another brand of fundamentalism. While living in Texas, I met a Marxist historian who taught me that old Karl, like Isaac Newton, had discovered a science true for all time – the tool for understanding history and for changing it. I read the Communist Manifesto and Capital, returned home to Cape Town as a convert, and immersed myself in 'the struggle', linking up with 'comrades' who took as given that what Marx had written applied to every branch of life. Arguments on current political concerns were laced with chapter and verse references to Marx, or to Lenin, or their late 20th century interpreters. To doubt one of the tenets of Marxism was to risk abstracting yourself from the argument and being treated as an apostate.

What these fundamentalisms shared was a sense of an inner circle blessed with the truth as revealed by a dead guru and passed down by live ones, up against a world infected with false consciousness.

## The Gospel According to St Charles

Which brings me to the odd phenomenon of ultra-Darwinism with its doctrinaire obeisance to the long-dead Master, its religious fervour and its obsession with gender. I am not for a moment suggesting that Darwin himself was anything other than one of the greatest biologists of his millennium, and I certainly don't want to compare him to men who got most of the big things wrong (like Saint Paul and Saint Karl), but there are parallels to be drawn about the behaviour of some of his more ardent disciples. The fundamentalism that infects genetic determinism can be traced to the aggressive proselytising by Darwin's late 19th-century bulldogs who helped equate evolution exclusively with natural selection, and natural selection exclusively with Darwin. This personification gathered steam in response to attacks from creationists, and in recent times, the terms of the debate have been cast as 'Darwin's theory of evolution' v 'intelligent design' or Darwin v God. The 200th anniversary of Darwin's birth, in 2009, heightened the tendency to conflate evolution with one man.

This individual focus is not restricted to mass media that inevitably offer personal narratives to complex tales. It is also stock-in-trade of biologists and psychologists who've taken a chapter-and-verse approach. For example, Richard Dawkins, the British socio-biologist whose version of evolution is a prime source of inspiration for evolutionary psychology, said: 'Charles Darwin really solved the problem of existence, the problem of the existence of all living things – humans, animals, plants, fungi, bacteria. Everything we know about life, Darwin essentially explained.'[1] Daniel Dennett, the American philosopher who faithfully follows in Dawkins's wake, wrote: 'Let me lay my cards on the table. If I were to give an award for the single best idea anyone ever had, I'd give it to Darwin, ahead of even Newton or Einstein and everyone else.²'

Underlying this praise-singing is a quasi-religious impulse – just as religious zealots preach obedience to God's laws as laid down in the Bible or the Qur'an, so neo-Darwinian zealots preach obedience to 'Nature's Laws' as laid down by Darwin. Anyone who diverges from the letter of Darwinian law has to be savaged – branded as 'PC' or as a soft-headed feminist, or as a politically-motivated fact-denier. To cite one example, Robert Wright, a prominent American journalistic cheerleader for evolutionary psychology, declared: 'There is not a single well-known feminist who has learned enough about modern Darwinism to pass judgment on it.'³

This more-Darwinian-than-thou evangelism might ring bells for anyone who has had a brush with, say, Islamism, or Pentecostal Christianity or Trotskyism. The difference is that these other isms aren't sciences – in fact, 'isms' are contrary to what science is about. And the overused phrase 'Darwin's theory of evolution' adds to the confusion. The 'theory' bit suggests it is something scientists *believe* in, which is hardly apt, and the 'Darwin's' bit suggests there are contrary evolutionary theories kicking around. It also contributes to a perception that he came up this idea all by himself and that it arrived complete, fully-formed and unimpeachable. None of this is remotely true – and it is more than a case of righting an historical distortion because this guru-worship distorts knowledge, freezing it in terms of interpretations of the master's voice. One needn't be a full-blown iconoclast to appreciate that this is not a healthy approach.

## Darwin, Wallace and the shoulders of giants

Isaac Newton, not a modest man by any means, nor a very nice one, famously wrote that if he had seen further it was only by 'standing on the shoulders of giants.'⁴ The same could be said of any great scientist, and the kindly Charles Darwin was no exception. For a start, the idea of evolution did not belong to him. To mention one predecessor, his grandfather, Erasmus Darwin, wrote in 1795: 'Would it be too bold to imagine that, in the great length of time since the earth began to exist, perhaps millions of ages before the commencement of the history of mankind ... that all warm-blooded animals have arisen from one living filament.[5]'

Charles followed in grandad's wake, absorbing the work of other pioneers including the French evolutionary theorist Jean-Baptiste Lamarck who wrote that the environment prompted changes in animals but mistakenly believed there was a tendency for them to move up the ladder and become more complex in a steady and predictable way. He also influenced Darwin's initial thinking on the 'transmutation' of species (the changing of one into another) although today Lamarck is best known for his belief in the inheritance of acquired characteristics – the notion that modifications made by an animal through use or disuse could be passed on to its offspring[6]. Darwin was also influenced by the ideas of several of his contemporaries[7] and drew a great deal from contemporary knowledge among farmers, breeders and pigeon fanciers who created new strains and breeds through selection.

Darwin's lasting contribution to evolutionary theory was his discovery that selection occurred in nature and that in animals this happened through sex. Those born with traits that made them better suited to their environment were more likely to survive and to pass those on to their offspring – a result known as adaptation. In this way all species, including human beings, evolved from common ancestors. As Darwin explained it: 'Can we doubt (remembering that many more individuals are born than can possibly survive) that individuals having any advantage, however slight over others, would have the best chance of surviving and procreating their kind? On the other hand, we may feel sure that any variation in the least degree injurious would be rigidly destroyed. This preservation of favourable variations and the rejection of injurious variations, I call Natural Selection.'[8]

This idea of Darwin's remains as valid today as it was when he wrote it more than 150 years ago – but even here he was not alone. If we insist on attaching a name to the 'theory" of natural selection then we should speak of Darwin and Wallace's theory.

Alfred Russel Wallace was a remarkable polymath whose discoveries on anthropology, ecology and biology made him one of the most innovative thinkers of his century. His most vital contribution came through independently proposing a theory of evolution through natural selection. Wallace, who was conducting research in the Malay Archipelago, had been developing his evolutionary theories over the previous 15 years. He corresponded with Darwin and sent him samples, and in 1858 sent him his paper[9] that demonstrated how, through natural selection, one species could diverge from another. He asked Darwin to forward this to the geologist Charles Lyell. Darwin, who'd been wary of publishing his theories because they might be seen to contradict Christianity, duly passed it on – but he was panicked into showing his hand because he was worried he would be 'forestalled' (beaten to the punch) and that 'all my originality will be smashed'.

The result was that Darwin, Lyall and Joseph Hooker ensured that Wallace's essay was presented alongside some of Darwin's unpublished writings, at the Linnean Society of London on July 1 1858 – the first public exposition of the theory of natural selection. So, even though Darwin had privately come up with the first strands of his evolutionary theories while on the Beagle, the first paper written on evolution by natural selection was not by Charles Darwin, but by Alfred Russel Wallace, and if it hadn't been for the unintentional prod from Wallace, Darwin would have waited longer before going public. Alternatively, if Wallace had sent it to a publisher rather than to Darwin, we might today talk of 'Wallace's theory of evolution'.

If we look at their work that followed, it could be said that despite Darwin's pre-eminence, in several areas Wallace's ideas have outlasted Darwin's. They shared the same theory of natural selection, but while Darwin focussed on competition between individuals, Wallace placed more emphasis on environmental pressures, which is now widely accepted. And while Darwin's notion of sexual selection focussed on females choosing males (he thought that females, including animals, had an aesthetic sense), Wallace focussed on what we would now call the better genes in the dominant males (such as bigger horns), an idea closer to the contemporary view. Also, when it came to explaining speciation, Darwin's 'principle of divergence' focussed mainly on competition within the same habitat, while Wallace focussed more on separation of populations, which is now accepted.[10]

On so many issues Alfred Russell Wallace was way ahead of his time (including his environmentalism, support for the liberation of women, opposition to eugenics, his socialism, anti-racism, anti-colonialism and anti-militarism), although his later life beliefs in spiritualism and in the spiritual origin of the higher faculties of human intelligence were very much of his time (and criticised by the agnostic Darwin).

Wallace was 14 years younger than Darwin, and being self-taught (he left school at 14), from a modest background, had neither the social status nor scientific standing and connections of the wealthy patrician scholar he so admired, and he worked in foreign forests rather than English fields. So despite the joint reading of their papers, Wallace was relegated to a supporting role, even though he received much acclaim during his long life (he died in 1913, shortly before his 91st birthday) – not only for his immense contribution to evolutionary theory but also for his other writings on his travels and on the natural world. However, once *The Origin of Species* hit the shelves, less than two years later, the term 'Darwinism' was coined and evolution became synonymous with one man.[11]

## What Darwin didn't know

This one man got many things right and some wrong, and, inevitably, there was much that he did not have the tools to understand. To call evolution 'Darwin's theory' is a misnoma – not only did evolutionary science predate him, but most of its key discoveries have been made since his death in 1882. Today when we talk of evolution we usually think of natural selection for traits that emerge through random genetic mutation[12] (selection occurs when those bearing the trait that is a product of a particular gene have more surviving offspring than those without that trait). Darwin and Wallace understood that evolution was driven by sexual selection but because they knew nothing of genetics, they had trouble explaining the source of the heritable variations that might be selected. Darwin assumed that offspring inherited adaptations made by their parents and believed this was strengthened or weakened through the extent a particular trait was used – and he mistakenly believed the characteristics of parents were evenly blended together.

While Darwin was writing *The Origin of Species*, Gregor Mendel, an Austrian monk who also happened to be a scientist, was conducting research in his monastery's garden on inheritance of traits in pea plants (29 000 of them). Mendel had studied Darwin and rejected his idea of the blending of traits, instead believing that microscopic particles were passed on whole, which he demonstrated through his pea plant experiments. These showed that a plant was tall or short according to the random combination of particles (genes) it inherited. Although his paper was published in 1866 it was largely ignored by the scientific community and it took until the start of the 20th century for his ideas on genetics to be rediscovered. It was only in the 1930s that biologists fully synthesised Darwin and Wallace's theory of natural selection with the theory of genetics that had started with Mendel.

Still, the notion of a relation between use and inheritance continued to resonate. Twenty years after Darwin's death Rudyard Kipling's *Just So Stories* were published, featuring 12 children's yarns. Just as Lamarck said that giraffes stretched their necks to reach the high Acacia leaves in trees, thereby lengthening them, and that this trait would be passed on, so it was with Kipling: the elephant got his trunk because a crocodile stretched his nose. Which might be fine for children's stories, but we expect something more scientific for adults. And yet today we see versions of evolution that sound suspiciously Lamarckian – claims of short-term behavioural changes prompting long-term evolutionary adaptation.

One particularly daft example was published in 2009 – on the evolutionary impact of Victorian novels. The Guardian's version was headed: 'Victorian novels helped us evolve into nicer people, say scientists'.[13] The 'scientists' were, in fact, nothing of the sort. They were, instead, a team of American evolutionary psychologists whose paper was published in their house journal *Evolutionary Psychology*[14]. Their research consisted of a questionnaire, sent to 500 academics who were asked to rate the personality traits of characters from 201 Victorian novels and comment on their emotional response to these heroes and villains. They concluded that the characters could be divided into groups mirroring the co-operative nature of Stone Age society, and claimed the novels 'fulfil an adaptive social function' and might 'stimulate impulses towards these real behaviours'[15]. They were quoted as saying that the novels serve 'some specific evolutionary function' rather than being mere 'by-products of evolutionary adaptation'.[16] And The Guardian's science correspondent went further: 'The despicable acts of Count Dracula, the unending selflessness of Dorothea in Middlemarch and Mr Darcy's personal transformation in Pride and Prejudice helped to uphold social order and encouraged *altruistic genes* to spread through Victorian society, according to an analysis by evolutionary psychologists.'[17] It goes without saying that while Darwin and Wallace were ignorant of genetics, they never descended to this kind of silliness.

## 'Survival of the fittest'

The error in viewing all human behaviour as a direct consequence of natural selection was amplified by Herbert Spencer's term 'survival of the fittest', used not just as a metaphor for evolution, but as a faux-Darwinian prescription for zones well beyond of the realm of biology. Spencer, a prominent British philosopher-economist, found parallels between his social theories and Darwin's evolutionary theories[18], while Darwin, in turn, started using 'survival of the fittest' in his own writing. But Spencer took it to places Darwin could not accept[19], using 'survival of the fittest' to explain economics, culture and politics.

What started with Spencer is now ubiquitous to the point where we have faux-academic disciplines like 'Darwinian Literary Studies'[20]. The term 'evolution' has long since burst its biological banks to be used for any manner of social development, while 'survival of the fittest' is embraced to advance unrestricted capitalism. The EP-backing journalist and Tory peer Matt Ridley, for example, has argued that evolutionary biology suggests that the best economic and political system is a libertarian one, with a minimal role for the state.[21] It is perhaps worth recalling that the term was once used for the opposite ends. Take, for example, Emile Zola's *Germinal*, published in 1885, where the 1860's strike leader Etienne Lantier blends Darwin and Marx, viewing the vigorous proletariat as ready to renew the world in its survival of the fittest battle with the decrepit bourgeoisie.[22] Logic should tell us that both the fictional Lantier and the all-too-real Ridley are over-reaching because there is no sense in equating selection for traits resulting from random genetic mutations with the way human beings organise their affairs. Even if you can claim to find some correlation or parallel between them, there is no causal link. To assume otherwise verges on metaphysics.

Darwin spotted the danger and rowed back from some aspects of social-Darwinism, but was certainly not immune to the prejudices of his day. Of particular relevance to this book, he adopted the conventional 19th century views on male and female attributes, believing that men were the superior sex, mentally as well as physically superior to women, just as he insisted the 'civilised races' were superior to the 'savage races'. In *The Descent of Man*, he wrote of how women differed from men in 'mental disposition' and referred to female 'powers of intuition, of rapid perception, and perhaps imitation', which he said were 'characteristic of the lower races, and therefore of a past and lower state of civilisation.[23] ' In this sense Darwin was a creature of his own time who reflected many of its values – a man of privilege who inherited wealth and married an even richer heiress, living near the apex of a tightly stratified nation that was also the world's premier colonial power, and he did not question many of its values, and reflected some of them in his writing.[24]

Wallace, on the other hand, was way ahead of his time in when it came to gender (and also, race[25]). He campaigned for women's suffrage and predicted the position of women would be 'far higher and more important than any which has been claimed for and by her in the past' and predicted that women would be 'placed in a position of responsibility and power which will render her his superior, since the future moral progress of the race will so largely depend on her free choice in marriage.[26] '

But these views were not widely shared and, instead, Darwininan theory gave birth to eugenics – the belief that the human species could be improved by breeding out, sterilising or eliminating those with undesirable traits, or by breeding those with desirable traits. Again, Wallace stood out – as one of the few prominent scientists to oppose eugenics, believing that society was too unjust and corrupt to decide who was fit or unfit , and he added: 'Those who succeed in the race for wealth are by no means the best or the most intelligent.'[27] But his warnings were ignored, and instead the rich and powerful followed the lead of the most ardent early proponent of eugenics, Darwin's fervently racist cousin Sir Francis Galton[28], who coined the term in 1883. From then-on it acquired a Darwinian gloss, attracting immense support from people in power[29] and from leading biologists of the day. However, after the second world war, the horror of the Holocaust gave eugenics, racial science and social Darwinism a bad name among Western intellectuals, prompting a shift away from explanations of behaviour based on genetics. The focus of public and academic discourse shifted towards the nurture side of that debate (and sometimes too far in the direction of blank slate behaviourism).

## Desmond Morris and the revival of social Darwinism

But a revived variant of social Darwinism emerged in the 1960s, starting a train of thought that led to evolutionary psychology a quarter of a century on. This new socio-biological innings was opened by the Nobel prize-winner Konrad Lorenz whose *On Aggression* was published in 1963.[30] Lorenz, a former Nazi party member who vocally supported eugenics, explained that 'the subject of this book was *aggression*, that is to say, the fighting instinct in beast and man which is directed *against* members of the same species' – behaviour that is part of human male instinct, through natural selection.

He was followed by Robert Ardrey, who wrote *The Territorial Imperative* in 1966 – a book that tried to explain the world in terms of the male fight over territory (an argument that led him to a virulent defence of apartheid South Africa, where he eventually settled). Our lot were 'killer apes' – particularly the highly aggressive males – and it was male violence over real estate, and male interpersonal aggression that prompted human evolution.[31] His fervent conviction about male supremacy led him to express his dismay about the desire of the contemporary woman for 'masculine expression' for which she possessed no 'instinctual equipment'. He despaired of the modern female desire to 'downgrade the care of children as insufficient focus for feminine activity' and claimed she was the 'unhappiest female the primate world has ever seen and the most treasured objective in her heart of hearts is the psychological castration of husbands and sons'.[32]

The most popular and prolific of this bunch was a one-time curator of mammals at London Zoo, Desmond Morris whose *The Naked Ape* was translated into 27 languages and was considered a publishing phenomenon. It started with the assertion that human nature evolved to meet the challenges of being hunter-gathers in Africa. His follow-up book, *The Human Zoo* [33] dealt with human behaviour in modern industrial society, showing how it resembled the behaviour of apes in captivity. Despite our bigger brains and penises, he argued, we men retain all our old simian instincts. In this way, he reduced human activity to zoology, setting a trend followed over the next four decades by academic socio-biologists and evolutionary psychologists.

Morris's prime obsession was the differences in male and female behaviour. In *The Naked Ape* he offered what was to become the familiar litany of genetic determinists – women talk more and are better with words, are more dextrous, less assertive and so on. And in his all-nature, no-nurture fervour, he noted similarities between the sexual signalling of female mammals at the start of oestrus, and the 'evolved' behaviour of human females in spending money on cosmetics. In juicy detail he tells of the evolutionary origins of lipstick, rouge, perfume, padded bras and 'bottom-falsies' for 'skinny females', while also asserting that males in all societies and at all times are attracted to the same hip-waist ratio. Along the way he offered readers titbits on female genitalia and on erotic stimuli used by naked apes.[34] For example, in one of his follow-up books, *The Naked Woman*, he enthuses about the full range of female genital waxing and trimming styles.[35] He argues it is contrary to human nature to mess with these laws because 'the naked ape's old impulses have been with him for millions of years, his new ones for a few thousand at the most, and there is no hope of quickly shrugging off the accumulated genetic legacy of his whole evolutionary past'.[36]

Morris's impact was considerable – fostering public interest in the idea of a huge, naturally selected and unbridgeable gulf in the minds and behaviour patterns of males and females. But his prurient-sounding claims about the intimate details of female adornment reinforced his reputation for quirkiness, and his inclination to write several books a year led to diminishing returns. His work has been widely criticised for its premises and conclusions (as hard evidence emerged that we are less like apes than he assumed, and that culture helps to shape our minds) and for its claims about instinctual traits in men and women, most of which have fallen to dust when subjected to more rigorous analysis.[37]

## The rise of sociobiology

In 1975 the Alabama-raised ant specialist Edward Osborne Wilson, wrote *Sociobiology: The New Synthesis,*[38] which was embraced by the media[39] with sales that were remarkable for a 697-page tome[40]. This was followed by three more books on sociobiology in the late 1970s and early 1980s[41], which drew strong backing from evolutionary psychologists like Steven Pinker[42].

Wilson came from an evangelical Christian background[44] and even today calls himself a 'deist', which might, or might not, have something to do with the fervour of his characterisation of the relation between the mortal body and immortal DNA and with his portrayal of human beings as nothing more than 'adaption executors'[45] (redolent of Calvinist pre-destination). In common with religious and Marxist fundamentalists Wilson regularly expressed the urge to contain just about everything under one banner – in his case the crusading standard of evolutionary biology. He insisted that *all* human behaviour arose from encoded genetic inheritance – governed by the need to preserve genes and pass them on, and believed that our minds were shaped far more by genes than by culture and, in any event, culture was biologically based. Talking of our 'genetic leash'[46] he said free will was an illusion, and insisted in offering biological explanations for war, racism, tribalism, entrepreneurialism and, most notably, for the different status of men and women.

Like the Mars-Venus-type self-help authors who followed in his wake[47], he claimed male dominance was hard-wired and unalterable. Even with identical education and equal access to all professions, men would 'continue to play a disproportionate role in political life, business and science'. He talked of the social costs of women entering these professions, concluding that gender equality went against human nature and could only be obtained by extreme social repression.[48]

And like Morris, he insisted that male appreciation of a particular forms of female beauty was innate. At one conference he showed slides of beautiful women before explaining what research revealed about the evolution of male preferences. 'Certain characteristics of the face found to be attractive give considerably more beauty when they are exaggerated .... high cheek bones, thin jaw, large eyes and a slightly shorter rather than longer distance between mouth and chin and between nose and chin. Few women approach this standard of facial beauty, which should be the case were it just the normal example of natural selection. ... Instead we have a *supernormal* exaggeration of those features which are signs of youth, virginity and the prospect of a long reproductive period.'[49]

These claims are challenged in later chapters but, for now, it is worth mentioning that while Wilson's writing was highly influential in the United States – extending beyond the academic community – he was also seen as a divisive figure and was particularly controversial on US college campuses with regular accusations of sexism, ethnocentrism and racism flung his way[50], at least until he recalibrated and turned his attention to his environmental concerns. However, Wilson succeeded in bringing biology back into the picture when human nature was discussed. He might have over-egged that particular pudding, but his point that our genetic inheritance is at the root of our humanity can't be disputed, and he has since made important contributions to debates about group-based evolution and about bio-diversity.

## Back to Darwin...

In the 1930s the biologists JBS Haldane, Sewall Wright and RA Fisher began to marry Darwin and Wallace's theory of natural selection with the rapidly advancing knowledge of genetics, work that was later built on by the geneticist Theodosius Dobzhansky, the ornithologist Ernst Mayr, the palaeontologist George Gaylord Simpson and others. This became known as 'neo-Darwinian synthesis' and it prompted what today seems like a hugely significant advance and, at

the same time, a rather limited model of evolution – one that confined it to natural selection through a slow and gradual modification
of gene frequencies. This morphed into a kind of ultra-Darwinianism
where evolution was seen as a one-horse show, restricted to this grad-
ualist notion. It is an outdated view that the likes of Morris cling to,
as do the evolutionary psychologists and, as we shall see in the next
chapter, popular science writers like Richard Dawkins.

Over the last 50 years evolutionary theory has moved on in a way
it could be compared to science after Newton. It built on Newton's
principles until the arrival of Einstein's theory of relativity, which
turned some dimensions of Newtonian physics on their head. Since
then, very few scientists have described themselves as 'Newtonians'.
With evolutionary biology, however, it is different. As we've seen,
there is still a determined posse on the fringes of science who insist
they're Darwinians and don't take kindly to even the most cautionary
words of criticism of the great man or any notion that things might
have moved on. And yet evolutionary theory has developed a great
deal since Darwin – way beyond Mendel's discovery of genetics. Ever
since the 'convergence' there have been fresh departures in evolutionary theory in a number of branches, some discussed in later chapters.

Today, when we look back at Newton, we might smile and shake
our heads at some of his obsessions (alchemy, for example, or the Holy
Trinity). We should do the same with some of Darwin's ideas (his sexism and racism, for example) and equally with the ideas that flowed
from early Darwinism (like eugenics). It follows that we should also
receive the notions of the contemporary neo-Darwinians with less
indulgence – their inability to see beyond a 'selfish gene' version
of evolution, their assumption that every common form of human
behaviour is a direct genetic consequence of natural selection, and
the bad ideas that followed in the wake of these errors including the
implicit misogyny of so much that emerges from the faux-science of
evolutionary psychology.

# CHAPTER THREE

# GAY GENES AND MYTHOLOGICAL MEMES

When my first daughter was born in 1990 I became interested in the politics and science of gender, and so it was that I became aware of a fresh wave of genetic determinism that was making its mark with emphatic claims about how male and female minds were moulded by gender-specific genes. As a first-time father of a baby daughter, this stuff worried me no end, and I began to delve further. I soon discovered when I burrowed beyond the headlines by absorbing the books and papers written by these gender-obsessed hereditarians that their favourite oracle was none other than the already famous Richard Dawkins. He had taken his place as their high priest, creating a bridge between socio-biology and this new variant of genetic fundamentalism, evolutionary psychology[1].

Unlike some of his predecessors in sociobiology, Dawkins was refreshingly free from any whiff of racism and while he periodically took swipes at feminists, he differed from his EP followers in that he was not exactly consumed by this issue. But more than any other sociobiologist, his views were used to give EP its biological underpinning. They also helped liberate this line of evolutionary thought from its more dubious connotations – for a while, anyway[2]. So it's worth taking a closer look at the premises and conclusions reached by this erudite and combative ultra-Darwinian.

Dawkins, the son of Kenya-based colonial officials, went through an intense religious spell as a teenager[3], but unlike EO Wilson, later rejected religion with a comparable intensity (on reading a book on Darwin, who, incidentally, was no atheist[4]). Citing St Paul, he said, 'scales fell from my eyes'.[5] Still, it took a while for his vision to clear. He showed little academic potential at school and none for biology, but, with a long family history at Balliol College, he went up to Oxford although he managed only a second class (2:2) degree. Today, that would be not good enough to study further at any Russell Group university, let alone Oxbridge, but things were different in 1962 and he was permitted to continue with his studies after discovering his passion for the then-obscure zoological discipline of ethology (the study of animal behaviour), and went on to lecture at Berkeley before returning to Oxford.

His life changed at the age of 35 with publication of *The Selfish Gene*[6]. From then-on, Dawkins became known for his role in popularising science and atheism rather than for any of his own theorising (let alone field research), and in 1995 this was given formal recognition when he was appointed the Simonyi Professor for the Public Understanding of Science, where his brief for the next 13 years was to give publicity to any scientific issues of his choice. Nine more books and a steady stream of articles, television programmes, radio interviews followed.

## The Selfish Gene

*The Selfish Gene,* which elegantly, simply and controversially explains Dawkins's view of evolution, was a huge publishing success.[7] The conceptual approach came mainly from his mentor and hero, the eugenics-backing Oxford biologist W D Hamilton, whose disputed theories of kin selection Dawkins enthusiastically endorsed.[8] Dawkins paints a picture of 'selfish' genes battling to survive within host organisms that are controlled by these 'replicators'. The 'selfish gene' is a metaphor (he wasn't implying they had little minds of their own – and later acknowledged that he should have taken his publisher's advice by calling it 'The Immortal Gene') but sometimes he meshed the metaphorical and the literal. As he put it in the book's introduction: 'Let us try to *teach* generosity and altruism, because we are born selfish. Let us understand what our own selfish genes are up to, because we may then at least have the chance to upset their designs ...'[9]

Explaining human interaction, Dawkins made a curious shift, arguing that because of our intelligence, we're capable of acting against the interests of our genes. 'We have the power to defy the selfish genes or our birth and, if necessary, the selfish memes of our indoctrination,' he writes. 'We are built as gene machines and cultured as meme machines but we have the power to turn against our creators. We, alone on earth, can rebel against the tyranny of the selfish replicators.'[10] I'll return to 'memes' shortly, but, for now, it's worth mentioning that his view of genes bending our wills until we tell them not to was enthusiastically embraced by some his EP followers who baulked at the idea of being no more than passive ciphers. Steven Pinker, for one, insists he's his own man: 'If my genes don't like it, they can go jump in the lake.'[11]

## The selfless gene

For all its undoubted catchiness, the notion of this metaphorically selfish gene dragging its literally selfish recipients on its leash in its single-minded drive for self-reproduction is not widely accepted by academic biologists. A particularly vociferous critic is the Stanford biologist and evolutionary theorist, Paul Ehrlich, who ridiculed Dawkins's metaphor, writing they are 'no more selfish than this information-containing sentence'[12] and that it would make as much or as little sense to describe them as 'cooperative' (because they need to act in concert with each other and with other parts of the cells to allow the right proteins to be produced[13]). He added, however, that it would be 'much less misleading to avoid such analogies altogether'.[14]

It is sometimes said that the 'selfish gene' version of evolution focussing on the survival of the fittest, tends to be confined to Anglo-American theorists while some of the departures have come from other parts of the planet.[15] However, the bete noire of the Englishman was the American evolutionary theorist Steven Jay Gould. Unlike Dawkins, Gould soldiered on throughout his life with his field research (on snails), work that informed his key contribution to evolutionary science, punctuated equilibrium, a theory he developed in 1972 with Niles Eldredge. They argued against the conventional wisdom that evolution could be explained by the drip-drip-drip of minute changes produced generation after generation by natural selection, instead showing that fossil records typically displayed millions of years of stasis followed by brief bursts of rapid change and said this was the 'dominant pattern of evolutionary change in the history of living organisms'.[16] Punctuated equilibrium has become widely accepted in a range of biological disciplines, partly as a result of new evidence from fossil records.

## Evolution: more than natural selection

After *The Origin of Species* was published the first litter of Darwin's bulldogs went into battle and natural selection was elevated from the Darwin-Wallace view that it was evolution's most important element to being the *only* element. Darwin did not know about genes and was therefore ignorant of most non-adaptive forms of evolution, but he was provoked to a rare display of anger against those claiming that natural selection was its sole cause. In 1872 he wrote: 'As my conclusions have lately been much misrepresented, and it has been stated that I attribute modification of species exclusively to natural selection, I may be permitted to remark that ... I place in a most conspicuous position ... the following words: 'I am convinced that natural selection has been the main but not the exclusive means of modification.' This has been to no avail. Great is the power of steady misrepresentation.'[17]

This misrepresentation, however, has persisted. One of the criticisms of the gene-centric approach is that it focuses too narrowly on natural selection at the level of the organism. The counter-argument is summarised by Gould: '(S)election cannot suffice as a full explanation for many aspects of evolution: for other types and styles of causes become relevant, or even prevalent, in domains far above and far below the traditional Darwinian locus of the organism. These other causes are not, as the ultras often claim, the product of thinly veiled attempts to smuggle purpose back into biology. These additional principles are as directionless, non-teleological and materialistic as natural selection itself – but they operate differently from Darwin's central mechanism. In other words I agree with Darwin that natural selection is 'not the exclusive means of modification'.'[18]

Biologists like Ehrlich, Eldredge, Steven Rose, Richard Lewontin, Ian Tattersall and many others joined Gould in stressing the importance of other non-adaptive factors that influence evolution and that can change its course. One of these is chance events like the meteors that wiped out the dinosaurs, prompting the rise of mammals, or changes in weather patterns or global or regional temperature, or natural disasters like forest fires. Another is the gene flow that occurs when one population comes into contact with another.

But the most significant is neutral evolutionary change through genetic drift, which is a result of random sampling within a relatively isolated population or within a population bottleneck[19]. Genetic drift occurs when changes in the frequency of an allele (gene variant) lead to a particular trait taking root, and then spreading more widely. These changes may incur no evolutionary advantage and may even be detrimental (the Ashkenazi Jewish genetic diseases like Tai Sachs and Gaucher's are examples). The Japanese geneticist Motoo Kumura, now regarded as one of the most important evolutionary theorists of the 20th century, argued that *most* genetic change was neutral (ie. not the result of natural selection for advantageous traits) —making it a primary factor in evolution.[20]

Another departure is the discovery that some evolutionary changes may be prompted at the level of the group, kin group or species: DNA sequences become fixed and spread within a population because they benefit the group (with the group acting as the vehicle for selection). If one group is better at cooperating than another, it may be better at reproduction.[21] This idea, also known as Multilevel Selection Theory, was revived, much to Dawkins's dismay, by EO Wilson and his colleagues Elliot Sober and David Sloan Wilson[22], and has long been advocated by others working in the field, including Gould.

Incidentally, in his later years EO Wilson diverged from Dawkins on a number of questions, to the point where he was questioned about his 'Dawkins dispute' as if they came from different poles of the evolutionary debate. Wilson was dismissive of this notion. 'I have no dispute with Richard Dawkins,' he said. 'My disputes are with other scientists and Richard Dawkins is a journalist'. Journalists merely 'report' what scientists do, he said, adding that he had long 'abandoned' the selfish gene notion. 'There might be a few scientists who still hold to it, but they have largely been silenced,' he said.[23]

Calling Dawkins a 'journalist' might sound like a catty insult, but it's not entirely misplaced. Unlike his scientific critics, Dawkins has not done anything resembling field work for several decades and is not credited with any major research-based breakthroughs, and his work on biology tends to repeat the discoveries of other scientists in fresh, well-written and exciting ways.

## Evolutionary spandrels

When it comes to gender, the most important riposte to genetic determinism comes from another evolutionary departure, first highlighted by Gould and his Harvard colleague Richard Lewontin in 1979: the notion of non-adaptive side consequences of evolution they called exaptations or spandrels[24]. They argued that spandrels were key features of human evolution, particularly relating to cognition.

For example, the human brain reached its current size and complexity at least 100,000 years before reading and writing developed, so the mental machinery for these capacities must have originated as non-adaptive side consequences that were later co-opted.[25]

This kind of example is uncontroversial because not even the most fervent genetic determinist would suggest that *all* human behaviour is evolved. For instance, one of EP's founders, Donald Symons, described female organism as a spandrel, insisting it could not have arisen through natural selection[26]. But Gould and Lewontin went further, arguing that *most* human mental capacities were spandrels. Gould took the example of religion, which some determinists see as adaptive. He adopts Freud's idea that fear of death acts as a key inspiration for religious belief, and says it is impossible to argue the human brain evolved consciousness to teach people they must die. He concludes that awareness of death is a spandrel that, in turn, inspired religion.[27]

In the nearly four decades since Gould and Lewontin first came up with this notion, neurological research has added ballast to it, with its focus on the plasticity of the human brain. Neurologists and cognitive psychologists now accept that the human brain's development is perpetually sculpted by its environment – it adapts to its cultural context and is shaped by it.[28] This emphasis on spandrels, and on the inclination of the brain to be moulded by environmental context, opens the space for considerations of culture. It questions the assumption that just because behaviour is widespread or even universal (as some say, incorrectly, that religion is[29]) it has a genetic root. As Gould put it: 'In pure numbers, the spandrels overwhelm the adaptations.'[30] The implication is that there should be no inbuilt assumption that differences between men and women are 'hard-wired'.

## Determinism and the decoded human genome

This perspective received further support when the Human Genome Project completed its work in 2003 although early media reports went in the opposite direction – based on the false assumption that the decoding of the human genome would lead to the discovery of genes for every kind of behaviour.[31] Craig Venter, the American scientist who headed the private sector side of the Human Genome Project, was irritated by such claims: 'There are two fallacies to be avoided: determinism, the idea that all characteristics of a person are "hard-wired" by the genome; and reductionism, that now that the human sequence is completely known, it is just a matter of time before our understanding of gene functions and interactions will provide a complete causal description of human variability.'[32] Venter specifically cautioned against the idea of finding genes *for* any behaviour. 'In everyday language the talk is about a gene for this and a gene for that. We are now finding that that is rarely so. The number of genes that work in that way can almost be counted on your fingers, because we are just not hard-wired in that way.'[33]

One discovery of the Human Genome Project was that the human genome contained only around 24,000 genes – less than a quarter the anticipated number. Some scientists said this was evidence of the limitations of a gene-centric approach. Even before this discovery, Ehrlich was arguing that the human genome had nowhere near enough genes to control the connections in our brain that control behaviour. 'People don't have enough genes to programme all the behaviours some evolutionary psychologists, for example, believe genes control,' he said.[34] He points out that people have more than one trillion nerve cells, with anything up to 1,000 trillion synapses between them. 'Given that ratio it would be quite a trick for genes typically to control more than the most general aspects of human behaviour. Statements such as "Understanding the genetic roots of personality will help you find yourself and relate better to others" are ... frankly nonsensical.'[35]

Others elaborated on the implications of these discoveries – even those inclined towards determinism. For example, the cognitive psychologist Robert Plomin and the geneticist Oliver Davis wrote that 'for most complex traits and common disorders the genetic effects are much smaller than previously considered: The largest effects account for only 1% of the variance of quantitative traits.'[36]

These findings coincided with new discoveries on epigenetics, which concerns the way genes are expressed through environmental factors, affecting the cell 'memory' but not the DNA.[37] Several studies have shown that these effects on gene expression can be passed onto the next generation, and in some cases the third or fourth generation. It could relate to the food we eat, how much we eat, the quantity of alcohol we consume, the levels of stress we face and even our sexuality,[38] complicating the assessment of the weighting of nurture and nature by adding a third consideration: environmentally-prompted non-genetic biological inheritance.

## Male sex crime genes?

This, however, does not mean there's no genetic link to the way we behave as males and females – we'd expect at least some individual genetic influence, however small, on a wide range of behaviours. For instance, recent studies suggest there is some heritability involved in the propensity of certain men to take part in sexual crime. In 2015 a Swedish-based study[39] concluded that men who had fathers who'd been convicted of sexual crimes were nearly four times more likely than the rest of the male population to do the same, and if their brothers were convicted, five times.[40] However, there are three substantial antidotes to the 'sex crime gene' idea:

First, more than 98 percent of the men whose dads were convicted of sexual crimes did *not* commit sexual crimes themselves (in contrast to 99.5 percent of men in the general population). As the study's lead author, Niklas Langstrom, cautioned: 'Importantly, this does not imply that sons or brothers of sex offenders inevitably become offenders too.'[41].

Second, it's hard to determine whether this is a result of genetics or shared environment. On finding that half-brothers were less likely to follow fathers in committing sexual crimes than full brothers, the researchers went in search of a heritability figure. They estimated that about 58 percent of the *difference* was due to factors in the wider environment, two percent to shared environmental factors (including parental attitudes) and 40 percent to genetics, but that is no more than a guess, which may well be wrong. We'd expect men to be influenced by their fathers' aberrant behaviour and it is certainly possible that the Swedish full brothers had different relationships with their sex crime fathers than did the half-brothers.

Third, the researchers make no claim to having found genes linked to their findings. Langstrom acknowledged there was no evidence at all for a sex crime gene. One of his fellow authors, the Oxford University psychiatrist Seena Fazel, reiterated this point: 'We are definitely not saying that we have found a gene for sexual offending or anything of that kind.'[42] Instead, he speculated that there might be a constellation of genes that could have some link to factors such as 'emotional lability and aggression, pro-criminal thinking, deviant preferences and pre-occupation with sex'.[43]

Finally, the finding that more than 98 percent of the sons (and 97.5 percent of brothers) of sex criminals did not follow in their wake should give some indication of the relative weighting of environment and genetics in prompting sex crimes, although the headlines relating to this research did not reflect these nuances. *The Daily Telegraph's*, for example, was: 'Sex offending is written in DNA of some men, Oxford University finds.'[44] In fact, all that was found was that there could be a family link to sexual crimes (and the research was Swedish-based, not Oxford-based). The scientific website, *Phys Org*, came closest to hitting the mark with its headline, 'Sex crimes more common in certain families'.[45]

## The testosterone dividend

Rejecting genetic determinism also does not imply a 'blank slate' where we are born utterly malleable, devoid of in-built mental content, and where the only innate gender differences between males and females are those we can see, which is the accusation frequently fired at those who critique evolutionary psychology – a point already discussed in chapter one. However, even in apparently unambiguous cases of male-female difference, it is not often clear where nature ends and nurture begins.

For example, it would seem that in all societies, men tend to be more violent than women (not the same thing as saying that they are always more violent – some women are more violent than most men). One possible cause is that for evolutionary reasons that go back millions of years before we became human, males produce more testosterone than females. Babies in the womb who get a big burst of testosterone at six or seven weeks become boys; those who don't, become girls and there are further testosterone boosts in males as they grow up, particularly during puberty. This contributes to their size and strength advantage and can contribute to aggressive behaviour when this is encouraged by some environmental conditions.[46]

But it is more complicated because testosterone levels measured in saliva or blood do not directly reflect the quantities of testosterone acting on the brain.[47] Other factors come into play, including the quantity of receptors for testosterone in the brain, and there has also been research indicating that women may be neurologically more sensitive to testosterone, and therefore to changes in testosterone levels. So while a woman with high testosterone levels will not have as much testosterone as a man, her relatively higher level may have more of an impact on her brain, possibly encouraging assertive, aggressive or competitive behaviour[48].

And that's not the end of it because even if we accept the relation between testosterone levels and violence, rates of violence vary hugely from time to time, community to community and country to country. The fact that men in South Africa, Lesotho, Swaziland or the Democratic Republic of the Congo are far more likely to commit murder than men in Malawi, Senegal, Liberia and Sierra Leone or that

El Salvadoran, Honduran and Venezuelan men are massively more inclined to kill other people than Algerian, Kuwaiti or Indonesian men, or that American men are 13 times more likely to kill you than Japanese men[49], has everything do with culture and nothing to do with hormone levels. If we restrict ourselves to southern and eastern Africa, Lesotho's murder rate relative to population is 21 times that of Malawi, or in Oceania the murder rate in Papua New Guinea is 26 times that of French Polynesia or in South and Central America, El Salvador's rate is 33.5 times that of Chile.[50]

In other words even in such an apparently clear-cut case as male violence (based on the presumption that most of these murders were committed by men), the relationship between behaviour and hard-wiring is a complex one, more strongly influenced by culture than by biology.

## The invention of 'memes'

Let's return to Dawkins who throughout his years as a popular science writer has focussed on culture from a very different premise – as a by-product of natural selection, requiring its own gene-related terminology to convey the idea of a 'unit of cultural transmission, or a unit of imitation.'[51] He came up with the word 'meme' – a cultural entity analogous to a gene. As he put it in the 1989 edition of *The Selfish Gene*: 'We need a name for the new replicator, a noun that conveys the idea of a unit of cultural transmission, or a unit of *imitation*.'Mimeme' comes from a suitable Greek root, but I want a monosyllable that sounds a bit like 'gene'... '[52] Memes could consist of ideas, practices or symbols and could be passed on from through speech, writing, gestures, rituals, melodies, fashions, skills or any other form of behaviour that can be imitated. Other examples include tunes, ideas, catch-phrases, ways of making pots or building arches, popular songs, stiletto heels, the idea of God and Darwinism itself.[53] These 'evolve' over time – in a way comparable to evolution through natural selection.

Dawkins was attempting to combine evolution and culture under a united neo-Darwinian banner, which can seem an attractive idea – so much so that it soon took off. For example, in a gushing tribute to Dawkins, the novelist Ian McEwan, excitedly noted that *The Selfish Gene* 'spawned a huge literature, and eventually a new discipline – memetics'. And, indeed, it had – a stream of psychologists began to write on the subject[54]. Soon, Dawkins's followers were using 'genes' and 'memes' in the same sentence as if they were both as concrete as each other. The philosopher Daniel Dennett, dubbed by Gould as 'Dawkins's lapdog'[55], took this furthest: 'According to Darwin's dangerous idea,' he wrote, 'not only all your children and your children's children, but all your brainchildren and your brainchildren's brainchildren must grow from the common stock of Design elements, genes and memes... Life and all its glories are thus united under a single perspective.'[56]

There is one key problem with the analogy between genes and memes: one is real, the other made-up. And when you make up a word and invest it with meaning, it should, at least, have some relation to the thing or process it defines – in this case to cultural transmission. But culture and thought do not come in particles and do not 'evolve' in anything approximating the biological sense. If we wish to apply similes or metaphors to culture then we might choose waves or currents rather than gene-like units – and when analysing the motion of waves and currents, we tend not to focus on the water's molecular structure.[57] 'Memes', therefore, do not help people to understand the ways they act – instead, they obscure it.

## Dawkins and selection for 'gay genes'

And finally, for an apt illustration of the limitations of the 'selfish gene' approach to evolution, we have Richard Dawkins on the 'gay gene'. His starting error is one all-too-familiar among neo-Darwinians: the assumption that any form of human behaviour that is widespread (such as homosexuality) must be evolved, and in Dawkins's view, this implies it evolved through natural selection and that a 'gay gene' must therefore be implicated. His problem comes in explaining why it is that this 'gay gene' survived when we'd anticipate that it would not be selected for the simple reason that homosexuals tend to have rather fewer children than heterosexuals. In an unintentionally funny YouTube interview, he offered three ways around this conundrum, two of which sound more like self-parody than biology.[58]

First, there's his 'gay uncle' theory: back in the African savannah 'butch men' went a-hunting, leaving children in the care of women and 'gay uncles'.[59] Even if this were so it doesn't explain why there would be selection for the genes of the gay uncles – because gay uncles don't do much reproducing.

Unless. ... and here comes his second thought, which he calls his 'sneaky fucker theory'. This time the uncles are *secret bisexuals* who merely *pretend* to be gay. So, the 'butch males' go on the hunt, leaving children in the care of their supposedly gay uncles, who have some action on the side with the mums. 'Being gay would have been a pretty good certificate,' Dawkins suggests. 'Now if they were bisexual this would have been a false assumption. Being gay was a convincing way of lulling the suspicions of dominant males.'[60] This implies the 'sneaky fuckers' were passing on bisexual genes through dangerous liaisons, but, needless to say, there's no evidence for this and scant evidence that being gay or bisexual is directly inherited (gay dads do not sire more gay sons or daughters) while evidence for an indirect link through the maternal line has yet to be proved, so it is unlikely that more 'sneaky fucker' bi-sexual uncles would equate to more gay children. But perhaps more pertinently, we might query whether 'sneaky fucker' uncles existed outside of Dawkins's imagination.

Third, he comes up with what he calls his 'esoteric' theory, explaining that 'when we talk about a gene *for* something or other... it is a gene for that thing under the right environmental conditions.' In other words, the gay gene that 'manifests itself now in an urban environment in a homosexual tendency might, in a very different environment, out in the African plain, have shown itself in another way that is quite different.' Straying into the zone of Gould's evolutionary spandrels, he speculates that perhaps this could have been something like being good at animal tracking, 'so there was nothing to stop it getting passed on because it was good for something quite different in those days.'[61] Which doesn't explain why it wasn't selected out of the gene pool once it emerged in its specifically gay form, or once animal tracking was no longer required. It also does not explain why homosexual behaviour is not just a human phenomenon, but can be observed among a rich variety of other mammals, birds and even insects too.[62]

That's as far as Dawkins has thought on the subject, which is not very far at all. If he'd read further, he'd have discovered that none of his gay gene theories hold up, and the question of what makes some people homosexual is rather more complex than this comic book version of genetics would suggest. The decoding of the human genome revealed no evidence of a 'gay gene' – and while homosexuality might be partially heritable, it is not directly inherited. This was the thrust of a substantial Swedish study, involving 7,600 adult twins, which found that the prime influences on the sexuality of males were environmental (including, most significantly, the environment of the womb) and that environmental influences were even stronger with female sexuality.[63]

It is worth noting that even though twin studies have been legitimately criticised for *underestimating* environmental influences[64], the Swedish study and other research shows that a key physiologically-based environmental factor that might influence sexuality is the amount of testosterone received in utero. This can affect the development of the foetal brain, which, in turn, can have an impact on sexuality.[65] The main reasons for differences in levels of testosterone absorbed between gay and straight males are not genetic – instead they relate to other factors such as the mother's immune system, her intake of various drugs and stress levels.

Which is not to say there is no genetic contribution to male sexuality. Recent research has found several genetic markers that might be implicated, although it is not conclusive, suggesting that if there is indeed a genetic link, it involves a combination of genes[66], contradicting the view of a single 'gay gene' that emerged from Dean Hamer's much-hyped research in 1993[67] – and that there may also be epigenetic factors (a view enhanced by the fairly frequent cases of identical twins where one twin was gay and the other not).[68]

As with so many aspects of human behaviour, the relationship between biology and environment is complex when it comes to sexuality. There is substantial research suggesting that predispositions towards male homosexuality (whether genetic, epigenetic or relating to the environment of the womb) may be triggered, or not, by experiences with parents, siblings and peers in early childhood, which is when gender identity is fixed. In other words, even when there is a biological inclination, there sometimes needs to be an environmental nudge.

Putting all this together, it appears that male homosexuality has a number of possible causes, mostly relating to the environment of the womb. Even those possible genetic influences that have been identified would not have evolved through selection for 'gay uncles' or 'sneaky fuckers' but rather for reasons unrelated to sexuality. With female homosexuality, evidence of any genetic link is weaker and the primary factors appear to be environmental – again, including testosterone levels influenced by the environment of the womb.

It would therefore seem that Dawkins made two fundamental errors in trying to explain homosexuality. First, he presumed a single cause involving a single gene. Second, in trying to explain selection for this gene he embarked on a backward looking, savannah-searching quest that assumed a direct, functional link between environmental cause and genetic result.

## What's all this got to do with gender?

The 'gay gene' example is pertinent because it provides a useful reference for the theory and methodology behind the gender-related claims made by genetic determinists. The only difference is that while there is some evidence that genes play a secondary role in homosexuality, there is no evidence of a genetic contribution to many of the other gender-related claims that will be discussed in the chapters that follow. What this example illustrates is that the faulty biology of the gene-centric approach can lead to faulty conclusions about human behaviour.

Gould and Lewontin's notion of evolutionary spandrels – non-adaptive side consequences – provides the tools to better understand the relation between biology and culture. This is especially useful when it comes to the evolution of the human brain, which, in turn, relates to human behaviour and male and female behaviour specifically. Instead of assuming that the way my daughters behave as females, and the way I behave as a male, are direct products of gender-specific genes, it allows for a more interesting alternative: that it is contingent, falling more under the banner of culture than of biology. Put differently, it suggests a versatile, flexible, spandrel-filled brain rather than one where every behaviour form is 'hard-wired'.

The hope of genetic determinists was that the Human Genome Project would expand proof of biologically-based differences in the brains and therefore the minds of men and women beyond obvious examples like the implications of higher testosterone production among males or the menstrual cycles of women. But the project produced nothing of the sort because there are no genes that enable men to read maps upside down or to prefer blue or to be nasty to their stepchildren, nor are there genes that prompt women to multi-task, or to prefer pink or to wear lipstick, or even for behaviour that would nudge them in those directions. Instead, the results show the opposite: that when it comes to understanding the male mind and the female mind, it is more to the immediate environment, starting with the environment of the womb and then the family, and then to the wider cultural milieu, that we should look.

# CHAPTER FOUR
# MEN, WOMEN AND MONKEYS

I had a quirky, greedy, guilt-ridden, low IQ black Labrador called Pedro, the son of a gentle and somewhat smarter golden Labrador called Rosie who, however, lacked a conscience. She, in turn, was a companion to a swaggering Jack Russell terrier called James who had a pronounced Napoleonic complex. And this pair succeeded a fiercely loyal Alpha male Staffordshire bullterrier called Ben, who had a psychopathic urge to maul other dogs. So you get the picture: lots of dogs with human names and all of them ascribed human characteristics. For instance, ever since Rosie died there was a sadness in Pedro's eyes because he missed her when he thought about it.

The reality, of course, is that dog brains don't work anything like human brains. They don't think in words or categories or concepts or abstractions and don't have self-awareness or human perceptions and emotions and memories or even a concept of past and present, but sometimes I like to think they do, perhaps because I grew up watching films and cartoons about talking animals, or just because they share my domestic space and the ups and downs of my life, or because I lack the imagination to conceive of consciousness outside of human categories. I know all this but I continue to indulge in little bursts of innocent sentimentality where my dogs are concerned and happily pass this affliction on to my children.

We'd expect people who study animal behaviour for a living to avoid the sin of anthropomorphism. And by and large they do, even though it's hard to shake off entirely, because of the conceptual limitations prescribed by the relationship between thought and language. Instead, however, some fall into the opposite trap – by ascribing animal characteristics to humans.

Ever since Darwin's *Descent of Man* revealed the evolutionary link between humans and animals, biologists and psychologists have been exercised by the behaviour of mammals and what it might tell us about ourselves. This interest morphed in the 1930s into its own zoological discipline, known as ethology[1], but it was only in the 1960s that this branch of research entered into popular consciousness, largely through best-selling books by Desmond Morris, Robert Ardrey and Konrad Lorenz, which I have already discussed. In each case they told their readers that we humans were no different from other animals and, specifically, that we should look at chimpanzees to find the clues about how human males and human females behave at work, at play and, in particular, in the bedroom. Under the veneer of culture, we were still, essentially, naked apes with deeply primitive instincts. In some of their writing the level of sophistication, rigour and common sense was hardly higher than that of the tongue-in-cheek Bloodhound Gang pop song of a few years ago, which had the wonderfully daft chorus: 'You and me baby ain't nothing but mammals / Let's do it like they do on Discovery Channel'.

## Kin selection and kin altruism

But while the likes of Morris and Ardry were making millions with their best-sellers, a new wave of academic ethologist was focussing research on understanding more specific aspects of animal behaviour – in particular kin selection. This was the basis of their explanation for altruism, which, they argued, was more common with kin than with unrelated individuals. Their reason was that we evolve to favour those who share our genes.

This notion of kin-based altruism has since become one of the key articles of faith of evolutionary psychologists who often draw their underlying theory from Richard Dawkins, who borrowed it from his late hero, W D Hamilton, who developed algebraic theories related to survival of the fittest. Hamilton in turn drew from one of the pioneers of evolutionary synthesis, J B S Haldane who famously quipped: 'I would lay down my life for two brothers or eight cousins.'[2]

The underlying argument relates to the evolutionary imperative for animals to pass on their genes by favouring the reproductive success of those who share them, meaning that children are favoured over siblings who are favoured over first cousins and so-on. Also, children are favoured over parents because one's offspring have more chance of passing on genes. Kin selection is said to happen either through direct kin recognition (animals identify relatives by sight or smell) or through 'limited dispersal' where 'viscous' populations are closely related and dispersal is rare. With the latter it is indirect – a consequence of living within a closely related groups.

Hamilton devised a 'rule' that went like this: kin selection causes genes to increase in frequency when the genetic relatedness to the actor of a recipient, multiplied by the benefit to the recipient, is greater than the reproductive cost to the actor. He believed natural selection favoured genes that enhanced their bearers' ability to reproduce, but also genes that encouraged bearers to support the reproductive efforts of kin.[3] This suggests that the care a father gives to his biological children increases his potential for passing on his genes (because healthy and safe children are more likely to breed).

But what about altruism that goes beyond family? At first blush, this *non-kin*-based altruism would seem to create problems for the idea that we, like all animals, are innately selfish, but Richard Dawkins offers a way out. He starts at the family level, using Hamilton's argument that if two animals share the same genes they will be more inclined to protect each other in order to protect those genes – for example, an animal defending her cubs to allow for the survival of their genes. In this way, the 'selfish' gene prompts the unselfish action of its host. They go all out to protect and promote other animals containing alleles that are most closely related to themselves – so they will fight to the death to defend their son, daughter or sister, but less furiously for their cousin, and so on.

Dawkins, however, extends his idea of altruism to reach beyond the family, but only when applied to humans: first, through reciprocation (giving favours in the hope of receiving them back); second, through acquiring a reputation for generosity and kindness; third, through 'buying unfakeably authentic advertising' through conspicuous generosity. He says kin-based altruism evolved when we lived in roving bands and this encouraged the development of the other forms of altruism. 'By any or all four routes, genetic tendencies towards altruism would have been favoured in early humans,' he concludes.[4]

Elsewhere, he talks of the 'big brain solution' to this peculiarly human problem of non-kin, 'misfiring' altruism: 'When we lived in small hunter-gatherer bands, the rule of thumb, "Be nice to everybody you meet" would have automatically singled out kin (huntergather bands are mostly family groups) and it would automatically have singled out long-term acquaintances with whom reciprocal altruism relationships are likely to build up. Just as we have sexual pleasure because sex in the wild leads to reproduction, so we have altruism pleasure 'because altruism in the wild leads to kin survival and reciprocation. ... Now we live in large cities so the premise of altruism pleasure is violated. So the altruism rule of thumb (Be nice to everybody) now misfires. But, just as we still take pleasure in sex when it misfires, so we still take pleasure in being nice (and feel pain at others' distress) although it mostly nowadays misfires.'[5]

But this explanation of 'misfiring' non-kin altruism can only work if we accept the Hamiltonian premise of biologically-based kin altruism – that all animals, including people, are innately drawn to those with genes most closely related to their own. There have been several criticisms of this underlying theory, which are beyond the scope of this book.[6] However, as a flavour, one riposte came from the socio-biologist E O Wilson[7], whom we met in the previous two chapters. He once embraced Hamilton's notion of kin-based altruism, but later recognised it as a dead-end, calling it a 'very seductive' idea that 'doesn't tell us anything decisive about how altruism originated'.[8] He now believes that altruism evolved more through ecological circumstances than genetic influences. Using theories of group-based selection, he argues that it occurs not because animals share genetic ties through kinship but because altruistic acts became useful for the overall survival of the group.[9]

It is certainly true that people are culturally disposed to caring for their biological children and other relatives, and also for their adopted children, and that this cultural bias is reinforced minute-by-minute by the time they spend with their biological or adopted kin, but no genes or parts of the brain have been identified as being implicated in kin-based affection, family love or altruism and evidence that we favour our children or siblings or cousins over strangers is not evidence of biologically-based kin selection. Paul Ehrlich, the Stanford biologist quoted earlier, notes that there is no data that allows genes for altruism to be demonstrated or measured, '[a]nd it is likely that much of human altruism has not been programmed into our genomes by selection but is a result of characteristics of the human mind that evolved for other reasons'. He adds that it is determined 'primarily by cultural influences'.[10]

In social animals like humans the key factors in acts of kin-based altruism include shared developmental environment, familiarity and social bonding, rather than simple genetic relatedness.[11] The fact of someone being kin is not the key consideration in why, for example, they often choose to live near their relatives, or help them when they are in trouble and there is no evidence that dads who are unaware that their children have different biological fathers treat these children any worse than those who are genuinely their biological spawn. Rather, the key considerations relate to the bonds we develop through childhood, including the time spent with relations and also, crucially, the mores we absorb about putting family first. As Bruce Springsteen's Highway Patrolman put it, 'Man turns his back on his family, well he just ain't no good.'[12]

Yet the notion of genetically-prompted kin-based preference, and its resulting altruistic behaviour, is one of the shibboleths of evolutionary psychology. As we shall see in chapter 14, misplaced faith in the existence of a kin-selection mental module pops up over and over again and has been used to underpin some of the wilder claims about the behaviour of men and women (such as that men are innately drawn towards abusing step-children[13]), which continue to attract considerable publicity in the media.

### What we can't learn from animals

A criticism frequently levelled at neo-Darwinians is that they draw too bluntly on studies of animal behaviour to make points about human behaviour, assuming that because we are mammals, observations about mammal behaviour will apply to people, especially when it comes to behavioural differences between males and females. Studies of animal behaviour can be useful if you can show common behavioural zones between particular animals and people that can fruitfully be compared. But there are several problems with analysing how animals behave and then applying the conclusions to us:

first, you can choose which characteristics to highlight because no two breeds behave in precisely the same way;

second, the interpretation of animal behaviour is so often influenced by the eye of the beholder;

third, in studying animal behaviour the adapted (instinctual) elements are often very hard to distinguish from the learnt elements.

### Boy monkeys, girl monkeys, cars and pans

One example of an experiment using animals to make points about people involved vervet monkeys being given supposedly boyish, girlish and neutral toys. The idea was to see if gender-related toy preference among human children was hard-wired as a result of the male brain receiving higher doses of testosterone (the point being, that if it was also found in monkeys, well then ...).

The researchers gave the monkeys six toys, one at a time (and here comes the funny bit): a police car and ball (boyish), a doll and a pan (girlish) and a picture book and a stuffed dog (neutral). Anyone with an iota of common sense would recognise immediately that while the gender basis of the toys might be culturally recognisable to a *human* child, they would have no such significance for a monkey. As far as I know, male monkeys don't drive cop cars, and female monkeys don't use pans to whip up soufflés on the stove.

In any event, the results were less decisive than sometimes portrayed. The males spent about a third of their time with each group of toys. The females, on the other hand, spent longer with the doll and pan than with the car and ball, which, naturally, was the result subsequently given all the publicity. However, when the researchers divided their toys differently, by comparing the male and female monkeys' inclination to play with object toys (pan, ball, book, car) and with animate toys (doll and dog), they found no gender-related differences at all.[14]

Nevertheless, this paper was picked up by evolutionary psychologists as offering proof of innate gender-based differences among people. For example, this is what the doyen of EP, Steven Pinker, said about this study: 'Among baby vervet monkeys, the males even prefer to play with trucks and the females with other kinds of toys!'[15] Incidentally, he used it to build his case that male dominance in mathematics, science and engineering academia could be explained by biology

A few years later a different group of researchers had another bash, this time choosing rhesus monkeys. They used a design that seemed to eliminate some of these problems, by giving them just two types of toy at once: a wheeled toy and a cuddly toy. The results were the opposite of the vervet study: the female monkeys showed the same interest in both toys, but this time the male monkeys stood out, preferring the wheeled toys. This, however, was enough to allow the researchers to entitle their paper, 'Sex differences in rhesus monkey toy preference parallel those of children'.[16]

Putting these two studies together, and taking their claims at face value, we might conclude that male *vervet* monkeys are equally inclined towards boys' and girls' toys, but females prefer girls' toys, whereas female *rhesus* monkeys have no preference between male and female toys but the males prefer male toys. How very confusing! Or rather, how very confusing if you are intent on finding only hard-wired reasons for behaviour.

So what other reasons might there be for these differences? If we took the vervet study, why is it that female might prefer a pan to a car, whereas a male might rate them equally? Those who have reviewed this research have suggested various possibilities ranging from the colour of the pan (red), which, for other reasons, might appeal to female vervets, to the design of the study (they were given the items on different days, when, for other reasons, they might have been more or less playful).[17]

If we're intent on using monkeys to find out about humans, the more academic papers we peruse the more confusing it becomes. Studies of some troops of wild Japanese macaque monkeys show extensive male involvement in raising babies (carrying them, grooming them, and protecting them), while other groups show less male involvement or none. Likewise, studies of the Gibraltar troop shows males, including young adult males, are intensively involved in the care of the infants, but the Morocco macaque males, less so.[18]

Levels of testosterone do not appear to differ between the troops, which raises the tricky question of animal culture: different norms of male and female behaviour prevail in different troops and these get passed on, down the generations. Baby monkeys, like baby humans, develop their gender identity early and have a strong inclination to

fit into the gender roles they observe, which, for males might involve nurturing or it might involve standing off. What this also illustrates is that different animals and even different packs, pods, schools or troops of the same kind of animal, can produce wildly varying results, which relates to the pick-and-choose point made at the outset.

A wide variety of animals have been used to draw analogies with people – from ants via blackbirds to monkeys to great apes. Lions are a popular choice when it comes to the conventional wisdom of self-help books on gender. But which lions should we follow as human models – the stay-at-home males whose role in life is to protect the pride and spread his seed among the pick of the females? Or the out-to-work females, who do all the hunting? You could, instead, choose the here-today-gone-tomorrow cuckoos or how about the mate-for-life gibbons, siamangs, swans and Canada Geese (who are monogamous, with both parents protecting the eggs and raising the goslings), or the prairie voles, where the males and females contribute equally to the parenting?

## Chimps, bonobos and human nature

First at the table when it comes to analogies with humans are chimpanzees because they are our closest relative, sharing either 98.8 percent of our DNA or around 95 percent, depending on how it is calculated.[19] But which chimps? The common chimp is aggressive and omnivorous and their communities are dominated by large alpha males who have first pick of females in oestrus within their group. They sometimes kill other chimps, they like to eat monkeys, tearing them limb-from-limb before munching away, and they engage in violent battles with each other and with rival troops. The smaller bonobo chimps on the other hand are mainly fruit eaters (with a bit of small game thrown in for good measure). Their behaviour is markedly less aggressive and violent, and their society is sometimes described as egalitarian and matriarchal. They have sex regularly with both males and females, not solely for reproduction and not only when the females are in oestrus but, it would seem, as a way of mediating potential conflicts.[20] So which chimp can teach us more about human sexual behaviour? The glib answer would be to say neither – because we aren't chimps.

However, most of those who work with great apes would plumb for the less-studied bonobo when it comes to human analogy. For one thing, these forest-dwellers look a bit more like us – shorter arms compared with the common chimp, thinner bodies, smaller teeth and more bipedal (they often stand upright). They are rather fond of the missionary position for sex and the males also have longest penises in the ape world (again, more human-like than ape-like). They are far less inclined towards inter-group violence than their cousins – and are often seen grooming and copulating with other bonobo groups they encounter. They regularly use male-male and female-female genital contact to resolve tensions[21] and are the only animal, other than humans, who copulate all the time (for all other animals, copulation is periodic). When it comes to size dimorphism (the gap between males and females, which is one sign of the level of male dominance), the degree of difference among bonobos, at around 15 percent, is the lowest of all the great apes[22] (slightly less than among humans, in fact). What about intelligence? Well, it's an open question but there are some bonobo skills that have not been recorded among common chimps. For example, a study of wild bonobos suggested they left symbolic damage in vegetation as markers to show the direction of group travel.[23] In captivity, a bonobo called Kanzi, known for his communication skills, also independently learnt to make flake tools by bashing one rock against another. He would use these to cut a cord that held a food box shut and to slice through a plastic sheet over the top of a drum. He then used his rock-bashing skills for hard-hammer percussion.[24]

So, if we insist on using simian models to tell us something about human behaviour, then the peace-loving, sex-loving bonobo would seem a more realistic candidate than the war-like common chimp. But really, that small DNA difference makes a huge difference when it comes to brains and minds. Even the most advanced bonobo lacks the tool-making skills of our earliest hominid ancestors. They can learn many words but their signs and grunts and squeaks have no suggestion of syntax and they have nothing comparable to our capacity for invention, imagination, self-consciousness and empathy. Human nature and chimp nature or bonobo nature are not alike.

## Chimp and blackbird cuckolds

The eye-of-the-beholder problem refers to the question of perception and bias on the part of researchers. As we saw with the vervet research, looked at in one way, there seemed to be sex differences in behaviour, but from another angle, there were none. In the days when field studies were all conducted by men, the focus was frequently on the role of the male and on sexual differences but as is shown by Anne Fausto-Sterling, a medical scientist from Brown University, the influx of women into this area shifted perceptions.[25]

Studies of baboons, which had previously focussed on the role of the alpha male, revealed that female kin groups were responsible for mediating and controlling their social lives.[26] Studies of blackbirds had once shown that the female was protected from predators by the vigilant male, while she laid eggs, kept nest, and gathered grubs. More recent DNA research, however, revealed a different picture: blackbird chicks in a particular nest all had the same mum – but several dads. In other words, while mum was home she was receiving gentleman callers.[27]

There were similar findings about chimps in the wild. It was once thought that the dominant males did most the mating and sired all the offspring, but a 1997 study suggested otherwise. DNA analysis revealed that seven of the 13 infants in the main group were not even fathered by males from within this group, even though males from other groups had not been spotted. The researchers concluded that the females were sneaking off for many of their copulations, without the main group males being any the wiser. They also found that of the four males who had achieved alpha status during their study period, two fathered no offspring.[28]

## The trouble with instinct

The third problem involves the concept of 'instinct', which means different things to different people, and is seldom used consistently (so when neo-Darwinians describe particular examples of human male or female behaviour as instinctual it is not clear which version of this amorphous term they are using.[29]) There is no dispute that some elements of animal behaviour emerge without learning (birds build nests, spiders spin webs, warblers who fly south in the summer want to do so even if reared in cages), but much of what is regarded as instinctual emerges from a complex relationship between the organism and its environment, which allows learning to take place. One of the world's leading ethologists, Cambridge University's Patrick Bateson, stresses that behaviour can't be neatly divided into two distinct types: learned and instinctive, and that apparently unlearned behaviour can subsequently be modified by learning after first use.[30] For example, newly hatched duck chicks get better at pecking their parents' bills with practice, birds and mammals of prey get better at hunting.[31]

On top of this, there are many examples of animal behaviour from the 'smarter' mammals and birds that fall outside of any definition of instinct – the kind of animal culture already discussed regarding the different troops of macaques. Studies among great apes, monkeys, elephants, dolphins, whales, parrots, crows, ravens and others have shown a considerable capacity for learnt behaviour, with the result that different groups behave differently. For example, studies of bottlenose dolphins and whales have found that groups tend to be clustered according to vocal dialects (such as whale songs), and that there are also differences in the way they forage and even their patterns of migration.[32] This occurs through imitation and social learning – with some members of the group able to manage the new skills and others not.[33]

This element of animal culture has been most observed among chimps and bonobos. For example, different groups of chimps in Africa have distinctly different ways of using tools, playing and communicating[34] – and a long-term study of chimps living in the Budongo Forest in Uganda showed them learning tool-making skills from each other.[35] The research team noted there were 39 distinct chimp behaviours thought to be culturally acquired. Until then this had been hard to determine in the wild but this changed when they observed one chimp using a new 'drinking vessel' out of sponge, made from moss. Another chimp copied and its use soon spread within this community alone. 'Researchers have been fascinated for decades by the difference in behaviour between chimpanzee communities,' said one of the team, Catherine Hobaiter, from the University of St Andrews. 'Some use tools, some don't, some use different tools for the same job. These behaviours have been described as 'cultural', which in human terms would mean they spread when one individual learns from another.'[36]

## Non-kin chimp altruism

Another challenge to Dawkins's idea of 'misfiring' altruism comes from recent developments in the studies of apes, which suggest that non-kin altruistic behaviour is not a uniquely human attribute (and therefore goes millions of years further back in the evolutionary cycle than the Dawkins view allows) – and also that its expression is culturally contingent.

Research by Felix Warneken at Leipzig's Max Planck Institute found evidence of altruistic behaviour (without hope of reward) towards non-related chimps and towards people. They found that out of a group of 18 semi-wild, unrelated chimps, 12 went to considerable lengths to help an unfamiliar human who was struggling to reach a stick. They did this for no reward, even when it required them to scale an eight foot high ropeway. Warneken said this was the first evidence of chimpanzees helping somebody they didn't know. They have also found evidence of chimps helping other, unrelated, chimps without hope of reward. For example, they taught the chimps to use a remote mechanism to unchain a door. When they saw an unrelated chimp struggling, they went to help him. They did this more frequently than when the other chimp was not trying to enter.[37]

The primatologist Frans de Waal mentions similar observations (young chimps helping an unrelated arthritic older female chimp to climb a frame; an adult male bonobo alerting zookeepers to the drowning of two young, unrelated bonobos), and as he puts it, 'Animals don't know much about genetic kinship or future return favours.'[38] De Waal challenges the much-publicised views on this subject of the evolutionary psychologist Jonathan Haidt who adopted a gene-centric approach to disgust, altruism and morality. Haidt said these evolved in humans through natural selection to suppress selfishness but De Waal points to the empathy and altruism shown by animals who have no 'moral' systems and, like Wilson, uses group-based evolutionary theory to explain it. 'For me, the moral system is the one that resolves the tension between individual and group interest in a way that seems best for most members of the group, hence promoting a give and take,' he said.[39]

This explanation takes the development of morality away from the exclusive terrain of natural selection and into the overlapping terrain of culture. And there is even more recent ammunition to strengthen this view. Studies of chimps in the *wild* show less unambiguous evidence of unrelated subjects helping each other. Warneken's explanation relates to the environment: 'They were in a completely different mindset,' he said, referring to their apparent lack of altruism in the wild. They were so concerned about finding food that 'they didn't appreciate that others needed help'[40].

De Waal agrees, arguing that chimps and bonobos show spontaneous altruism more readily when the constraints of the wild are removed.[41] In other words, simian nature is not set in stone: environment affects culture which, in turn, affects behaviour. For Dawkins, altruism is uniquely human, rooted in kinship, and only 'misfires' because of our human intelligence and because we no longer live in societies where kinship is at the core. The chimp studies suggest a different conclusion: that this capacity for altruism is not uniquely human and therefore goes back far further in the evolutionary chain, and that it is culturally contingent.

There is certainly persuasive evidence that cultural contingency with regard to altruism also applies to humans. One example comes from studies of Romanian orphans cut off from human contact during their early years of life. The brains of those orphans who were most isolated and who were abused for the longest period showed unusual developmental patterns[42], affecting, among other things, their capacity to love and respond to love and affection.[43] There is also psychological research on people displaying 'Narcissistic Personality Disorder' '(and related 'Borderline Personality Disorders') showing a possible link with early childhood chaos, abuse and neglect. So it would seem that narcissism, like altruism, is simply one possibility in the human range, at least partly contingent on the way we are raised and on environmental conditions we face in the early years of life.

The point is that a great deal of what is said to be 'hard-wired' or 'instinctual' in the way men and women behave– from territorial imperatives to altruism, from hip-waist preferences among men to 'retail therapy' among women – is nothing of the sort. And the same could be said of other examples of human behaviour, many falling into Mars and Venus categories. These are frequently bolstered by reference to the behaviour of non-human animals – which makes no more sense than my sentimental tendency to smother my dog, Pedro, with a doggy version of my own thoughts, categories and emotions.

# CHAPTER FIVE

# PENIS ENVY AND THE SOLAR PHALLUS MAN

For just about as long as men have been writing, they've been giving each other instructions on how to treat women, and they've been giving women instructions on how they should behave. But the origins of separate spheres for men and women, and of female subservience, go back far further, although just how far and in which direction, we can't be sure. We know very little about the way hunter-gatherer groups organised their lives in the Stone Age, and next to nothing about the nuances of the sexual division of labour that must have existed, so we have to tread very carefully in making any assumptions about how it might have worked way back when (a favourite parlour game for evolutionary psychologists).

Using contemporary hunter-gatherer tribes as proxies proves very little – first, because of the huge variety in their cultural forms, and second, because they don't represent cultural cul de sacs. Their lifestyles are not static – they change over time, albeit more gradually than communities in agricultural and industrial societies. So we can't assume that the way they live now has much relation to the way their ancestors lived tens of thousands of years ago. Population pressures, attacks, and competition from other tribes, migration, accumulated innovations, the influence of other communities and civilisations, loss of territory, natural disasters and climate change can all have a huge impact on the way people live, including hunter-gatherers. We would make very different assumptions about the lifestyles of the earliest humans if we assumed they were hunting game in the savannah than if we assumed they lived primarily off fish at seaside caves or at rivers and creeks (which, in fact, was the case with some of the earliest modern humans we know most about[1]). Either way, it is folly to assume today's hunter-gatherers live the same way that hunter-gatherers (and fisher-gatherers) did tens or hundreds of thousands of years ago.

The best we can say is that if we look at some of the older hunter-gatherer tribes in Africa, the sexual division of labour and authority is far less absolute than evolutionary psychologists would have us believe, and the assumption that hunter-gatherer men are invariably promiscuous hunters and their women are homemaking gatherers, also does not fit the evidence. For example, as will be discussed in more detail in chapter 14, the women of the Aka pigmy tribe take part in hunting, even when pregnant, and the men play a major role in nurturing babies and children. Among the San (Bushmen) of southern Africa, at least when they were still able to pursue a traditional lifestyle, women were described by one anthropological researcher as being 'relatively equal'[2] and having high social status. They could be leaders of clan groups and at times they also took part in hunting (and the men in gathering).[3] The San are said to have the oldest continuous culture in the world, so we could tentatively suggest that aspects of their traditional way of life *might* have resembled that of *some* Stone Age Africans, but we can take it no further. What we can say with confidence is that while there is no evidence of any matriarchal societies in pre-history, the Flintstones version of life on the Pleistocene savannah favoured by evolutionary psychologists represents a clear case of imposing contemporary mores on pre-historical people.

## Agriculture and the origins of patriarchy

The biological basis of the division of labour within hunter-gatherer societies came from two physical differences between males and females. First, men are, on average, are bigger and stronger than women and therefore did most of the hunting, or at least the big game hunting, and most of the fighting against rival groups; second, periodic nine month pregnancies followed by long periods of breast-feeding meant that, on average, women played a bigger role in child-rearing.

However, the origins of the forms of patriarchy we know today are relatively recent and lie within the transition from hunter-gatherer lifestyles to agricultural lifestyles, which started around 10,000 years ago (or about 190,000 years after our lot first emerged with brains like ours[4]). Over time, as agricultural communities led to the formation of villages and, eventually to towns and cities, social structures became more stratified. The ownership of property and domestic animals became synonymous with wealth and power, and the idea that women were part of this property system was consolidated. In most of these agricultural societies, ownership of property was passed on through the male line – and 'ownership' of women also passed from father to husband. In this sense, at least, women became a commodity, and we still see a residue of this in some of our customs (for example, the father 'giving away' the bride to the husband as part of traditional western wedding ceremonies).

However, just as no two hunter-gatherer societies are identical, so there were huge differences between ancient agricultural societies. For example, according to Herodotus the position of Egyptian women was very different from that of Greek women. Unlike their more subservient Greek counterparts, wealthier Egyptian women sat on local tribunals, took part in property transactions and were permitted to witness legal documents and more generally, women attended markets and were allowed to trade.[5] And if we can draw any wider significance from the power wielded by the female pharaoh Hatshepsut (who ruled for 15 years and was known as a prolific builder), or from that of the Greek-speaking Cleopatra (69BC to 30 BC) as the last Egyptian pharaoh, there seemed to be acceptance of female leaders.[6] Another example would be the apparent popularity of the Syrian queen, Zenobia after conquering Egypt from the Romans in 269 AD to declare herself Queen of Egypt. She was known as the 'Warrior Queen' and is said to have led her army on horseback while sometimes walking several miles with her foot soldiers.[7] Likewise, according to the Greek historian Strabo, the Nubian archers were led by a one-eyed warrior queen when they repelled the invading Romans in 24BC.[8]

And the position of what we now call Celtic women in England differed significantly from that of Roman woman, which was one of the underlying reasons for Boudica's revolt against the Romans in 61 AD. According to Roman historians, Boudica's husband, the ruler of the Iceni tribe, left his property to his daughters, but under Roman law female property ownership was forbidden. When Boudica objected, the Romans flogged her, raped her daughters, annexed her kingdom and sold much of her family into slavery, after which Boudica, who, incidentally, was not the only female Celtic leader of her time[9], led 100,000 warriors, who probably included women[10], against the Romans, sacking Camulodunum (Colchester), burning Londinium (London) and Verulanium (St Albans) to the ground and killing at least 70,000 men, women and children before being defeated.

But in most ancient agriculturally-based societies the position of women was more emphatically subservient and they were excluded from most aspects of public life including politics, the military and property ownership – largely confined to the domestic sphere and to certain categories of labour.

## Patriarchy, 'sacred texts' and fairy tales

When we look at contemporary misogyny our critical gaze often focuses on cultural sources such as the way women are depicted and judged as objects of desire in advertising and other media and the ubiquity of pornography, much of which depicts women as receptacles for male fantasy and fetish. But the roots of patriarchy go far deeper – into the realm of the ideas, ancient and modern, that form of the glue of our culture.

For example, male dominance is reflected in the texts of almost all religions – particularly, but by no means only, the Abrahamic religions[11], which continue to have an over-developed impact on the position of women in contemporary society, most notably among their conservative and fundamentalist advocates for whom opposition to women's advancement is a major part of the raison d'etre – with the various Islamist strands taking this significantly further than any of the others.

How the subservience of women in ancient agricultural societies found its way into various scriptures, and how this rippled and reverberated down the centuries, is way beyond the ambit of this book, but it goes without saying that the historical and contemporary impact of these 'sacred texts' has been a significant factor in moulding and entrenching perceptions that men and women have about each other's roles in life. In the Judeo-Christian tradition, this starts at the very beginning, with the Adam and Eve story (which also appears in different tones in Islam and the Bahai'i religion). After Eve succumbs to the evil serpent's temptation, eating the forbidden fruit and persuading Adam to do the same, God passes sentence: 'To the woman he said: "I will greatly increase your labour pains; with pain you will give birth to children. You will want to control your husband but he will dominate you." '[12] This version of the creation story was probably written nearly 3,000 years ago[13] and yet its influence persists.

When you are raised, as I was, with the notion of your creator as a man, of the first woman being a product of the first man's spare rib and the first woman being a temptress who led the man astray, of the messiah and all the prophets and priests and disciples being men, and of a natural domestic hierarchy ordained by the creator – or when you thank God 'for not having made me a woman'[14] or you read that 'men are guardians over women'[15] or that women should not be allowed to 'teach or exercise authority over a man, but to remain quiet'[16], or when your prophet is quoted as saying: 'If I were to allow prostration to anyone other than the One God, I would have directed women to prostrate to their husbands'[17] – well, this kind of instruction is likely to have some impact on self-perception, quite aside from the more specific instructions and injunctions in the Torah, Bible and Qur'an about how men and women should worship, behave and dress. Certainly if we were to examine the impact of these scriptures over the millennia, it would be hard to dispute the contention that the supposed divine authority of such views on men and women, as reflected in chapter and verse, has been used to impose patriarchy.

And this is reinforced by other mythological stories we inherit and pass on, including the fairy tales we read, or which are read to us, with their 'ladies' who are either pretty and docile, or plain wicked. The virtuous ones go through necessary trials to get their reward of the robust, active husband – in the Grimm brothers' tales, Snow White's ribs crack when she is squashed into her corset; Cinderella gets her man after a life of subservience because her desirably tiny feet can fit into the glass slippers. But those who step out of line are sentenced to grizzly deaths, like Hans Christian Andersen's peasant girl Karen in The Red Shoes, who goes against the instructions of the rich old woman, gives vent to her vanity and buys the red shoes – and as soon as she puts them on, they won't stop dancing. Eventually she persuades a woodman to chop off her feet with the shoes on, and then she dies. The end

But if we want to understand how modern men and women perceive their roles in life and their relation with each other and towards their children, it would also be worth looking at the mythology of more contemporary prophets and their sacred texts, and the way they prod and tweak and guide and sometimes govern our behaviour. Here, the founders of modern psychology can take a bow – and, in particular, Sigmund Freud and Carl Jung.

## Freud: penis envy and the Oedipus complex

Freud was determined that his perceptions on the unconscious should enjoy the status of a science, as was Jung (who somehow managed to combine this with his belief in supernatural mysticism). In this sense, they were no different from so many others working in what are inappropriately called the 'social sciences'. Karl Marx, for example, gave birth to what was dubbed 'scientific socialism' and his followers considered his 'historical materialist' theories to be new science. That tradition continues today with everyone from economists to evolutionary psychologists claiming the scientific mantle for theories that relate more to understanding human thought and behaviour than to the potentially provable stuff of scientific inquiry[18]. But in addition to posing as scientists when it suited them, the men who founded the various schools of psychology – not just Freud and Jung, but others like Lacan who followed – also took on the self-promoted status as leaders of cults, with followers fervently devoted to their demi-god gurus, fiercely defending their legacies and fighting off critics or those who strayed even a little bit from the doctrinal purity of the hallowed texts, giving rise to what, in a different context, Freud called 'the narcissism of small differences'.[19]

But for anyone well beyond the fold, the writings of the founders of various schools of psychology might reasonably be considered as no more than ideas – some good, some silly but all representing a very different form of knowledge than the discoveries of scientists. The existence of atoms and quarks and gravity and DNA molecules and genomes can be demonstrated in experiments in the laboratory or in the field, which means, like any genuinely scientific theory, they must also be potentially falsifiable. But the putative existence of, say, the id, the ego and the super ego, cannot be tested in this way. At best they are words that denote concepts that have some bearing on reality; at worst they have no relation to reality. In other words, the faith their founders shared in the absolute truth of their 'discoveries' does not make them 'scientific' and the no less fervent faith of so many of their disciples does not make them true. Freud and his followers would have done well to reflect on his wise words of advice when writing about the mythology of others: '[W]e will call a belief an illusion when a wish-fulfilment is a prominent factor in its motivation, and in doing so we disregard its relations to reality, just as the illusion itself sets no store by verification.'[20]

Yet the ubiquity of Freud's ideas has had a profound impact on the way many people regard themselves as males and females. Over the last century his theories have entered the marrow of a substantial section of at least Western middle class consciousness, and like Biblical texts, they channel and reinforce deep-routed cultural perceptions. His theories are all too often taken as facts, rather than what they really should be: metaphors used to describe patterns of behaviour he observed, and which he often incorrectly assumed to be universal and innate. It is worth making the point that the evidence for most of these ideas was gleaned largely from treating a small sample of supposedly neurotic Viennese women and their children, and this research was superimposed on his own Victorian pre-conceptions, which included heavy doses of Mars and Venus prejudice about the very different ways the minds of men and women worked (for example, that men were rational, unemotional creatures and women were emotional, irrational creatures).

Two core, interconnected Freudian ideas have raised the most concern among feminist psychologists and social theorists: the Oedipus complex and penis envy. To give a very brief and no doubt inadequate summary, this package involves the notion that boys become sexually fixated on their mums (and want to kill their dads) during their 'phallic stage'. This prompts a 'castration anxiety' where they develop fears of their penises being cut off by their fathers. The successful resolution of this complex involves boys identifying with their fathers. Its unsuccessful resolution leads to homosexuality, paedophilia and neuroses.

Girls in their phallic phase want to possess their mothers and therefore develop 'penis envy', but this is then redirected towards their fathers, which allows the girl to progress to normal, hetero-sexual development, concluded when she has a child of her own (a substitute for her missing penis). Freudian theory suggests this is more intense than the process with boys and could result in a woman becoming submissive and insecure, or, alternatively, if unresolved, it could lead to a woman wanting to dominate men.

The implications of these views for the supposed intellectual inferiority of women were spelt out in a paper written by Freud in 1925, entitled 'Some Psychological Consequences of the Anatomical Distinction Between the Sexes'. He notes that when a girl becomes aware of the 'wound' to her narcissism (a product of the knowledge that she is a castrated male who will never obtain a penis), 'she develops like a scar, a sense of inferiority'. At first she takes this punishment as personal before realising that it is a universal condition, after which 'she begins to share the contempt felt by men for a sex which is the lesser in so important a respect ... .'[21]

Freud goes on to say that the effects of this penis envy may go deep into the female psyche: 'I cannot evade the notion ... that for a woman the level of what is ethically normal is so different than it is for men. Their superego is never so inexorable, so impersonal, so independent of its emotional origins as we require it to be in men. Character traits which critics of every epoch have brought up against women – that they show less sense of justice than men, that they are less ready to submit to the great exigencies of life, that they are more often influenced in their judgements by feelings of affection or hostility – all these would be amply accounted for by the modifications in the formation of their super-ego.' He closes the deal with a warning against the feminism of his era: 'We must not allow ourselves to be deflected from such conclusions by the denials of the feminists who are anxious to force us to regard the two sexes as completely equal in position or worth ...'.[22]

When I first dipped my toes into Freud's ideas, studying psychology at university, they struck me as utterly bizarre. 'Surely, he can't really have believed all this, literally?' I asked friends who were more advanced in Freudian studies. 'Well,' I was assured by one neo-Freudian, 'You have to bear in mind that he was forming his ideas a long time ago, so the language might seem sexist to our sensibilities but the general principles apply.'

But do they really? For example, are the mother-son and father-daughter relationships inevitably as sexually charged as Freud suggested? When I read beyond my undergraduate reading lists, I found that subsequent studies suggested that the Oedipus, negative Oedipus and castration complexes were not as culturally universal as Freud had claimed. What he came across from Victorian mothers and nurse maids, who might have been horrified about their children masturbating, perhaps threatening to cut off their boys' penises if it continued, does not necessarily apply in cultures where sexuality was less taboo than the Vienna of more than a century ago. When re-examined in the light of what we know about men and women today, his views on their profoundly different mental and emotional capacities of suggest that he was falling into that oh-so-familiar failing of social theorists – of assuming the transitory world they observe is natural and normal and universal and shaping their ideas to fit it. His notion of the relation between his Oedipus complex and his Penis Envy and the supposedly innate rationality and emotional distance of men and innate irrationality and emotionality of women spring from this fundamental ontological error.

It is worth adding that Freud (and Jung) were both 'recapitulationists' who followed Ernst Haeckel's fantastical idea that the evolutionary history could be 'read' directly from the embryological development of 'higher forms' – in other words, each individual, as he or she grows up, passes through the stages representing the adult ancestral forms in their order of evolution. So, for example, the gill-like slits of a newly conceived human embryo were thought to represent an ancestral adult fish, and the embryo's temporary tail, its mammal ancestor's tail.[23] Freud used recapitulationist ideas when coming up with his notion of the Oedipus complex, arguing in his book *Totem and Taboo* that the urge of boys to kill their fathers must reflect real parricide once upon a time – that ancestral sons must have killed their fathers to secure the favours of women.[24]

Evolutionary biologists have long-since dismissed the notion of recapitulation, while anthropologists have long warned against the habit of assuming the customs and cultures of our own worlds are universal, but I don't want to leave the impression that I am dismissing all the foundations of 20th century psychology. Querying the universality of the Oedipus complex and penis envy and suggesting they are based on rocky biological and empirical ground, does not necessarily imply a rejection the entire rubric of Freudian theory. Rather, I would suggest that the best way to treat Freud is how we might treat any other social theorist from a century ago: with a sceptical interest and an eclectic sensibility. We might for instance, accept that the spread of his ideas helped us all to extend our inner reach, and we might even embrace some of his 'discoveries' about the unconscious and about the significance of sexuality, and his explanation of religion, and some of his ideas about psychoanalysis, while rejecting many others.

## Chodorow: learnt gender identity

One of the critiques of Oedipus complex theory that most appealed to me when I began to read beyond Freud came more of less from the inside – from the Berkeley psychoanalyst and clinical psychology professor, Nancy Chodorow, who has written several books on psychoanalytic theory and gender. Freud believed gender roles were routed in nature and that the different responses of boys and girls to the phallic stage was universal – and in this way the natural became cultural. Chodorow, in contrast, believes these roles are socially constructed from the start, and culturally contingent.

As soon as boys and girls become aware of their masculinity and femininity, which, she says, happens earlier than Freud realised, they begin to identify with the parent of their own sex. Most boys, she says, develop their masculine gender identification without the same kind of personal relationship they have with their mothers because their working dads are more distanced figures, so they begin to learn to be male without a continuously available male role model.[25] This identification is therefore less intensely personal than a girl's constantly mediated identification with her mother.

Chodorow believes that boys resolve their Oedipus complex by rejecting the feminine world and learning to be masculine more consciously than girls learn to be feminine – and this happens at an earlier stage than with girls. One result is that their ego boundaries are often more firm than those of girls.[26] Put differently, most girls come to think of themselves in relation to others (the ever-present mother) while most boys perceive themselves as unconnected individuals (the often-absent father).

According to Chodorow, the continual close identification of girls with their mothers may also mean that their inner lives are more intense than men's, with the result that they may seem to be more empathetic and personally engaged than males (although, as will be shown in later chapters, the actual gap between the ability of men and women to display empathy and to 'read' other people's emotions is miniscule and perhaps non-existent)[27]. For males, on the other hand, the experience of separation from the mother without the same kind of intense relationship with the father, can lead to them wanting to deny their need for love and ultimately to become intolerant of those who express a need for love.[28]

But Chodorow presents an important exception: she insists this would not be so if fathers were more intensely involved in nurturing their children. In other words, the greater inclination towards emotional engagement shown by many girls and women, and the emotional disengagement displayed by many boys and men, is a product of nurture and not, as Freud believed, of nature. And nurture is a good deal easier to change than nature.

When I look at this now, I still find it an attractive and intellectually intriguing idea, but I wonder if it might be pushing things too far in the Freudian direction, and whether it would be better to abandon the Oedipus notion altogether and embrace a more simple, non-biological explanation for the greater emotional and social engagement shown by girls and women. There are numerous studies showing that parents treat baby girls differently from baby boys, even when they are trying their best to treat them equally. For example, a 2006 study of mothers' speech and play patterns with babies at six, nine and 14-months-old, showed that they interacted and talked to girls more than boys, even though the boys were equally responsive their mothers' speech and equally eager to remain at their side.[29] There has also been research showing that mothers react more to changes in facial expressions of happiness in unfamiliar six-month-olds when the baby was labelled a girl than when the baby was labelled a boy.[30] What these studies suggest is that from very early childhood girls are being conditioned into a more intense and consistent level of emotional engagement and social interaction than boys.

If we take the Oedipus concept too literally, whether in the innate version of Freud or the nurture version of Chodorow, it would raise uncomfortable implications for *Silas Marner* girls raised only by their dads, or for all those boys raised by single mums, or, for that matter, for the girl children of gay male couples or boy children of lesbian couples, especially when these children don't have nurturing role models of their own sex in their early years. You would expect that such children would, necessarily, end up thoroughly confused and profoundly damaged as a direct result, and yet I have not come across any studies that reliably confirm this. And although I am aware that anecdotal evidence counts for nothing, the many children of single and gay parents I've come across over the past 35 years or so seem to come in more or less the same range as those of heterosexual couples – some seemingly happy and well-adjusted; others less so.

An interesting caveat in this regard, drawn from a 2013 University of Bristol study of 5 631 children, is that the absence of a father in early childhood (the first five years) seems to have more of an impact on depressive symptoms in adolescent *girls* (at the age of 14) than on adolescent boys.[31] These results seem to complement a 1998 Finish study that suggested that men are more likely than women to experience depression in old age as a result of the loss of their *mothers* in early childhood, and the same applied to elderly women who lost their fathers in early childhood.[32]

## Jung: gender archetypes and the collective unconscious

The other 20th century theorist of the mind often credited with a significant impact on our conceptions of ourselves as men and women is Carl Jung, whose Swiss-German patriarchal prejudices about gender roles are found throughout his oevre. A glance at his life history and some of his stranger views might give pause to anyone inclined to accept uncritically his claims to have been a scientist. One could mention the affairs he had with his patients, his belief in the occult, in Germanic paganism, alchemy and the spiritual realm more generally, his temporary descent into psychosis, his flirtation with the Nazis, and the depth of his racism[33], as well as his views on curing homosexuality. None of this, however, is sufficient to dislodge his core theories of individuation and of universal archetypes within the collective unconscious. But perhaps more damning is the evidence that has fairly recently emerged that he engaged in what might be called scientific fraud (if we were to accept Jung as a scientist, which, really, we can't).

Jung believed we all inherit what he called 'a second psychic system of a collective, universal and impersonal nature which is identical in all individuals'[34] and that this innate collective unconscious consisted of archaic pre-existent archetypes, which pop up in dreams, visions, religious experiences and psychotic episodes. At times he would suggest this had evolutionary roots; at others that it was of divine origin. Many of the examples of archetypes and of archetypal forms he cited were gender-specific – the anima (the threatening feminine spirit within a man), the animus (the threatening male spirit within females), the great mother, the maiden, the wise old man, the wise old woman, the hero, Apollo and so on.

His favourite example, when claiming proof of his ideas, was a story relating to the 'solar phallus'. He enthusiastically told this tale for much of his working life to illustrate his claim about the universality and timelessness of his archetypes. Here's his story: In 1909 one of his assistants interviewed a male schizophrenic patient who said he'd seen visions of the sun with a penis and that this was the origin of the wind. Jung, who knew that similar images were found within the cult of the ancient Greek god Mithras, claimed this case proved beyond all doubt that all humanity shared these archetypes – his point being that the patient could not possibly have known about this obscure Greek cult, so therefore .... .

In fact, prior to the 1909 interview, several German authors had written prominently about the cult, so the likelihood is that the solar phallus man was merely hallucinating on something he'd read. When Jung was alerted to this inconvenient truth, he juggled the chronology by claiming a date for the interview with the solar phallus man three years before it really occurred (in other words, that the interview with the schizophrenic patient was conducted before the publication of the solar phallus books). This allowed him to continue claiming that the man could not possibly have known about the cult and his audiences were suitably impressed. In addition, Jung later falsely claimed that he himself had interviewed the schizophrenic man[35]. According to the Harvard University academic Richard Noll, who investigated this case, the Jung family refused him permission to see the notes taken on this issue by Jung's assistant[36], which might have added further proof of Jung's deceit.[37]

Despite this revelation, the popularity of Jungian ideas and Jungian analytical psychology has continued to spread, riding the wave of the post-60s explosion in 'alternative' religions, therapies and philosophies. And this includes his views on gender identity – such as his notion that masculine energy was creative, rational and active and feminine energy was receptive, passive and irrational, or his castigation of women who pursued 'a masculine calling'. This pursuit, he insisted, 'can even grow into downright daemonic passion that irritates and disgusts men' and could 'smother the charm and meaning of femininity' and lead to neurosis[38]. Or to take another example, his attitude can be seen in his archetypical image of the father as the diametric opposite to that of the mother. As he expressed it: "Fatherland' implies boundaries, a definite localisation in space whereas the land itself is Mother Earth, quiescent and fruitful.'[39]

One might think that anyone not of a religious or 'spiritual' bent would dismiss a mystical-sounding notion of universal gendered archetypes within an inherited collective unconscious as pure hocus-pocus. But some contemporary Jungians have tried their best to find little scraps of scientific credentials for their faith. The Jungian analyst and author Devon Anthony Stevens, for example, drew on Noam Chomsky's increasingly disputed notion that all humanity inherits a universal grammar as a kind of parallel example of the sort of thing Jung was referring to. And, inevitably, he made common cause with evolutionary psychology and its notion of inherited patterns of behaviour that evolved in the Pleistocene era and lodged themselves in the human psyche as discreet, universal, mental modules. Stevens writes about the 'congruence' between evolutionary psychology and Jungian archetypical theory,[40] which would horrify most evolutionary psychologists.

## From Jung to EP

This brings us back to the subject of EP and its faith-based obsessions about gender. In their popular science and self-help forms, these too have also had a significant impact on public consciousness. The reason evolutionary psychologists claim the male mind has evolved so

differently to the female mind is rooted in their conceptions of evolutionary biology, which, as we have already seen, is flawed because
of its rigid genetic determinism, its obliviousness to genetic drift and
its failure to embrace the implications of evolutionary spandrels. At
the heart of their perceptions about the differences between the 'male
mind' and the 'female mind' is their notion that men are driven by
their genetically-induced urge to spread their genes as far and wide
as possible, whereas women are driven by their genetically-induced
urge to choose their mates carefully, to ensure the best genes are
passed on. Our minds, they believe, were moulded by these gendered
imperatives, and our intellectual, practical and emotional capacities
ultimately relate to them.

In this sense, they have a different starting point than Freud and
Jung (whose grasp of evolutionary theory was even more flaky – Jung,
for example, favoured Lamarckian ideas), but their conclusions about
men and women very often echo the same prejudices. Where they
differ more substantially from Freud, Jung and Lacan, and, in fact,
from all previous schools of psychology, is that their views are, in
essence, *anti*-psychological. They believe that the genes we share are
far more important to the way we turn out as individuals than any
factor in our socialisation, including our family backgrounds or social
circumstances. Or to put it differently, genes trump life. As Steven
Pinker, the poster boy for EP, expressed it: 'We must see culture
as a product of human desires rather than a shaper of them.'[41] He
believes that upbringing has little role in determining how a child
will emerge: it is all down to genes. And if parents can't influence
how their children will turn out, then what chance do psychologists
and psychiatrists have in helping adults sort out their lives?

Evolutionary psychologists therefore tend not to be the sort who
spend their time listening to patients or clients. Instead, as will be
illustrated with specific examples in the chapters that follow, they
are the sort who do research, usually conducted exclusively among
their own students (partly because psychologists don't get the kind

of funding that real scientists draw from drugs companies, which enable them to conduct large-scale, randomised, double blind trials). And the reason they do all this research among their students is because they have far grander ambitions than the apparently futile stuff of helping patients whose minds have already been moulded by their genes. Their research projects usually have a single aim: to win kudos within their own world, and publicity within the media, through seizing upon yet another aspect of human behaviour and demonstrating that this is sufficiently universal to be placed within the 'hard-wired' column. Pinker, for instance, tells us that the heritability of milk and fizzy drink intake is *high* but of fruit juice and diet drinks is *low*[42].

To close the circle and add a causal narrative to their hypotheses, their conclusions frequently include another component – beyond the data their questionnaires deliver from their students. This involves asking the *how* question – how did women get to prefer the colour pink, or to relish a lovely long shopping trip, or get to be so damn chatty, or to be so empathic, and how did men evolve to be so mean to their step-children and get to prefer their maternal cousins, or to develop their capacity to read maps upside down and to parallel park, and get to be so single-minded? They start with the assumption that these supposedly universal behaviours must have evolved biologically, and that this biological evolution is expressed in mental modules (as we shall see in more detail in the next chapter, they assume the mind – as opposed to the brain – has a modular structure, much like the body organs and limbs and so on)[43].

They cast their own minds back to a savannah in an indistinct period of time in an indistinct part of Africa. The image they conjure up is one of tribal hominids on the cusp on modern humanity moving around in small hunter-gatherer bands, and from this they start their guessing game about how women and men came to behave like this or that. They consider the different roles their males and females supposedly played all those hundreds of thousands of years ago, and how this created a predilection for male and female ways of thinking and acting, which remain rooted in our modern brains – a view that does indeed have parallels with the 'ancient or archaic' archetypes of Jung's collective unconscious. For example, as we have seen, the activity on the ancient African savannah that somehow prompted a selection for pink-preference traits among women was the supposedly exclusively female activity of fruit-picking.

Sometimes they talk of their pet examples as being illustrative of a kind of problem – a problem of us trying to solve our 21st century issues with minds that evolved in the Pleistocene. As two of EP's founders, Leda Cosmides and John Tooby, put it: 'Our modern skulls house a Stone Age mind.'[44] They delight in this inversion of the Flintstones (where Stone Age cartoon people were created to resemble white, middle class America of half a century ago) because they like the idea that modern men and modern women have Stone Age minds. Except, of course, when you think about it, this is not really an inversion at all, because, as illustrated at the start of this chapter, we know very little about how men and women behaved way back when, but from the few hints at information we can glean from African caves from tens of thousands of years ago, it seems unlikely that the version of the stone age African past dreamed up by the evolutionary psychologists to create an ancient fit for their student survey results is any more realistic than a television series that died in 1966 because its take on the past no longer resonated with the present.

# CHAPTER SIX

# SWISS ARMY KNIFE MINDS AND
# BALANCED BRAINS

The evangelical Christianity of my childhood explained the world according to God's plan, Satan's treachery, the sin of 'man' and the redemption offered by Jesus. Everything that happened in the world was seen in this context. The Marxism I first absorbed in my late teens explained it in terms of a perpetual class struggle over production relations. All history and every societal structure and social change was viewed in this light, which was why all the 'social sciences' had to be re-interpreted through a 'historical materialist' lens. I finally abandoned Marxism in my late twenties, partly because its attempt to explain everything in terms of production relations came to seem absurd, after which I was drawn toward an intellectual eclecticism and even empiricism that I'd previously shunned.

So when I first came across evolutionary psychology in the early 1990s, I have to acknowledge my hackles were already raised, and one of the reasons was that it soon became clear that EP, like fundamentalist religion and like Marxism, had a grand ambition to colonise the humanities under its own rubric by demonstrating that human behavior was a direct product of shared evolutionary adaptations.

Their big idea was (and is) to create a kind of framework within which all psychology and all the other 'social sciences' operate. Leda Cosmides and John Tooby, often cited as the founders of the faith, put it like this: 'Evolutionary psychology is an *approach* to psychology, in which knowledge and principles from evolutionary biology are put to use in research on the structure of the human mind. It is not an area of study, like vision, reasoning, or social behaviour. It is a *way of thinking* about psychology that can be applied to any topic within it.'[1] Elsewhere they go further: 'Evolutionary psychology is the long-forestalled scientific attempt to assemble out of the disjointed, fragmentary, and mutually contradictory human disciplines a single, logically integrated research framework for the psychological, social, and behavioural sciences.'[2] It has to be said that after a couple of decades of proselytising, networking, publishing and preaching, they have had considerable success in reaching this goal, at least within the worlds of psychology, the mass media and self-help publishing where their influence and impact has steadily expanded.

## The Swiss army knife mind

Evolutionary psychologists want us all to see the world like this: our dim-distant ancestors had to learn to communicate, choose places to live, select fertile mates, fend off competitors for these mates, protect and provide for their kin, avoid poisonous plants, poisonous snakes and dangerous predators, identify edible plants, hunt, fish, forage and so on, and for each of these demands, and many others, they evolved discreet brain circuits for the specific coping mechanisms required. The human mind is therefore a Swiss Army Knife (their phrase, not mine) made up of highly specialised tools, which emerge from psychological adaptations to problems we faced in the Pleistocene era. As one of EP's leading lights, Donald Symons, put it: 'There is no such thing as a 'general problem solver' because there is no such thing as a general problem.'[3] Instead, he talks of an 'array of psychological mechanisms that is universal among homo sapiens'[4] Tooby and Cosmides call these evolved modules, 'the psychological universals that constitute human nature'.[5]

Steven Pinker encapsulated this perspective: '(T)he mind is organised into modules or mental organs, each with a specialised design that makes it an expert in one area of interaction. The modules' basic logic is specified by our genetic programme. Their operation was shaped by natural selection to solve the problems of the hunting and gathering life led by our ancestors in most of our evolutionary history.'[6] Much of the energy of these EP advocates goes into what they call 'evolutionary functional analysis' and what others call 'Just So Stories' – the impossible task of guessing about which particular stone age problems might have produced their chosen modules.

## Pink and blue 'modules of the mind'

Most important for evolutionary psychologists is that these modules of the mind or 'instincts'[7] can only deal with a specific aspect of the world and not with information about other things.[8] They are therefore discreet – isolated from the rest of the mind's processes. They operate independently. Just like the ear can only do sound and the eye, sight, so these mental modules can only do the stuff they have evolved to do. They also develop of their own accord, although it may be necessary for them to be 'triggered' by an environmental stimulus. And, a bit like Jung's archetypes, these mental organs mystically arrive with inbuilt knowledge and innate procedures for applying that knowledge, and this can be done quickly and efficiently without having to sort out all the information available in the brain – special purpose 'mini-computers' dedicated to solving a single problem.[9]

An oft-cited example is the notion of innate universal grammar punted by the linguist Noam Chomsky and embraced by Pinker – that a child exposed to speech will develop a very specific set of universal grammatical rules by the age of five, after which he or she will be able to understand complex sentences (whereas 'feral children', whose early years are devoid of human contact, never learn these rules because they would not have been 'triggered'). They believe these ready-made, brain circuitry-induced rules apply to all of humanity (like Jung's archetypes) – an idea that is losing ground in the world of linguistics.[10]

## Why brains aren't modular

Now to the critique: No-one who deals with the brain would claim that its plasticity is infinite – obviously different parts of it deal with different needs and problems, and not just at the physical level (sight, sound, smell, touch, movement, reproduction etc.) but also with language, cognition, face-recognition and so-on, particularly as we approach adulthood when the brain becomes more specialised. There is a huge difference, however, between parts of the brains that relate to specific mental or physical functions, and the more abstract notion of evolved, mind-based modules. More specifically, do the vast range of modules proposed by evolutionary psychologist really exist?

In a debate with Stephen Pinker, the British neuro-biologist Steven Rose made a point about the specificity of the visual cortex, and then went on to argue: '(I)t's a mistake to have to think in terms of modularity, to an excessive degree, when one's concern is much more complex functions than simply visual analysing functions.'[11] Yet evolutionary psychologists like Pinker have no such qualms and their list is potentially endless, currently including modules for things like kin-oriented motivation, sexual attraction, friendship, social exchange, cheater detection and many, many others.[12] They talk of 'Darwinian algorithms' that somehow transform such problems into evolved solutions in the form of mental modules.[13]

Many of these modules are said to have developed substantially differently in males and females because of their different impera-tives. As evolutionary psychologists see it, males and females are alternative adaptive forms who must solve their own sets of problems to reproduce, creating distinct selection pressures and therefore dis-tinct psychological outcomes. Pleistocene men faced competition for females, which involved learning to fight for them and to court them and to retain them, and they would therefore have developed specific

modules for these purposes. In the course of this modular evolutionary journey, males developed an innate preference for young, nubile
females – another module – whereas females developed an innate
preference for older, high-status males – another module. Their point
is that on a gendered basis we all possess these adaptations within
our psyches, which is part of the reason why they argue that cultural
diversity among humans is over-stated[14] but distinctions between
men and women are understated.

EP's mission includes a quest to find more and more of these
putative modules that come in distinct pink and blue forms to
explain what they regard as innately gendered behaviour, and many
take it further, suggesting that their conclusions should have policy
implications. Robert Wright, an American journalist who became
one of EP's prime cheerleaders, proposes that our legal systems adjust
to innate, module-based, genetically-determined imperatives[15], and
that glass ceilings can't be broken because women are hardwired to
have less ambition, drive and risk-taking inclination. 'Evolutionary
psychology sees … some clear differences between the male and female
minds,' he says. '[M]any of the differences between men and women
are more stubborn than most feminists would like, and complicate
the quest for – even the definition of – social equality between the
sexes.'[16]

## Neural plasticity and the non-modular mind

Evolutionary theory tells us that the particular problems faced by
Pleistocene people would need to have been stable for a very long
time for these evolutionary solutions to gel. It also suggests the
resulting selections for advantageous mutations would need to alter
the physiology of the brain. And yet EP proponents talk of 'hundreds
of thousands'[17] of these modular mental mechanisms.

Let's, for a moment, swallow any incredulity about whether
being nasty to stepchildren or being inclined to rape (men), or being
inclined to seek out older men or to shop-shop-shop (women) really

have genetic origins, and assume that there are, indeed, hundreds of thousands of mental modules like these, all of which evolved through natural selection. This would require, in turn, hundreds of thousands of genetic mutations because the logical implication of the EP view is that each of their mental modules would have evolved independently. So, as more and more of these modules evolved, the number of brain-based genes would have had to increase proportionately.

However, as mentioned in chapter 4, the human genome project found that there were only around 24,000 human genes, less than a quarter of the expected number. Roughly half of these are implicated in the functions of the brain, but this includes the genes for our sensory receptors – seeing, hearing, smelling, tasting and touching – which require greater genetic specification than our cognitive functions. As the philosopher of science, David Buller puts it: 'Given the complexity of the brain, it appears that its higher cognitive structures are vastly *underspecified* genetically compared to its more peripheral sensory structures.'[18] And, as we've seen in chapter three, this view is backed up by leading geneticists like Craig Venter and Paul Ehrlich, who stress our gene shortage (we have fewer than a mouse, which suggests there is no relation between the size of our genomes and the complexity of our brains). Quite simply, we do not have enough genes for the EP model to work.

But even if we did, or if evolutionary psychologists had vastly over-estimated the number of modules while getting the basic concept right, the EP idea of genetically discreet brain circuits evolving to cope with specific adaptive problems in the Stone Age does not square with what we now know about the human brain's sensitivity to environmental influence, particularly as it develops during childhood and the teenage years. One of the most remarkable aspects of the human brain's evolution is this plasticity. The most recent part of it in evolutionary terms, its neo-cortex (which is implicated in most of the functions related to EP's modular model – including consciousness, thought, language, memory and perceptual awareness), is also its least modular and most flexible part, with capacities to perform a variety of functions – one part sometimes taking on another part's function. In other words, most of our brain circuits are not restricted to particular domains.

The term neural-plasticity also relates to a subject I have touched on already – the fact that the brain's development is mediated by its cultural context and not via hard-wired 'triggers' to activate certain modules. Put differently, there is a constant process of sculpting and moulding. The brain's cortex has a 'proliferate and prune' process where the neurons and connections that respond most to the environment of their bearer will be those selected to help to structure it.[19] The circuits that emerge from this interaction are therefore not 'hard-wired' evolutionary adaptations – which is one reason why the analogy between human brains and computers is so off-the-mark. The wet, organic brain is nothing like a computer.

Although this plasticity is most marked during childhood, it is by no means confined to those early, developmental years – the adult brain also changes constantly through environmental stimulus, which is one of the many reasons why snapshots showing differences between male and female brains do not present a definitive picture (because they don't take account of the different cultural influences absorbed by these males and females). This is clearly at odds with the notion of the EP notion of mental modularity – of these evolved 'mini-computers' processing information at high speed in isolation from the rest of the brain. As the language acquisition expert Annette Karmiloff-Smith puts it: '(I)f we want to hang onto the Swiss army knife metaphor, then we need to shift focus from the end product, the clever little knife sold in the shops, to the account of its development.'[20]

But there is one more bullet in the EP barrel, which goes something like this: if you reject the idea of a modular brain and insist on domain-general learning, how do you explain our capacity to choose the essential things to learn rather than useless data? For example, if a new-born baby did not have an evolved face-recognition module, how would it know to choose to focus on its parents' faces rather than, say, the wall? In other words, the range of options it would have to choose from to survive would be too vast, which is why it requires the specialised, innate knowledge of these domain-specific modules.

One problem with this argument is with its conflation of innate knowledge and modules. But, actually, we don't need either to explain how our minds get channelled in particular directions. The fact that the baby's brain shows an inclination to look at faces rather than walls by no means implies that it possesses a discreet, evolved, mini-computer for facial recognition, or for any of the other hundreds of thousands of things picked out of the hat by evolutionary psychologists. Nor, for that matter, does it imply that the baby's brain contained innate knowledge of faces. Rather, it suggests that the brain has a head-start in learning about certain vital things, which prompt it in the right developmental direction.

Buller explains this in terms of initial biases in the mechanism 'which channel attention to particular environmental inputs more than others' – a predisposition to apply learning to particular things.[21] Evidence for this comes from the fact that it takes quite a while for babies to show preference for human faces. At first, they're more interested in three high-contrast blobs on a triangle, and at six months they are just as interested in monkey faces as human faces.[22] So their initial bias (in this case, originating in a sub-cortical devise in the brain) has nothing to do with faces. Instead, it is a bias towards looking at triangular shaped objects with blobs on them. But this interest soon becomes more specific, until, by using another devise, in the cortex, the babies focus on human faces and learn to distinguish between them and to discern their emotions and so on. And as they learn, the circuitry of their brains changes, until their brains specialise in human faces. If they were primarily exposed to monkey faces, or cow faces or dog faces, they would similarly become experts in these. This is a very different notion to that of an evolved, discreet face-recognition module.[23]

So the picture that emerges from contemporary neuro-science and contemporary genetics is of a brain that evolved to be highly flexible, full of non-adaptive capacity and perpetually sensitive to environmental input, and of a mind that is closer to 'domain general' ideas, moulded into specialisation by experience, than to the 'massive modularity' notion of EP. Face recognition, along with voice recognition and language acquisition, are specific areas of learning that do, indeed, appear to have an evolutionary bias that prompts the brain in a particular direction, provided it is exposed to the right environmental stimulation. But there is no evidence for an evolved bias for most of the other domains dreamed up by EP – including their big gender-based ones such as male preference for nubile women and for rape, female preference for high status older men, and their big kin preference ones such as the male inclination to be mean to stepchildren. On the contrary, as we shall see in later chapters, there is convincing evidence that none of these inclinations are 'hard-wired'. They are, instead, products of a relation between specific environmental inputs and brains that have evolved towards extraordinary flexibility and plasticity.

## Baron-Cohen's male and female brains

But the evolutionary psychologists are not finished yet. If their specific claims about pink and blue modular minds turn out to be a bit dodgy, what about their wider claims about the differences in male and female behaviour? In later chapters dealing with IQ, intellectual inclination, empathy, language skills, sexuality, parenting and adornment, I will look in more detail at some of the specific claims made by evolutionary psychologists, but, for now, I will touch on the more general claim made by the Cambridge psychologist Simon Baron-Cohen that there is such a thing as the 'male brain' (single-minded, systematising, capable of analysing complex systems) and the 'female brain' (empathetic, caring, good at communication). His point is that there are significant, hard-wired, gender-based differences in the way these two distinct brains work and what they are likely to produce in terms of thought, emotion and action, and that these differences have implications for the kinds of careers that should be chosen.

Baron-Cohen, a University of Cambridge-based evolutionary psychologist who happily owns up to biological determinism[24], helpfully suggests that people possessing the female brain 'make the most wonderful counsellors, primary school teachers, nurses, carers, therapists, social workers, mediators, group facilitators or personnel staff', whereas people with the male brain 'make the most wonderful scientists, engineers, plumbers, taxonomists, cataloguists, bankers, toolmakers, programmers or even lawyers.'[25] This career selection is a perfect fit for those jobs that happen to be populated mainly by women and for those by men, rather than for the tasks they cover. Lawyers, for example, do all sorts of 'female brain' things like communicating empathetically and nurses have to do plenty of 'male brain' things like measuring medicines. But perhaps the more telling difference in Baron-Cohen's career advice service is that most of his male brain jobs pay considerably more than the female brain jobs, and most are more intellectually challenging.

In Baron-Cohen's partial defence he does acknowledge that there is not a neat fit between men and male brains and between women and female brains – in fact the majority of his respondents had a 'balanced brain', with less than 50 percent of women having a 'female brain' and only 60 percent of men, a 'male brain' (while 17 percent of men had a 'female brain' and the same percentage of women had a 'male brain'[26]). But whatever the breakdown, how does he decide which brain is which? Through brain scans? Genetic profiling? Behavioural observation? Actually, none of the above. Instead he asks his males and females a whole lot of questions and makes his classifications on the basis of their answers alone. His 'Empathy Quotient' questionnaire asks respondents whether they like caring for others, or whether they can tell if someone wants to enter a conversation. His 'Systematising Quotient' asks them if they could fix the wiring at home and whether they like to read football league tables and stock market indices in the newspaper.[27]

The most obvious problem here is that self-assessment of this kind is notoriously inaccurate. All it measures is people's perceptions of themselves, which tend to be way off the mark. People are not very good at reading their own minds, or at understanding their own motivations and capacities. Ask men if they are good at male-type accomplishments such as systematising, or maths and science, and they will tend to over-rate themselves; ask women the same question and they will tend to under-rate themselves[28], and the opposite is true with questions relating to empathy and kindness. Because most men like to think of themselves as masculine and most women like to think of themselves as feminine, their self-perception all-too-often conforms to accepted gender stereotypes of masculinity and femininity. Reviews of the literature show that self-reporting questionnaires have, in particular, little or no value when they ask about emotional capacity (such as empathy, sympathy and social sensitivity).

With Baron-Cohen's tests the questions so obviously relate to perceived masculine and feminine attributes that it is likely that respondents would be aware of this, which might further colour their self-perception (for example, the female edge in empathy is increased in self-perception tests where it is apparent what is being tested and is reduced to almost nothing in those that disguise what is being tested).[29] So the fact that Baron-Cohen's men were more likely to rate themselves highly on systematising and his women were more likely to rate themselves highly on empathy, has no bearing on whether these men were more systematic and whether these women were more empathetic, let alone whether these inclinations were hardwired. In other words, his male-brain/female-brain categorisation is worthless, and the only surprise is that his test results were so ambiguous.

For Baron-Cohen the story starts with testosterone, which shapes the brains of males in the womb and in childhood, and helps make up their minds. As he puts it, 'the more you have of this special substance ...., the more your brain is tuned into systems and the less your brain is tuned into emotional relationships'.[30] In other words, if you absorb lots of testosterone in the womb you will end up with one of Baron-Cohen's hard-driven, single-minded male brains, and if you get not-so-much you will get one of his touchy-feely female brains and just kind-of average amounts will give you a 'balanced brain'. The essence of his claim is that the higher levels of testosterone absorbed by the male in the womb create a more cramped left hemisphere, but, like so many of the gendered claims about our brains, this one has since been thoroughly debunked. For example, a 2007 neuro-imaging study of 74 newborn babies' brains found no evidence to support it (in fact, with both newborn boys and girls the left hemisphere was larger than the right).[31]

He also believes that *really* high doses of foetal testosterone will give you an 'extreme male brain', his other word for autism. However, there is reason to question Baron-Cohen's notion that autism represents an 'extreme male' pole on the gender spectrum, prompted by high doses of foetal testosterone. First, increasing numbers of girls are being diagnosed to be on the autistic spectrum (including Asperger syndrome), and experts in this area believe that there is also significant under-reporting of female Asperger's – with the ratio of boys to girls now thought to be around 2:1, whereas it was once thought to be around 16:1.

Second, autistic people have problems with cognitive empathy (they struggle to discern other people's intentions and emotions), although as the neuro-psychologist Cordelia Fine points out they don't have the same problems with sympathy.[32] Yet in Baron-Cohen's schema it is sympathy that is lacking in those with a male-brain and not so much empathy. To be effective, the hard-driven business executive, or barrister, or political leader, needs to be able to 'mind read' (discern what his colleagues or opponents are thinking or planning). What he might lack, however, is real compassion in the well-being of others – the opposite of the problems faced by those on the autistic spectrum.

Third, there has been recent research suggesting that a high level of foetal testosterone doesn't cause autistic symptoms directly, as suggested by Baron-Cohen. Rather it 'reduces the threshold' at which the symptoms of autism begin to manifest themselves.[33]

Baron-Cohen, however, is not put off by neurological evidence against his pet theories. His bid to establish the connection between testosterone and his systematising male-brain involved a Systematising Quotient test for children. But this one was no more reliable than his adult version. His method involved comparing levels of amniotic testosterone with the results of his questionnaire, filled in by the children's mothers. The reliability of his results has been queried because of his small sample sizes[34] but the more substantial query is whether mothers are likely to report accurately on their children's behaviour patterns, particularly when gender-type questions are asked (such as whether the child can figure out the controls of the video or DVD player).

There is the added problem that some of his questions had little relation to systematising. For example he asked if the child became annoyed when things weren't done on time and whether he or she noticed whether something in the house had been moved, prompting Fine to wonder whether 'some items from the Fusspot Quotient accidentally found their way into the SQ'.[35] His own argument is that systemising 'needs an exact eye for detail'[36], which is no doubt true, but then again, so does effective empathising because it requires a focus on the subtle nuances of someone else's behaviour patterns. And a successful systemiser would require not just an appreciation of detail, but also a sense of perspective – to understand the relation between the system and its component parts. When you look at it like this it would seem that systemising and empathising are not opposites: there's a big overlap.

Baron-Cohen's most cited study involved looking for gender differences among 102 newborns aged one-and-a-half days old, who were given the choice between a face (of his graduate student, Jennifer Connellan) and a mobile to look at. The hypothesis was that empathetic girls were hardwired to look more at faces and that systemising boys were hardwired to look at mobiles (and because they were newborns the influence of socialisation could be ruled out). The babies were filmed and then analysed and the results seemed to bear out the hypothesis, albeit by a small margin. The males spent more time focussing on the mobile (51 percent compared with 41 percent for females) and the females spent longer looking at Connellan's face (49 percent compared with 41 percent for males).[37] This study has been very widely quoted by those arguing for innate gender differences, both in the media and by authors of books on popular science. For example, the single sex education advocate, Leonard Sax says that its results suggest that 'girls are prewired to be interested in faces while boys are prewired to be interested in moving objects'.[38]

What its advocates did not get around to considering was the methodology of this study, which wasn't up to scratch, making the results impossible to interpret with any degree of certainty. First, when testing newborns for visual preferences, the standard procedure is to present the two stimuli simultaneously because of the babies' very low attention span. If you present them consecutively then, as Fine puts it, 'you don't really know whether the baby looked at stimulus A more because she genuinely found it more interesting, or whether she was irritated by some internal rumblings, about to fall asleep, or simply a little tired of life when stimulus B was on show'.[39]

Second, as we've already seen, newborns are a long way from being interested in actual human faces – a triangle with three bright dots will do the trick even better than a squishy face. And because their eyesight is wobbly at one-and-a-half days old, it just doesn't work unless all of them are presented with the stimuli from precisely the same angle, which was not the case with this study (some babies were tested on their backs, others in their parents' laps, but we don't have a gender breakdown for this difference).

Third, and most important, was the team's failure to take heed of Heisenberg observer effect principle – that measurements of certain systems cannot be made without affecting the systems. To reduce the risk in this kind of study, it would be essential to create a gender-neutral environment. But in this case, the researcher, Connellan, who was also the stimulus, would have been aware of the gender of most of the babies and we can't be sure that this knowledge didn't sub-consciously affect her behaviour towards them. This is because there was no attempt to neutralise the environment in the maternity ward. Any pink (or blue) balloons, cards, babygrows, blankets, flowers or decorations would have given the clue, aside from the possibility of the parents referring to 'him' or 'her'. A slight difference in Connellan's behaviour which she might not be aware of (such as jangling the mobile a little bit more for boys or looking more directly at girls) could explain small differences in results.[40]

So what would happen with a better-designed study of this kind, set in a gender-neutral environment? Well, a subsequent study conducted four years later, also testing for gender difference in eye gaze, did just that, going to elaborate efforts to create an environment where the researcher was unaware of the sex of the infant, and, low and behold, no gender differences were found among the newborns[41]. This result is consistent with several other studies in this area, whereas Baron-Cohen's results have not been replicated.[42]

# CHAPTER SEVEN

# THE COLOUR–CODED BRAIN

If you don't believe the minds of boys and girls are fundamentally different, for god's sake, just take a look *inside* their brains, will you? That's the nub of challenge so often used to challenge those rowing against the pink and blue tide of genetic determinism. The supposed evidence is displayed in pictorial form in magazines, websites, self-help books and television programmes, and repeated in everyday discourse: men are left-brained; women are right-brained or both-brained – that sort-of thing.

When I first dipped my toes into the confusing world of gender science I was continually confronted by images of brains, showing differing areas lighting up for men and women. One that struck me so forcibly that I cut it out and preserved it for 17 years was a story in The Observer Magazine, written by their science editor, entitled 'Girl Power', although it was really about boys. And in case you were confused by the main brain scan illustrations, one with just a bit of one side lighted up in red, orange and yellow (boy brain) and the other with bits of both sides lighted up (girl brain), the stand-first explained: 'It's all in the head: Robin McKie on the differences between girls and boys.'[1] The story went on to encapsulate the essence of an argument still trotted out today by genetic determinists.

It begins with our old friend testosterone, which descends in an 'avalanche' on boy brains when they are in the womb. From then-on, their brains develop differently from girls'. It goes on to remind us that our brains come in two hemispheres, one handling language and reasoning, and the other, emotion (plus movement, and our sense of space and position). These halves communicate with each other through a large bundle of nerves, the *corpus callosum*, which, we are told, is thinner in a man's brain than a woman's, 'a weaker connection that possibly explains why men usually attack certain problems by using only one side of their brain, while women use both sides'.

Drawing from this picture, it quotes the Oxford scientist Professor Colin Blakemore as saying: 'Men tend to tackle problems in a linear way; women approach them in a more holistic way.' McKie suggests this prompts the conclusion that boys 'are therefore better at sequential thinking, girls better at seeing the whole picture. This explains male predominance in mathematics, female superiority in the arts.' He rows back for a moment by quoting another scientist as saying that, actually, the brain's prime job is to control the body and that most of the difference between male and female brains reflect their different reproductive roles, but he quickly returns to the subject of testosterone – the 'cascades' that happen, for boys, in the womb, and again at the ages of four or five and once more at puberty. And from there he leaps onto the central case of evolutionary psychology: 'Men would have been driven by an instinct to father as many children as possible ...' while 'women would have benefited if they were able to hold on to their mates and get them to stay to provide for their babies', which, it is implied, explains the whole testosterone, brain development shebang.[2]

When I read this feature 17 years ago, I wondered: how do we explain those brain scan pictures showing different areas lighting up in the brains of males and females? Or the bigger corpus callosum in women? Do these not provide physical proof that men and women have evolved to think differently – of a male brain that in many crucial areas is distinct from a female brain, producing different thought and emotional patterns? Then again, what also struck me about this story was the leaps of logic it encapsulated. Did the thickness of the *corpus callosum* really have anything to do with 'linear' or 'holistic' thought, or with the way boys and girls performed in maths or the arts, or was it just another example of over-interpretation or misinterpretation? And what did that have to do with these avalanches of testosterone? And was there really such a direct relation between testosterone surges and the male 'instinct to father as many children as possible'?[3]

Clearly, there were plenty of questions to be answered, but what I soon discovered, on reading more about this subject, is that there is nothing new when it comes to extrapolating meaning from the differences in male and female brains and skulls.

## Brain weighers and skull-fillers

In the 17th century a view emerged that the delicacy of female brain fibres explained their inability to indulge in abstract thought.[4] In the 18th, brain scientists would compare women and the 'primitive races' by measuring their 'facial verticality', which led them to conclude that only white males were capable of higher logic and all that entailed.[5] Victorian scientists would empty skulls and fill them with barley or bird shot and draw conclusions on the amount it took to fill the skull. They would measure skulls of men and women (and black people and white people) this way and that, comparing length and width, and they would weigh brains. And because men had slightly bigger, heavier brains, they would talk about the 'missing five ounces of the female brain', claiming that this explained why men were smarter than women and why women were incapable of coping with analytical thought.[6]

Eventually scientists were forced to abandon this notion because it dawned on them that bigger brains tended to come with bigger skulls, which, in turn, tended to come with bigger bodies, and that this said nothing about intelligence. So they transferred their efforts into analysing ratios (brain weight to body weight, muscular mass, size

GAVIN EVANS

of the heart and even size of the femur') One Victorian evolutionary biologist explained women's 'marked inferiority of intellectual power' as a consequence of the fact that 'the general physique of women is less robust than that of men – and therefore less able to sustain the fatigue of serious or prolonged brain action ...'[8] Another focussed on the relative size of different parts of the brain in men and women. He decided men had bigger frontal lobes and women bigger parietal lobes and assumed therefore that the frontal lobe was where abstract, intellect thought resided. Later, he changed his mind and decided that the intellect was situated in the parietal lobes, after which he measured again, and found that men had bigger parietal lobes after all.[9] Early in the 20th century, another view emerged: that the profound differences between men and women, including women's inappropriateness for politics or the law, were explained by the fact that the brain stems of women were larger and the brain mantles smaller, and because the upper half of women's spinal cord was smaller.[10]

It goes without saying that no-one in the *scientific* community believes any of this stuff anymore (although, as we shall see in chapter 8, the evolutionary psychologist, Richard Lynn, still clings to this view). Most are inclined to shake their heads and chuckle wryly because they know very well that what the brain scientists of the 17th, 18th, 19th and early 20th centuries were doing was taking perceived differences in male and female behaviour, presuming they must be physiological in origin, and then searching for differences in the brains of men and women, assuming a causal link between the differences and the behaviour. In each case, as it turns out, the scientists of the past were wrong. So when contemporary evolutionary psychologists and some neuro-scientists extrapolate from evidence of small differences in the male and female brains to explain what they regard as huge differences in thought and behaviour, we should treat their claims with similar caution.

Two other points I discovered from my reading on the brain, both suggesting further caution: I've already referred to the view that because men's brains seem to be more lateralised, men are better at homing in on specific tasks, and because women's brains seem less lateralised they are better at multi-tasking – a view that I will dispute shortly. It is therefore also worth noting that, as the socio-medical scientist Rebecca Jordan-Young put it, 'left-handers seem to be lateralised differently from right-handers'.[11] For example, with most right-handed people over the age of six language and speech functions are based in the brain's left hemisphere, but with left-handers there is a significantly higher occurrence of language being located in both hemispheres.[12] In other words, left-handers are less lateralised than right-handers. But, as far as I know, no-one outside of the political sphere has suggested that righties are from Mars and lefties from Venus.

And one more: we all know that men have bigger brains than women – mainly because they have bigger heads and bodies. We also know that some people have bigger heads than others, and therefore bigger brains. What is less widely known is that bigger brains create engineering problems, partly related to higher energy requirements, which means a slightly different organisation of brain structure.[13] Women also have, on average, slightly more grey matter relative to total brain size than men. But recent studies have shown that such differences are not essentially male-female; instead they are big brain-small brain differences related to confronting cognitive challenges 'using differently sized neural machinery'.[14] Put another way, bigger brains reach the same cognitive outcomes using slightly different pathways. But no-one claims that big-heads think differently from pin-heads and there are no proposals that classes should be divided on the basis of head size. Gina Rippon, a neuro scientist from Aston University in Birmingham, stresses this point: 'There are differences in rates of development of brains, but they are due to differences in size – if you got a whole lot of brains and divided them by sex you'd find some differences, but if you divided them by size you'd find substantially more differences.'[15]

The more general point here is that apparently significant neural differences may not, in fact, be significant at all because they may represent no more than alternative means to the same conceptual or behavioural end. Or, differences in the brains of men and women may suggest the opposite to what the contemporary brain weighers propose: they may be compensatory in nature. As the neuro-endocrinologist Geert de Vries puts it, 'They may prevent sex differences in overt functions and behaviour by compensating for sex differences in physiology'.[16] He cites the example of the equal parenting contribution made by male and female prairie voles. In the female, this is prompted by hormonal changes during pregnancy, while with the male, a part of the brain called the lateral septum is responsible (the males have more receptors for a particular hormone, which prompts this nurturing behaviour).[17] Or they could be the result of different lifestyles, a point stressed by Rippon who notes that male and female brains develop differently because of different experiences. 'Give a woman six or seven weeks of practice in Tetris and her brain will change.'[18]

### The corpus callosum and the holistic brain

Let's pursue the corpus callosum claims in more detail, including those I referred to from *The Observer* – that its less substantial presence in men explains why they 'usually attack certain problems by using only one side of their brain', while women 'use both sides' and the extrapolation from Professor Colin Blakemore that, therefore, men 'tend to tackle problems in a linear way; women approach them in a more holistic way.'[19] Claims about the vital role played by the more bulbous female corpus callosum (and particularly its splenium) in encouraging 'lateral' or 'holistic' thinking, and multi-task capacity (and the less substantial male corpus callosum encourage more single-minded, focussed behaviour) have been regularly repeated by some neuro-scientists and evolutionary psychologists, and widely aired in Mars and Venus-type books over the past two decades. So is there any truth in this? Do men and women (or, if we prefer, big-brained and smaller-brained people) really think and act differently as a result of the size and complexity of the corpus callosum?

The first question is whether the corpus callosum in females really is larger than that in males (thereby allowing for better connections between the two hemispheres of the brain), a claim first made in 1982 and published in the journal *Science*, based on a study of just five female brains and nine male, after which the talkshow host Phil Donahue announced that the biological basis for 'women's intuition' had been discovered.[20]

In 1997, two years before the publication of The Observer's report, 50 such studies were reviewed and the conclusion drawn by the scientists was that there was no size difference in the corpus callosum of adults[21]. Needless to say, this research did not attract the same publicity as the 1982 study. Three years later, the biologist Anne Fausto-Sterling published the results of further meta-analysis of studies of the corpus callosum and delivered the definitive conclusion that there are no sex differences in the size or shape in this area (neither in absolute nor relative terms).[22] Other studies have shown no difference in the size of the corpus callosum in boys and girls, and between male and female foetuses.[23] A 2009 review of all the scientific literature in this area by the neurobiologist Mikkel Wallentin came to the same conclusion – that 'the alleged sex-related corpus callosum size difference is a myth', one which he blames on studies with sample sizes that were too small.[24] Yet educationists, journalists and Mars & Venus authors continue to repeat the original, discredited claims and use it as the basis for treating girls and boys differently (such as separated learning in the version proposed by single-sex learning advocate Leonard Sax[25]).

### Neuro-imaging and the colour-coded brain

But what of those brain scans, such as the one displayed in *The Observer*, showing different parts of the brain lighting up – surely they tell us something profound about the different ways that men's and women's brains work?

It is worth pointing to the problems with using colour-coded pictures from neuro-imaging to illustrate difference:

First, it's a relatively new technology, one where the specialists are still finding their feet – both in terms of the technology itself and in terms of how to analyse the statistical data. As a result, single studies should come with a health warning: the raw data may be wrong and the interpretation of this data may be wrong.

Second, what you see is not quite what is happening in the brain. As neuro-psychologist Cordelia Fine points out, the colour patches seen on brain scans 'don't actually show brain activity'.[26] Scans don't measure brain activity directly; instead they reflect changes in the blood oxygen levels. The coloured spots therefore represent 'statistical significance at the end of several stages of complicated analysis – which means there is plenty of scope for spurious findings of sex differences in neuro-imaging research'.[27]

Which raises a third problem: as already discussed in the introductory chapter, in most areas of psychological research at least one in 20 studies will throw up a rogue result that occurs by chance, and the smaller the sample the higher the chance of such a false result – and neuro-imaging studies tend to come with small samples because they are costly. They are also more prone to rogue results because all sorts of variables can have an impact (ranging from caffeine intake to menstrual cycles)[28].

Fourth, if the study involves male and female participants, it is likely the researchers will check for gender difference. If no difference is found they're unlikely to report it. However, if the research does show gender difference, it's certain to be reported and published, because gender difference is newsworthy. So it is quite possible to have 100 studies in this area, with 95 showing no gender difference, and none of these are publicised. But the five showing gender difference, as a result of chance or faulty sampling or caffeine or menstrual cycles, are trumpeted in the journals and in the media. And this is how the publicity for a false outcome from a small sample neuro-imaging study showing gender difference, (such as with the early reports on corpus callosum being larger in women) begins.

But even if the neuro-imaging reflects something real and sub-stantial – that men and women are using different parts of the brain to respond to some stimulus or other – it does not imply a different conceptual or emotional result. As we have already seen, men and women can reach the same results in terms of thought and behaviour using different neural pathways, and this may relate, in part, to the size of their brains. So, the pictures from brain scans showing dif-ferences between men and women, which still are so widely used, as 'proof' of male focus and female multi-tasking, in fact prove nothing of the sort.

And yet, they keep on coming. The latest to create a stir was a much-publicised study on the different 'wiring' of male and female brains.[29] It provoked a deluge of headlines all over the world. This time I will choose *The Independent*, which went with 'The hardwired difference between male and female brains could explain why men are better at map reading'. It came with colour coded illustrations on male and female brains (men in blue, women in fawn), while their intro announced: 'A pioneering study has shown for the first time that the brains of men and women are wired up differently which could explain some of the stereotypical differences in male and female behaviour, scientists have said.'[30] The American media also got in on the act. CBS went with: 'Different brain wiring in men, women could explain gender differences' while the LA Times chose: 'Brains of women and men show strong hard-wired differences.' But pride of place when it came to over-reaching went to the BBC Radio 5 news, which announced: 'It has now been *proved* that men really do come from Mars and women from Venus ... .'[31]

The researchers begin their abstract with this assertion: 'Sex dif-ferences in human behaviour show adaptive complementarity: Males have better motor and spatial abilities, whereas females have superior memory and social cognition skills.'[32] As is shown later in this book, there is strong evidence to dispute both of these assertions. But it then goes on to link these supposed differences in ability (that don't actually exist) with 'unique sex differences in brain connectivity during the course of development' as children go through adolescence, concluding: 'Overall, the results suggest that male brains are structured to facilitate connectivity between perception and coordinated action, whereas female brains are designed to facilitate communication between analytical and intuitive processing modes.'[33]

They used a brain-scanning technique called 'diffusion tensor imaging' to measure the flow of water along a nerve pathway, and in this way measured the 'connectivity' between nearly 100 regions of the brain, drawing up a brain map they called the 'connectome', which, they said, showed that in the *typical* female brain the connections ran from side-to-side between the brain's two hemispheres, while in the *typical* male brain it ran between the back and front of the same hemisphere. They decided these 'hard-wired' distinctions were implicated in behavioural differences between the sexes, with men's brain being better equipped for perception and coordinated action and women's for social skills and memory, making them better adapted for multi-tasking.

One of the researchers, Ragini Verma, professor of psychology at the University of Pennsylvania in Philadelphia, explained: 'These maps show us a stark difference – and complementarity – in the architecture of the human brain that helps to provide a potential neural basis as to why men excel at certain tasks, and women at others. What we've identified is that, when looked at in groups, there are connections in the brain that are hardwired differently in men and women. Functional tests have already shown than when they carry out certain tasks, men and women engage different parts of the brain.'[34] She added that the left side of the brain was wired more logical thinking and the right for intuitive thinking. 'So if there's a task that involves doing both of these things, it would seem that women are hardwired to those better. Women are better at intuitive thinking. Women are better at remembering things. When you talk, women are more emotionally involved – they will listen more. I was surprised that it matched a lot of the stereotypes that we think we have in our heads.'[35]

Perhaps the most cogent of the many scientific critiques prompted by this paper relates to its assumption of a causal link between the differences in the neural pathways in male and female brains and perceived differences in behaviour – yet another case of falsely assuming that correlation equals causation. In fact, as most neuro-scientists caution, we have little idea of the nature of the link between cognition and the complex interactions between the neurons in our brains. The New York University neuroscientist J. Antony Movshon says the authors exaggerate what we know about the human brain: 'The relationship between the pattern of anatomical results and the paper's claim that ... male brains are structured to facilitate connectivity between perception and coordinated action, whereas female brains are designed to facilitate communication between analytical and intuitive processing modes' strikes me as fanciful at best, because we actually have no clear idea what connections are involved in connecting 'perception and coordinated action' or 'analytical and intuitive processing modes."[36] Rippon agrees, noting that while the authors may have shown differences between male and female brains, they failed to prove that those have any connection to how people live: 'Any relationship with behaviour can only be speculative at this stage,'[37] she said.

As we've seen, the differences in human brain connectivity can relate to a number of factors not implicated in behavioural differences. So, the mere fact that men and women may, on average, use different parts of the brain to respond to some stimulus or other does not imply a different conceptual or emotional result. Men and women, big brained people and small brained, left-handers and right-handers, can reach the same results in thought and behaviour using different neural pathways. And we also know that some men and some women use a-typical neural pathways when presented with the same cognitive stimulus (which seems to be borne out in this study, which suggests that not all male brains connected the *typical* male way, and not all female brains worked the *typical* female way).

A related problem is with the authors' use of terms like 'hard-wired' and 'architecture' to describe the brain. The term 'hard-wired' has been drawn from computer science but the brain is not a computer. It does not even resemble a computer in a metaphorical sense, nor an architectural design for that matter. The neural connections change according to the way the brain is used, and these changes start in utero and continue throughout our lives but may be more marked at some stages than others. It is claimed by the paper's authors that the way the neural pathways are 'hard-wired' along gender lines occurs mainly during adolescence (although they show no statistical connection between age and sex). But this also happens to be the age when males and females consolidate the differences in their gendered identities. Could it be that differences in behaviour are prompting differences in the way the brain is used, rather than the other way around – and that this is the reason why not all brains follow typically gendered lines? The answer is that we can't be sure because we don't yet know enough about the human brain.

What we can say with more certainty is that the authors are way off the mark when it comes to their assumptions about differences in male and female behaviour. For example, as we shall see in later chapters, the claim that women are more 'verbal' has been decisively demolished , and the idea that men are innately better at reading maps than women or that women are better at 'multi-tasking' has also been discredited. If we start from the opposite assumption to that of the authors of this paper – that male and female potentials relating to perception, coordination, social skills, memory and multi-tasking are very similar – then we have to come to opposite conclusion about the relevance of their use of different parts the brain: that whatever the reasons for average gender distinctions in terms of the use of neural pathways they appear to have little or no implications relating to behaviour.

## Male-female brain overlap

A huge 2015 study, involving MRI brain scans on more than 1,400 men and women, strengthened the view the differences between male and female brains have been exaggerated and that the blue brain/ pink brain dichotomy was off the mark. Instead, human brains have a patchwork of forms, some more common in females and others in males and many common to both. The differences between individuals of either sex are more profound than the average differences between the sexes. Overall, male brains and female brans are the pretty much the same and individual brains rarely show all-male or all-female traits.

The study, conducted at the University of Tel-Aviv and published in the American journal *Proceedings of the National Academy of Sciences*, dealt with anatomy – the sizes of various parts of the brain. The researchers considered how often each of these parts was consistently at the 'female-end' or 'male-end' if the scale. The methodology involved creating a continuum of femaleness to maleness for the whole brain (with the male end consisting of features more typical in men and the female end with features more typical with women). With each brain analysed, they then came up with a score, region-by-region. For example, they found that the left hippocampus (associated with memory) was typically larger in men, but that some women had a larger left hippocampus and some men a smaller one.

However, overall, their results revealed 'extensive overlap' between males and females for all the grey matter, white matter and connections assessed, and that brains with features consistently at one end of the 'maleness-femaleness' continuum were rare (only six percent could be categorised this way). Instead, the researchers wrote, 'most brains are comprised of unique "mosaics" of features', some more common in females, some more common in males and some more equally prevalent.[38] And they concluded that 'human brains do not belong to one of two distinct categories: male/female brain'[39]. As the head researcher, the behavioural neuroscience professor Daphna Joel, put it: 'We show there are differences but brains do not come in male and female forms. The differences you see are differences between averages. Each of us is a unique mosaic.'[40]

The researchers compared these results to those of two earlier psychological studies involving more than 5,500 people who were assessed in a number of stereotypically male or female personality traits, attitudes, interests and behaviours, and again they found that males and females had similar results, with only 0.1 percent of subjects showing uniquely 'male' or 'female' behaviours. Joel said their results suggested there were 'multiple ways to be male and female – there is not one way and most of these ways are completely overlapping'[41] and there was 'no sense in talking about male and female nature'.[42]

## Men, women and multi-tasking

The claim about gender differences in the size of the corpus callosum and the claim about the different 'wiring' of male and female brains have both been used to back the view that women are innately better at multi-tasking. In fact, it turns out that the evidence that women are better than men at doing more than one thing at a time is extremely iffy because different surveys and tests have produced conflicting results – and where differences have been found, they have been too small to draw definitive conclusions. For example, a Swedish study found that men performed better than women when it came to multi-tasking but a British one found the opposite. In both cases, however, the differences were marginal.

The Swedish study, published in the peer-reviewed journal *Psychological Science,* involved 160 men and women aged 20 to 43. They were instructed to keep track of three digital clocks or counters that displayed different times at different speeds, while also having to watch a scrolling ticker featuring common Swedish names, pressing a button when one of the names was repeated. The researchers found that men had a small advantage over women who were ovulating, but that they were otherwise equal. Still, the overall average gave men a slight edge. Timo Maentylae Stockholm University, the head researcher, commented on the popular perception that women had the edge in multi-tasking: 'On the contrary, the results of our study show that men are better at multitasking than women,' he was quoted as saying.[43]

However, a University of Glasgow study involving 120 men and 120 women found that while they were equal when the tasks were tackled one at a time, women had a miniscule advantage when they were mixed up (they were 69 percent slower than in the initial test, compared with 77 percent slower for men). 'We'd never claim that all men can't multi-task, or that all women can,' said one of the co-authors of the study, Keith Laws of the University of Hertfordshire.[44] However, there is also no implication that the slight female advantage found in the Glasgow study (as opposed to the Stockholm one) was the result of evolution. It could be a rogue result or it could reflect differences in the lifestyles of Glaswegian men and women, with women having to juggle career, child care and housework more than was the case with men.

## Brizendine and the brain's sex hub

This, however, does not quite close the show. There have been numerous other, very specific, and sometimes quite extreme, claims made about the differences between male and female brains, and of the significance of these distinctions, and most of these coagulate in a book by the American psychiatrist Louanne Brizendine, published in 2006 and still widely cited. It is not worth discussing *The Female Brain* in any detail because, as we will see again in chapter 11, her claims have been substantially discredited.[45]

However, for now, just one: her idea that the 'sex-related centres in the male brain are actually about two times larger than parallel structures in the female brain'.[46] She compares the male brain's 'hub for processing thoughts about sex' to Chicago's hyper-active O'Hare airport while the female equivalent is 'the airfield nearby that lands small and private planes'.[47] Now, I concede this is quite funny but it turns out that her similes have no bearing on reality because there is no biological basis for them. The hub she is referring to is the hypothalamus, which, indeed, is larger for men than for women but her claim that this has some kind of sexual purpose is nothing more than wild speculation. Rebecca Jordan-Young points out that no-one knows its function yet (although she speculates it may relate to something non-psychological). She adds, however, that 'there's certainly no evidence that it has anything to do with processing thoughts about sex'.[48] She also presents evidence directly contradicting Brizendine's notion that its greater size among men relates to their O'Hare-sized libidos, noting that some studies have found that its nucleus is also smaller, on average, in gay men when compared with heterosexual men. 'Brizendine's theory would predict that gay men have lower, more "female-type" libidos than heterosexual men, but this suggestion would go completely against behavioural evidence'.[49]

Finally, despite this difference in hypothalamus size, it is worth pointing out that when presented with a human brain, without any other biographical detail, scientists are unable to discern with any degree of certainty whether it is a male brain or a female brain because the differences are too subtle to know for sure.[50]

## Testosterone revisited

Which is not to say that foetal testosterone and oestrogen and other hormones have *no* impact on shaping brains and minds, directly or indirectly. I've already discussed the relationship between testosterone and male aggression and violence, but to take just two other more uncontroversial examples, it also affects the risks of some brain-related diseases and affects subsequent sexual preference. By the time they are born, testosterone levels of boys and girls show only a slight difference – but the two bursts in the womb are enough to masculinise male babies' sex organs and to have an impact on subsequent behaviour (although the impact of testosterone on the foetal brain is frequently over-stated, partly because it matures more slowly than any other organ).

We know that male rats and monkeys are more inclined to engage in rough and tumble play than females soon after birth, and that this might be influenced by testosterone among other physiological factors, but people aren't rats or monkeys. As the neuroscientist, Lise Elliot, puts it: 'The bigger the brain, the less instinctive the behaviour and the more the brain's abilities are influenced by learning.'[51] So while boys tend to engage in more robust play than girls, we can't be sure whether that is primarily a product of testosterone or primarily a product of socialisation, and because little boys aren't rats we can't remove their testicles to find out. Also, by the time children are old enough to play, they are already aware of their gender, and are rapidly becoming aware of what activities and toys are associated with their gender. So where hormones end and culture begins is hard to say.

One way of assessing the impact of pre-natal testosterone is to consider the cases of boys who have been re-assigned as girls because of circumcision disasters or other accidents to their penises, or congenital abnormalities, but the results are not conclusive. One review showed that by 2005 there were records of 77 such cases, and only 17 of them had reverted to being male, although several of those who remained female were attracted to women and showed signs of masculinity. It appears the longer the gap between birth and re-assignment, the higher the likelihood of reversion.[52] 'These data do not support a theory of full biological determination of gender identity development by prenatal hormones and/or of genetic factors,' said the reviewer, Heinz Meyer-Bahlburg, a Columbia University psychologist. And he added that 'social facts have a major influence on gender outcome'.[53]

Another route is to study girls raised in the opposite way to what their hormone exposure in the womb would suggest. About one in every 16,000 girls is born with a disorder called congenital adrenal hyperplasia (CAH). This involves a lack of an enzyme, which prompts their bodies to produce an excess of adrenal hormones, including testosterone, from very early in the pregnancy. This masculinises girls, producing a small penis and something like a scrotum, while not affecting their internal feminine organs (meaning they can still have children). Usually, they are operated on at birth, and later, and are raised as girls, while being treated with hormone supplements.

The research on these girls suggests they behave in a more typically masculine way than most other girls – more fond of robust play, more inclined to play with boys and boys' toys, and less inclined to dress up or play with typically girly toys, and this continues into adulthood when they tend towards stereotypically male professions.[54] However, the studies of whether CAH girls are more dominant or aggressive are more ambiguous, with the results differing according to which measure of aggression is chosen.[55] Their communication ability and mathematical skills are no different to that of other girls, and one study of girls with CAH found that they showed *less* attention to detail than other girls – the opposite of what Baron-Cohen's schema would suggest.[56] Most of the CAH girls have no problem with being identified as girls, and later, as women (but on average, they tend to have less sexual attraction towards men than control females, and more inclination towards lesbian or bi-sexual attraction).

At first blush these ambiguous results would suggest a significant but not overwhelming influence from this flood of pre-natal testosterone, along with several other hormones, but, as ever, it's not so simple. We can't discount the possibility that at least some of their parents and elder siblings, knowing their condition, might permit or encourage more boyish behaviour than they would with typical girls.

It is also possible that some CAH girls, already aware of CAH, would identify more with boys than would other girls, and that this would prompt them to want to play with toys and games associated with boys, whatever they happen to be, or as Fine puts it, 'they are drawn to what is culturally ascribed to males'.[57]

Yet another approach is to focus on girls who have boy twins. The reason for this interest is that these girls are exposed to higher doses of testosterone than singleton girls (or girls who have girl twins). The studies show that as a result of this testosterone exposure, there appear to be slight physiological differences between these girl twins and other girls (larger teeth, minor differences in hearing, for example) but no differences when it comes to behaviour or cognitive skills. And the same applied in reverse – the behaviour and cognitive skills of the boys who had twin sisters was not appreciably different from those in the control groups. A few studies suggested the girls who have twin brothers are more inclined towards risk-taking and aggression, but this could well be a result of growing up with a male twin, and, anyway, these results were not replicated in most of the studies, including those with the largest samples. Intriguingly, however, studies of girls with *older* brothers showed they were more likely to play with boys' toys and to enjoy sport, and less likely to play with girls' toys. This suggests that the inclination towards masculine behaviour in girls may have more to do with nurture than with nature.[58]

So, to summarise the evidence, testosterone does appear to be a factor prompting boys to engage in rough and tumble play, and it also appears to affect levels of physical aggression and perhaps of risk-taking, and possibly also the inclination to choose toys associated with boys. But it does not appear to have any influence on male or female linguistic or mathematical abilities, nor to their inclination towards empathy or sympathy, nor to their ability to multi-task — which takes us a very long way from the claims made in the previous chapter, including Simon Baron-Cohen's male brain-female brain

divide, and from the pink and blue modular minds of the evolutionary psychology mainstream. As Eliot put it: 'While testosterone is
clearly a factor in males' greater aggressiveness, this behaviour is far
more plastic in humans than in other animals. Males are not slaves to
their circulating steroids, nor are women immune to the aggressive
impulses fostered by similar hormonal chemistry.'[59]

But to come back to the starting point, how much of the science
behind that Observer story survives 17 years later? The answer is:
none. It would seem that the 'avalanche' of testosterone that boys
experience in utero, is not an avalanche at all, and its prime function
relates to the development of male sexual organs while its role on
the development of the brain is comparatively minimal. We have
also seen that a woman's corpus callosum is no thicker of bigger in
a man's, and the idea that men use just one side of their brain and
that this prompts focussed, single-minded thought whereas women
use both sides and this prompts a more 'holistic', multi-tasking mind
just doesn't hold up with what we have already seen in the previous
chapter about the flexibility of the human brain and to its suscepti-
bility to environmental influence. In short, the differences between
male and female brains, and, more particularly, what they produce in
the mind, have been hugely exaggerated.

# CHAPTER EIGHT
# EP AND WOMENS IQS

When I was a young child, I relished the idea that boys were better than girls – and better meant smarter as well as stronger and everything else. This had everything to do with being part of the boy team, the tribe of boys, and because I went to a boys' school and followed in the wake of my older brother. So, for a few years I tended to regard girls as foreign objects. But then my sister, Karen, arrived in the world, and, soon after, I had my first crush on a girl. The boys-better notion dissipated. When I finally went to a co-ed school in Texas, I couldn't help noticing that while girls and boys came with more or less the same range of intelligence and stupidity, girls, on average, seemed to do a little better than boys, and there was a slight majority of girls in most of the advanced classes I chose. By then, if anyone had suggested to me that boys were the brainier sex, I would have shaken my head in bemused wonder.

Today, most people, at least in advanced industrialised countries, believe that males and females have no advantages over each other when it comes to innate brain power. This is also the view of almost all of those regarded as experts on the subject. But almost all is not all. There are a few evolutionary psychologists who answer the question, 'Do men and women have the same average intelligence?' in the same way as I did as five-year-old, with a big fat no. And then there are rather more who answer it with a, 'well, yes, but ... .'

GAVIN EVANS

## Lynn, Irwing and the 'men are smarter' thesis.

In the first, category we have Richard Lynn, an octogenarian University of Ulster evolutionary psychologist and his ally Paul Irwing, a Manchester Business School evolutionary psychologist. Irwing's best-known foray into this terrain came in 2012 when his paper, entitled, 'The Distance Between Mars and Venus: Measuring Global Sex Differences in Personality' concluded that men and women shared only 10 percent of personality traits (discussed in more detail in the introductory chapter). None of the newspapers who trumpeted his absurd Mars and Venus findings bothered to look any closer at his 'research'. If they had, they would have found it was based entirely on a 19-year-old American survey that asked participants to assess their own personality traits, which, as every social researcher knows, is useless as an objective measure of behaviour.

Lynn is better known for another obsession: his view that black people are innately less intelligence than white and Asian people and for his 'IQs of Nations' schema that has 'Bushmen' and Pygmies at the bottom of the intelligence pile with Ashkenazi Jews at the top. I disputed Lynn's views in detail in my book, *Black Brain, White* Brain[1], showing why there are no innate differences in intelligence between population groups, but he pops up again here because he (and Irwing) also cling to another 19th century prejudice: that men, with their bigger heads, are intrinsically more intelligent than women, and that the higher we go up the intelligence pole, the more these big-heads dominate.

This pair wrote a paper in 2005 (which followed their earlier, similar account of IQ scores[2]), claiming on the basis of analysing 22 tests that men are, on average, 4.6 points ahead of women when it comes to IQ results. They also say this IQ difference only kicks in at the age of 14 (before then, no difference), and that once you get to the upper reaches of the IQ stratosphere, it becomes more marked – for instance, there are 5.5 men for every woman at the 155 IQ mark.[3] It is worth stressing that Lynn and Irwing, like all evolutionary psychologists, hold to the view that IQ is an accurate measure of general intelligence, so they equate higher IQ scores with higher intrinsic, genetically-induced intelligence.

Lynn continued to pump out papers and newspaper articles propagating his pet obsessions and some newspapers were only too willing to indulge him. In 2010 the *Daily Mail* saw fit to publish a prominent story by 'PROFESSOR RICHARD LYNN' (their capitals), which carried this headline: 'Sorry, men ARE more brainy than women (and more stupid too!) It's a simple scientific fact, says one of Britain's top dons'.[4] The story included nuggets like: 'One of the main reasons why there are not more female science professors or chief executives or Cabinet ministers is that, on average, men are more intelligent than women.' Lynn added that 'not only is the average man more intelligent than the average woman but also a clear and rather startling imbalance emerges between the sexes at the high levels of intelligence that the most demanding jobs require. For instance, at the near-genius level (an IQ of 145), brilliant men outnumber brilliant women by 8 to one. That's statistics, not sexism.'

Lynn blamed 'political correctness' for the lack of attention to these 'facts' and he continues: 'Ever since the Frenchman Alfred Binet devised the first intelligence test in 1905, study after study has confirmed the same result. When it comes to IQ, men and women – at least once they've gained adulthood – simply are not equal. Boys and girls may start out with the same IQ but by 16 or so boys are starting to inch ahead. The ever-growing success of girls at GCSE, A-level and now at university would seem to refute this – but the blame lies with our exam system, with its emphasis on coursework, which rewards diligence more than it does intelligence. The undeniable, easily measurable fact remains that, by the time both sexes reach 21, men, on average, score five IQ points higher than women.'[5]

He went on to say that the 'field of evolutionary psychology' provides reasons for males being the brainer sex – hunters were faced with more complex problems than gatherers/child carers and were therefore 'clearly the most intelligent'. Also, men, with their testosterone boosts, were more competitive. They therefore developed bigger brains and higher IQs, and he insists this advantage is more marked the higher one goes up the IQ scale although he adds that there are 'far more stupid men around than there are stupid women' (but fails to offer an EP-based reason for this, noting there is 'no simple, or, indeed, totally convincing explanation as to why this is'[6])

Lynn and Irwing's work was savaged with vigour in the science journal *Nature*, which branded its methodology and conclusions as 'deeply flawed', noting they failed to weight their tests according to sample size. In a separate article, *Nature* reviewer and intelligence testing specialist Steve Blinkhorn assessed their approach and declared: 'Their study ... is simple, utter hogwash'.[7] He lambasted their statistical analysis and pointed to a vast body of research showing no differences in male-female IQ scores. As he explained: 'Studies with no significant or substantial results never find their way into a journal, with no reporting of separate statistics for each gender when there is no difference. My own file drawer turned out to contain an analysis of data from 752 applicants for places on one degree course during the 1970s, tested on the advanced matrices [an IQ test], which were designed for the top 20% of the population. This yielded an advantage of 0.07 standard deviations for females. The sample is larger than all but five of those found by Irwing and Lynn.'[8]

Blinkhorn explained why such research is under-reported. 'Psychologists often carry out studies that find no differences between men's and women's IQs but don't publish them for the simple reason that finding nothing seems uninteresting. But you have to take these studies into account as well as those studies that do find differences. Lynn and Irwing did not, which skewed their results.'[9] He specifically mentioned a massive Mexican study they ignored, showing virtually no difference between male and female IQ scores. Such was its size that it would have comprised 45 percent of their data. 'Had it been included, as it should have been, it would have removed a huge chunk of the differences they claim to have observed,' Binkhorn said.[10] He added that where there are sex differences to be found, 'detailed study of the internal workings of the test tends to show why. That's not based on instinct, but on my professional experience in designing gender-fair tests.'[11]

### Pinker: more male geniuses, more male idiots

When it comes to the second, 'yes, but ...' category, we are spoilt for choice. Take, for example, the LSE philosopher and EP punter Helena Cronin, who rivals the most fervent evolutionary psychologists when it comes to pink and blue advocacy. 'Females are much of a much-ness,' she has noted, 'clustering round the mean. But, among males, the variance – the difference between the most and the least, the best and the worst – can be vast. So males are almost bound to be over-represented both at the bottom and at the top. I think of this as "more dumbbells but more Nobels" ...'[12]

Still, Cronin must make way for exhibit number one, the doyen of evolutionary psychology, Steven Pinker, who has long earned his epaulets when it comes the all-nature-no nurture view of the world – particularly regarding gender difference. This is the tone of contempt for those who see a substantial role for parenting: 'It is said that there is a technical term for people who believe that little boys and little girls are born indistinguishable and are moulded into their natures by parental socialization. The term is 'childless'.' The childless Mr Pinker shares Lynn's view that males are the more variable gender and that men produce more geniuses than women, but also more idiots. (Incidentally, he also shares Lynn's views that different human populations may differ genetically when it comes to 'average talents and temperaments'[13] and is strongly inclined towards Lynn's view that Ashkenazi Jewish men are more intelligent than everyone else.[14]) Pinker, it should be said, is an Ashkenazi Jewish man who rates his own intelligence highly. For example, he once wrote that he'd had his IQ tested and that the results were 'above average'[15] and after having his genome sequenced he asked: 'Who wouldn't be flattered to learn that he has two genes associated with higher IQ?'[16] (In fact, claims previously associating higher IQ with two particular genes have since been thoroughly discredited – the genes have no bearing on intelligence[17]).

In 2005 the president of Harvard, Larry Summers, an economist by training, got into a spot of bother by claiming that the under-representation of women in tenured science and engineering positions at top universities was explained mainly by 'intrinsic aptitude' at the 'high end'. This speech prompted a wave of condemnation and a series of apologies from Summers who later resigned[18]. His cheerleader was Pinker whose crusade involved debating fellow Harvard cognitive psychology professor Elizabeth Spelke. Unlike Lynn and Irwing, he stressed there were no differences in *average* intelligence. As he put it: 'Men and women show no differences in general intelligence or $g$ — on average, they are exactly the same, right on the money.'[19] But he insisted that 'males are the more variable gender' with the result that they produce 'more prodigies, more idiots', and like Lynn and Irwing he argued that the differences at the prodigy level only emerged at puberty.[20]

To illustrate his prodigy point, he turned to a long-term study of mathematically precocious children selected in the 7th grade for being in the top one percent of maths ability. These super-bright 13-year-olds were given the SAT mathematics test, devised for college-bound students. Speaking in March 2005, Pinker reported a male-to-female ratio of 2.8 to 1 for those achieving the elite-level score of 700 or above, and he went on to suggest the only feasible reason was innate mathematical ability. But here comes the crunch: he had to admit what he called the 'interesting' fact that 25 years earlier the male-to-female ratio at the 700-plus mark for the same test was 13-to-1. So which is more significant: the fact that 11 years ago girls formed 26.3 percent of the mathematical elite among American 13-year-olds, or that in 25 years the representation of girls among this elite rose by 346 percent? And what does this rapid increase in female representation suggest? Obviously there were no genetic changes between 1980 and 2005, so it must come down to environment. The question then becomes one of whether the 2.8–1 ratio is the biologically-induced final limit, or whether that too might change in another 25 years, suggesting other factors are involved.

In her response, Spelke drew attention to this rapid rate of female improvement and explained the remaining, shrinking, gap mainly in terms of the socialisation of girls and boys on mathematical and scientific terrain, but also in terms of a gender bias in the SAT mathematics questions, which, she said, under-predicted the performance of women in the talented sample.[21] It is worth noting that the SAT does not purport to be an intelligence test and most experts concede that performance in this test relates as much to the way mathematics is taught and learnt as to natural ability.

If, like Pinker, you are determined to 'prove' that men are over-represented at both the prodigy and the idiot end of the intelligence scale, and that this relates to the greater 'variability' of the male gender, then you need to find a way of measuring innate intelligence. Pinker, like Lynn, believes that such a method has existed for 110 years: IQ testing. He has declared IQ to be 'highly heritable' and believes it really does measure intrinsic general intelligence[22] and so he turns to IQ tests to make his point – or rather to one IQ test conducted in Scotland 85 years ago, which he claims, in italics, was administered to *the entire population of Scotland* (actually, it wasn't – it was administered to 87,498 children born in 1921). He tells us that 'at both extremes, males slightly predominate'.

The results showed that while the average IQ of this cohort of Scottish girls was slightly higher than for boys[23], the boys represented 57.7 percent of those with IQs of 130 or more and 58.6 percent of those with IQs of 60 or below.[24] Incidentally, Steven Pinker's sister and fellow evolutionary psychologist, Susan Pinker, uses the identical graph in her book *The Sexual Paradox,*[25] based on the same study, to show that 'men are simply more variable'. But the authors of the paper they drew from were more cautious. They noted that the conclusions of American gender-based studies reporting that males show greater variability in some abilities (e.g. mathematics) 'are not consistently found in other countries'.[26] For example, a 1994 cross-cultural study that compared sex differences in variability in verbal, mathematical and spatial abilities found that in each of these areas there were countries where the female score was more variable than the male.[27]

An interesting meta-analysis, involving 7-million children, was conducted by the University of Wisconsin-Madison psychology professor, Janet Shibley-Hyde, who found that the prediction that males would always score higher than girls at top percentile levels was wrong. An example comes from Minnesota 11th grade students, whose results were analysed to see how many boys and girls scored in the high 90s. Among white children Pinker's thesis held. About twice as many boys scored above the 99 percent mark. But with Asian children there was a different result – a lead for girls at the 99 percent mark.[28] A study of mathematical ability at the top five percent of ability found that in four countries (Indonesia, Britain, Iceland and Thailand) there were either more girls than boys at the elite level or they were equal[29] – an outcome mirrored in two other large cross-cultural studies.[30]

Girls also feature in maths tests designed to find students who are not just 'highly gifted' but 'profoundly gifted' – girls like Sherry Gong who won the gold medal at the gruelling International Mathematical Olympiad (IMO) in 2007. The cognitive psychologist Cordelia Fine also points to the huge variation in female representation in the IMO from country to country. For example, a profoundly gifted female mathematician in Slovakia has a five times higher odds of being included on her country's IMO team as her counterpart in neighbouring Czech Republic. And in the United States, Asian American girls are not under-represented in the IMO relative to their proportion of the US population.[31]

So it appears the pattern in mathematical tests for the profoundly gifted is similar to that in IQ tests: in most populations there are more boys at the top percentiles, but in some countries and populations there are the similar numbers and in some there are more girls. This suggests that the reason has nothing to do with biology and everything to do with culture. Quite simply, some cultures nurture mathematical ability in girls more than others.

## 110 years of IQ

Before we draw conclusions based on IQ results, we need to answer three questions relating to IQ: First, do IQ tests measure 'general intelligence'? Second, is IQ mainly a product of genetics or of environment? Third, when considering the IQs of the male and female populations, are there environmental factors that might influence their average sores and the distribution of their scores?

The story begins with a modest French psychologist who didn't believe his tests measured intelligence and worried that others would get the wrong idea. In 1904 Alfred Binet was commissioned by his government to find students who'd benefit from special education. He devised several tests and assigned an age level to each. Later, mental age was divided by real age to create an 'intelligence quotient' (IQ), although Binet was uncomfortable with this acronym because he felt intelligence was too complex to be expressed as a single number and could not be measured 'as linear surfaces are measured'[32], and he was not convinced that the number expressed anything 'congenital'. He feared that if given too much significance 'it may give place to illusions'.[33] But Binet's fears were realised – as soon as American and British psychologists got their hands on his tests. For Binet the IQ number expressed no more than a rough guide to the average result for the mini-tests. For his successors, it expressed something momentous – innate general intelligence.

Let's begin with the intelligence bit. If Binet was right, and these tests don't measure intelligence, what do they measure? The man regarded as the most important intelligence theorist of the past half century, Jim Flynn, said they measured a form of 'abstract problem-solving ability'[34] and 'correlate with a weak causal link to intelligence'[35]. In other words, what we understand by intelligence covers a far wider and ambit and more diverse range than the abstract problem solving ability measured by IQ tests. The braininess that will help you get an A* in maths might also help you get a high IQ score, but has little relation to the kind that will help you understand the nuances of human inter-relation or the emotional pain someone is experiencing, or that will prompt you to paint a masterpiece or view the world in existential terms, or work out quickly what is wrong with a machine and how to repair it, or for that matter with the kind that will attract the epithet, 'wise'.

Some intelligence theorists have tried to find alternative tests to measure a wider range of intelligence-type abilities. One was the American psychologist Louis Thurstone who disputed the notion of 'general intelligence' and developed an alternative model based on his belief that there were a number of largely independent 'primary mental abilities' (verbal comprehension, word fluency, number facility, spatial visualisation, associative memory, perceptual speed and reasoning). Then in the 1980s a Harvard developmental psychologist Howard Gardner came up with a theory of multiple intelligences, independent of each other – linguistic, logic-mathematical, musical, spatial, bodily/kinaesthetic, interpersonal, intrapersonal and naturalistic. 'These multiple intelligences constitute a better description of a range of human cognitive capacities,' he said. 'Just because a person is smart in one area, we simply can't predict how they will do in other areas of life.'[36]

This view is supported by recent cognitive research. One study involved 100,000 people taking 12 mental tests. Results suggested three distinct intellectual components – short term memory, reasoning, verbal ability. A sample of the volunteers then had MRI scans and it was found that these three corresponded with distinct patterns of neural activity, involving different nerve circuits.[37] 'A person may well be good in one of these areas, but they are just as likely to be bad in the other two,' said one of the paper's co-authors, Roger Highfield. 'For a century or more, many people have thought that we can distinguish between people, or indeed populations, based on the idea of general intelligence which is often talked about in terms of a single number: IQ. We have shown here that's just wrong.'[38]

But within a few years of Binet's first tests, his US followers had decided that what they measured was nothing short of biologically-defined general intelligence. They declared this be a science, and used it to rate the supposedly innate intelligence of races and populations, to keep waves of immigrants out of America, to separate 'morons' from society and to sterilize 'feeble-minded' people. One psychologist in particular was responsible: Colonel Robert Yerkes managed to persuade the US army to test 1.75-million recruits during the First World War. With his assistant, Captain Boring, and a team of researchers, he divided soldiers into two groups – the literates, who were given the Army Alpha test and the illiterates, given Army Beta. The former included knowledge-based questions about geography, food products, baseball stars, advertising characters and even 'the number of legs on a Kaffir'. The latter required soldiers to identify light bulb filaments, tennis nets and record player horns. They were often administered in a slap-dash way, but Yerkes, Boring and their disciple Carl Brigham decided that what they measured was innate, and they ranked the races accordingly – northern Europeans at the top, Jews and other eastern Europeans in the middle and blacks at the bottom. These results were later used to help keep Eastern European immigrants out of America, including Jews fleeing the Nazis.

Meanwhile an Englishman Charles Spearman was embracing the new mathematical technique of factor analysis and applying it to IQ testing, which provided a way of correlating the matrices from each of the verbal and arithmetical mini-tests involved. The general factor between them – known as $g$ – was said to reflect general intelligence, which he insisted was intrinsic. '$g$ is ... determined innately,' he said, adding that 'a person can no more be trained to have it in higher degree than he can be trained to be taller.'[39]

Most of these early IQ pioneers eventually recanted. Boring admitted that the hereditarian conclusions about the army tests were 'preposterous', and Brigham agreed that comparative tests of racial groups were invalid, adding: 'One of these comparative racial studies – the writer's own – was without foundation.'[40] But perhaps the most remarkable volte face came from Spearman who conceded that his factors had no necessary relation to physical reality and that anything outside of hard science was 'mostly illumination by way of metaphor and similes', adding that it was 'all the folly of youth and that it was pleasant to act foolishly from time to time'.[41]

But the IQ missionaries steamed ahead, undeterred. The most fervent was Spearman's batman, Cyril Burt, an Oxford-educated psychologist who was so convinced by the biological qualities of IQ that he decided that poverty was caused by low IQ rather than the other way round, or as he put it: '[T]he backwardness seems due chiefly to intrinsic mental factors ... that extend beyond all hope of cure.'[42] Burt claimed to be testing separated identical twins in his bid to determine just how innate these scores were and he used the claimed results to push for the introduction of 11-plus exams, which were then used in English state schools (1944 to 1976). The idea was that the top-20 percent of 11-year-olds would be sent to grammar schools; the rest to trade-based secondary modern schools, although the results were tilted towards boys because there were more grammar school places in boys' schools.

After Burt died in 1971, his reputation unravelled through a series of revelations about his methods and results. The coup-des-grace came from his close friend and admirer Leslie Hearnshaw whose official biography declared that Burt's early work was haphazard, sloppy and biased, and his later work – including all of his twin studies – was fraudulent (he had invented his separated identical twins). Some hereditarians leapt to Burt's defence, saying he was guilty of no more than carelessness but the more credible view is that he fabricated his results. None of this had any impact on the ubiquity of IQ testing, particularly within the United States where it was used as a way of deciding who should get which jobs.

## How to increase (or reduce) your IQ

Most contemporary tests divide *g* into 'fluid intelligence' (the ability to solve novel problems through reasoning) and 'crystallised intelligence' (knowledge-based), with fluid intelligence seen as being more '*g*-loaded' (innate). In fact, most hereditarians insist that fluid intelligence (*Gf*) is set for life at an early age and cannot be raised although they allow one exception: practicing IQ tests, which, when you think about it, is really a concession that 'fluid intelligence' is anything but fixed (if doing lots of IQ tests raises your 'fluid intelligence' score, then, clearly, learning is part of the *Gf* package).

Recent research contradicts this faith in the innate properties of *Gf* – showing that learning can increase results in these tests. For example, in 2008 a team of researchers exposed volunteers to a computer game designed to improve short-term memory. All of their fluid intelligence scores increased and those who did the most practicing improved the most.[43] There have been claims that other forms of learning can also increase IQ scores, including music lessons and reading to your child every day from the age of three,[44] and, as we shall see, the expectation of doing well can, it itself, be a significant factor in performance in all sorts of aptitude tests, while the expectation of doing poorly will have the opposite result. In addition, there are several health-related ways of improving IQ, with research indicating that breast-feeding for at least nine months can raise your baby's IQ by seven points (although this might have more to do with the additional close contact with the mother). Other claims have been made for certain fish-based diets, for exercise during pregnancy, and, more definitively, for iodine supplements taking during pregnancy.[45]

On the other hand, there are many IQ-diminishing possibilities including drinking alcohol during pregnancy, smoking cigarettes and/or cannabis during pregnancy and 'spanking' your child regularly. A recent study of 328 mothers and children found that pregnant women exposed to chemicals found in phthalates (found in products such as lipstick, nail polish and air freshener) had IQs of seven points lower than those with least exposure.[46] More generally, there is a huge body of research showing that poverty and growing up in chaotic surroundings can have a long-term negative impact on IQ.[47]

But none of this has stopped the hereditarians of IQ theory from persisting with their claim that IQ results reflect a high level of heritability, at least when considered within a given population. Their 'proof' in this regard comes from twin and adoption research.

## Twins, adoption and IQ

There are two ways of using twins to prove your point. The first is to compare single egg (identical) twins and fraternal (non-identical) twins on the basis that they share the same environments equally. The idea is that if the IQs of identical twins are similar and of non-identical twins less so then we can devise a percentage figure for the heritability of IQ (because fraternals are in same genetic position as other siblings while identicals share the same genes).

The problem with this is its premise: the assumption that fraternal twins share their environment in the same way as identical twins. Fraternal twins frequently look no more alike than ordinary siblings (which might mean they look nothing like each other). They may do their best to distinguish themselves from their twin siblings and they are often treated differently by teachers, peers and parents. As they grow up, they tend to move further apart, sometimes in ways that could have a direct impact on IQ – one twin might be more studious, the other might drink more alcohol and smoke more cannabis. So the underlying environmental assumption behind these studies is flawed.

The second way of using twins is the method falsely claimed by Cyril Burt: comparing separated identical twins. But these also come with an inbuilt problem (aside from the fact that they are hard to find): if raised in similar backgrounds in terms of education and social class how can we decide whether the similarity in IQ scores is the result of genes or environment? Put differently, if a pair of twins who have the same genes are separated at birth and raised in the same kind of middle class home how could they possibly end up with IQs that are anything other than similar? This was a point made in a 1981 book by the clinical psychologist Susan Farber who studied previous research on separated identical twins (95 sets) and found that most were actually not separated at birth and had spent several years together both before and after adoption. Many were adopted by family members and most were raised in the same kinds of families. When she examined their IQs, she found that the more separately they were raised, the greater the IQ gap.[48]

However, this by no means ended the reign of the twin studies industry. A very determined hereditarian, Thomas Bouchard, got down to business, generously bankrolled by an overtly racist funding organisation, the Nazi-inspired Pioneer Fund (whose current aim includes promoting eugenics and 'human race betterment'). Bouchard lucked out when he read reports of the 'Jim Twins', Jim Springer and Jim Lewis. They were separated at one month old but had all sorts of life story overlaps: both once worked as deputy sheriffs, took holidays in Florida, drove Chevrolets, had dogs called Toy and ex-wives called Linda and Betty. One had a son called James Allan; the other James Alan – and they drank the same beer, smoked the same cigarettes and bit their nails. Their story made headlines all over the world and seemed to confirm the idea of the astonishing impact of genetic inheritance.

But there are several problems with using this case as being representative of separated identical twins. First, in the more than 150 pairs studied by then, they were the only ones showing anything close to this level of coincidence. Second, they were raised in the same kind of family in the same area, which might explain their life choices. Third, closer examination showed that while the similarities were cherry-picked, the differences were understated. For most of their lives they had different kinds of jobs, they had different ways of presenting themselves, different hairstyles and facial hair and there were marked differences in personality. One was better at speaking; the other at writing; one was 'more easy-going' the other 'more uptight'. And, oddly, we were never told whether their IQs were similar. As for the rest: pure coincidence. Not even the most ardent genetic determinist would claim there were alleles for the names of wives, children and dogs.

But the 'Jim Twins' helped launch Bouchard's 'Minnesota Study of Twins Reared Apart', which analysed data from 56 separated identical twin pairs who'd lived together for an average of just over five months prior to separation and were re-united an average of under two years before being interviewed. From these results he decided that adult IQ was 70 percent heritable but he reached this conclusion through a questionable assumption: that although almost all were raised in similar white middle class families, there was 'no environmental similarity'. Yet he acknowledged that only a few of his initial cohort of 56 were raised in poverty and none were 'retarded' (sic) and he recognised that that non-middle class environments might increase environmental percentages.[49]

Actually, his results raise the odds well above 'might'. Read beyond the headlines and you come across a Bouchard case where one identical twin was adopted by a fisherman, raised in a home with few books and only schooled up to the 10th grade while his brother was adopted by a cosmopolitan family, lived all over the world and became an electronics expert for the CIA. The brother's IQ was 20 points higher. In another, the twins' IQs were 29 points apart.

The impact on environment can be seen from another celebrated case, highlighted in the *New York Times* magazine. A hospital error meant that two pairs of Colombian identical twins were mixed up and therefore raised separately as two pairs of fraternal twins – one pair in a poor rural area and the other in a lower middle class urban area. When they found out the error as young adults and met up, initial reports focussed on the similarities. Then the California State University professor, Nancy Segal, who had once been Bouchard's head researcher, subjected them to interviews, questionnaires and IQ tests. She expected similar results for the identical twins but although their IQ results were not released, she acknowledged they were less alike than anticipated. 'I came away with a real respect for the effect of an extremely different environment,' she was quoted as saying.[50]

Geneticists warn against trying to come up with hereditability figures for social phenomena. The Stanford biologist Paul Ehrlich stresses that even under experimental conditions, where one can come up with mathematical data about the comparative contributions of genes and environment, 'it can't be done completely because there is an "interaction term". That term cannot be decomposed into nature or nurture because the effect of each depends on the contribution of the other.'[51] With IQ in particular this quest for a hereditability percentage has always seemed quixotic. There is the unknown number of genes that might be implicated in ways we don't know. Then there are environmental factors directly affecting IQ. And there is the impact of the environment on the genes – in the way they express themselves. Finally there's the impact of genes and environment on each other (in the way smart people seek out smart environments). Nature works through nurture, genes are expressed within an environment and their expression is influenced by that environment.

It is also worth noting that while research by psychologists tends to focus on zones of similarity between identical twins, geneticists are more interested in differences. These may related to chance differentiation in the womb (different placentas, for example), epigenetic influences (relating to differences in the expression of genes), different experiences in the womb (in positioning, for example) or different experiences during birth or in early life. The result is that even when raised together one identical twin might be gay but not the other, or they may die of different diseases at different ages, or they might have different IQs. The point is that whether looking at similarities or at differences the relationship between genetics, epigenetics and environment is far trickier to discern than previously realised.

Another way of trying to unravel this riddle is to look at children who are not twins who have been adopted into different kinds of families. The results illustrate that at least when it comes to IQ, home environment plays a huge role. In one French study, children from poor families adopted by poor families had IQs averaging 92.4; those from poor families placed in wealthier families averaged 103.6. In another French study of severely under-privileged and abused children, average IQ at the time of adoption was 77. Nine years on they were tested again. Those adopted by farmers and labourers averaged 85.5; those adopted into middle class home averaged 92; those who went to upper middle-class homes averaged 98.[52] As you vary social conditions substantially, particularly regarding social class and education, IQ scores pull apart, and these gaps continue into adulthood.

Yet evolutionary psychologists insist that parental influence and socialisation counts for next to nothing regarding IQ. This is how Steven Pinker put it: 'There may be effects of parental expectations and parental treatment on young children while they're still in the home, but most follow-up studies show that short of outright abuse and neglect, these effects peter out by late adolescence. And studies of adoption and of twins and other sibs reared apart suggest that any effects of the kinds of parenting that are specific to a child simply reflect the pre-existing genetic traits of the child, and the additional effect of parenting peters out to nothing.[53]' In fact, twin and adoption research shows the opposite, thoroughly discrediting the notion that genes will always trump parenting – and this applies particularly to IQ.

## Male and female IQs

But what of the different average IQ scores of different populations? A few IQ theorists – those of a racist bent – cling to the idea that genes play a part in these gaps. But the overwhelming consensus is that the differences are explained *entirely* by environment. The key evidence comes from the 'Flynn effect', named after Jim Flynn, who showed that IQ scores were rising consistently, which is why the tests need to become ever-more challenging if the 100 mean is to be maintained.

There were two essential points in Flynn's discovery. First, the reason IQ scores rise has nothing to do with genetics. He showed that the key environmental factor was exposure to abstract logic, which is what IQ tests assess. Second, IQ scores of some groups rise faster than others – the US Ashkenazi Jewish average early in the 20th century was well-below the 100 mean, whereas now it is well above, and recently it's been the Kenyans who've shown the fastest average IQ growth – a rise of 26.3 IQ points in 14 years.[54] If different populations are subjected to different environmental influences (diet, styles of parenting, educational input, discrimination and prejudice, familiarity with aptitude testing and, in particular, access to various forms of abstract logic), then their IQ averages will differ.

How does this relate to gender? Well, although girls and boys have the same ranges in terms of class and family background, we cannot assume they are raised in identical environments in all IQ-related respects. Clearly, in some families in some eras and some parts of the world, it is assumed boys are to be the bread-winners, and that boys' education is more valuable and that boys are more naturally inclined towards maths, science, computer programming and business, and therefore need to be steered in those directions. On the other hand, in more recent years, in just about every subject in every school year, girls outperform boys in most advanced industrial and developing states, which might be explained partly by gender-related learning cultures.

Any of this could have an impact on average IQ, and on IQ scores at the upper and lower ends of the spectrum. For example, if, putting effort into school work is considered girly or swotty then this is likely to have an impact on academic grades, which it certainly does do in the UK where white, working class boys have long been right to the bottom of the academic ladder at all levels of schooling (below white working class girls and well below working class boys and girls of other ethnic groups). British state education thankfully no longer invests in IQ testing (beyond the entrance exams of a few grammar and private schools), but we'd anticipate that this kind of anti-learning culture would have an impact on average IQ scores. On the other hand, if some boys are hot-housed from early childhood to excel in maths and science, and are told these are masculine subjects, and are tutored in them, and if, in addition, they also play ever-more-challenging computer games, their IQs could be raised accordingly. And if more boys than girls are pushed and prodded in this way, one might anticipate that more of them would have IQ scores in the higher percentiles.

On the average IQ question, Flynn accepted the point made by Lynn (but rejected by other IQ theorists), that through much of the 20th century adult males marginally outperformed adult females, although unlike Lynn his explanation relates entirely to environment. He diverges more pertinently from Lynn by showing that in recent years average IQ scores of women have *overtaken* those of men. 'In the last hundred years, the scores of both men and women have risen,' he says, 'but women's have risen faster.' The reasons relate to changes in the workplace and in education in the second half of the 20th century. 'This improvement is more marked for women than for men because they have been more disadvantaged in the past. ... The full effect of modernity on women is only just emerging.'[55]

This would also help to explain why the male-female gap at the upper percentiles of tests like the SAT is narrowing. But the results will vary from area to area, country to country, and may relate to the position of women in society and in the professions. In places where the proportion of girls taking advanced mathematics, physics, chemistry, statistics, computer science and so-on increases and where families encourage girls in these directions from an early age, it seems likely that these gaps at the elite level will continue to close. In other words, to return to Steven Pinker's obsession, the reason the male gender appears to produce 'more prodigies, more idiots' is the same reason why the prodigy gap is narrowing: it has all to do with cultural factors and nothing to do with genes.

# CHAPTER NINE

# LADY DRIVERS AND GENTLEMAN PARKERS

I'm regarded as something of a joke within my running club when it comes to finding my way. I get lost – frequently – and new members are routinely warned that they should never follow me if they hope to get back to base. Every time I take a wrong turn in a cross country or triathlon or training run (which is often), the round of hilarity is resumed.

No doubt my inclination to wander off-piste is mainly genetic in origin. I inherited it from my mum, and passed it onto my eldest daughter (although my father showed no problems with finding his way – nor my brother, sister and younger daughter). Mums and daughters are the expected inheritors of any shortfall in what was once termed the 'bump of vocality'. But boys and men? They're supposed to know where they are going, and to be able to read maps upside down if in doubt. But I can do neither – and I should add that the rest of my practical skills extend no further than being able to assemble Ikea furniture packages. Not very manly!

It is often claimed that 'male brain' activities like being able to find your way and read an A-Z standing on your head are a by-product of the package that comes with the testosterone dividend – part of the largesse of being born with a pair of testicles. If this were true, it would suggest men like me should be scraping the testosterone barrel. But, as it happens, for unrelated medical reasons, I've had my testosterone levels tested twice over the last decade and there was no shortfall, so it would seem that low testosterone levels is not the cause.

Which raises another possibility: the observation that it is primarily women who are destined to be unable to parallel park, read maps upside down and find their way has nothing to do with testosterone and everything to do with self-reinforcing cultural prejudices. From another angle, we might then say that the finding-your-way genes are distributed in a gender-neutral way but tend to be ignored when they are put to use by women and remarked upon when absent. A women who struggles to parallel park, or who hesitates in taking a narrow gap in the road or who gets confused at a roundabout, might be branded a 'typical women driver'. A man with these problems might, instead, be branded simply as a 'bad driver' or an 'over-cautious driver', or even one who 'drives like a woman'.

## Pinker: men are better at rotating shapes

I've previously discussed the view in EP circles that the mental 'modules' of men and women evolved differently, leading to different intellectual and emotional inclinations and capacities. Steven Pinker is a fervent advocate of this notion, which he uses to explain why men are more prevalent in some intellectual pursuits and women in others. He summarises his perspective like this: 'Men are better at mentally rotating shapes; women are better at visual memory. Men are better at mathematical problem-solving; women are better at mathematical calculation.'[1] More specifically, he tells us that 'for some kinds of spatial ability, the advantage goes to women but in "mental rotation", "spatial perception" and "spatial visualisation" the advantage goes to men'. These, incidentally, are the kinds of assets that help people find their way and read maps outside down.

He believes these gender-based predilections are 'hard-wired', reinforced by similarly innate social and intellectual concerns – greater female interest in people and living things; greater male interest in inanimate objects. Such inbuilt inclinations result in women being more naturally inclined towards studying education and the social sciences and men more towards studying the physical sciences and engineering.[2] In addition, he says men are the more reckless, risk-taking sex, and that includes intellectual risk-taking. So, not only do men and women have different intellectual capacities, but they have different inbuilt motives, which prompt them to pursue different academic and career paths – a similar perspective to Baron-Cohen's male brain-female brain dichotomy with its suggested gender-directed job choice.

Pinker's emphasis in explaining why men are more prevalent at the elite academic levels in maths, science and engineering is that they are inherently better at them. As he puts it: 'In psychometric studies, three-dimensional spatial visualization is correlated with mathematical problem-solving. And mental manipulation of objects in three dimensions figures prominently in the memoirs and introspections of most creative physicists and chemists ... '[3] Further, he tells us that 'men score better on mathematical word problems and on tests of mathematical reasoning, at least statistically.'[4] But these differences do not exist until puberty and the data requires him to acknowledge that in mathematical reasoning 'there has been a decline in the size of the difference'. He does not explain why this gap is narrowing.

Despite these lacunae, Pinker insists on his all-nature-no-nurture case, noting that gaps between male and female performance are culturally universal and stable over time. To forestall the argument that they might *reflect* gender roles, he insists that social forces are over-rated as an explanation for gender differences in academic achievement, that parenting has little impact on the way children turn out, and that in contemporary America, parents and teachers treat boys and girls in exactly the same way, particularly when it comes to encouraging academic achievement. Where stereotypes exist, he says, they are not the cause of different outcomes but rather *reflect* different innate abilities and he adds that 'the error people make is in the direction of *under*predicting sex differences.'[5]

## Pinker on the nullity of 'several generations of feminism'

In a rather odd diversion, Pinker tells us that despite several generations of feminism, there is 'famously, *resistance* to change in communities that, for various ideological reasons, were dedicated to stamping out sex differences, and found they were unable to do so'. Examples he dismissively cites include 'the Israeli kibbutz, various American Utopian communes a century ago, and contemporary androgynous academic couples'.[6] As an explanation for why there are not more women in tenured positions in the sciences, this is, well, rather an odd departure – and his use of 'famously' and emphasis on *'resistance'* suggests an undertow of contempt. His decision to include the paragraph does nothing for his core case, but it does seem to say a fair amount about his mindset on questions of equality.

So then, a spot of diversionary comment of my own, from the shallow well of personal experience: In my late teens and early 20s I lived in a series of communal houses in Cape Town with people dedicated to social change, including stamping out sex differences – people whose mode of behaving and dressing might have appeared as 'contemporary androgynous' to Pinker. In one form or another, this lifestyle persisted throughout my undergraduate and early postgraduate years – for about seven years or so. But, as Pinker would have predicted, it sort-of faded after this. However, the reason was not because it defied biology but rather because it didn't fit the wider world. More specifically, work took over, and the financial need to live communally no longer existed. In the decades that followed, those of us who'd lived 'androgynously' in these communal houses had to make our accommodation with this wider world. Most of us got married, had children, bought our own houses. But through all this, the impact of those gender-equal years was never extinguished.

Most of the women kept their own surnames after marrying and, more significantly, continued to work after having babies, while most of the men played a significant role in child nurturing. And without exception these parents felt it part of their role in life to raise children in a way that reduced the impact of sex differences.

## Spelke: why men learn to be better at rotating shapes

Anyway, back to the core subject: responding to Pinker in their Harvard debate, Elizabeth Spelke picked Pinker's core arguments to pieces by getting down to the specifics of children's performances in a range of mathematically-relevant tasks. She disputed his point that from birth boys are inherently more interested in objects and mechanics and girls in people and emotions, citing 30 years of research (some of which has already been discussed in chapter six). 'Do we see sex differences?' Spelke asked. 'The research gives a clear answer to this question: We don't. Male and female infants are equally interested in objects. Male and female infants make the same inferences about object motion, at the same time in development. They learn the same things about object mechanics at the same time.'[7] She added that common paths of learning continue through pre-school years, using the example of children manipulating objects to see if they can get a rectangular bloc into a circular hole. 'If you look at the rates at which boys and girls figure these things out, you don't find any differences. We see equal developmental paths.'[8]

Spelke considered whether males enjoyed an inbuilt advantage when it came to mathematical reasoning by looking at the mathematical foundations that emerge in childhood – first, the system of distinguishing between one, two and three objects; second the system for distinguishing large, approximate magnitudes; third, the system for verbal counting; fourth the system for determining the geometry of a surrounding layout and fifth the system for identifying landmark objects. 'We can ask, are there sex differences in the development of any of these systems at the foundations of mathematical thinking. Again, the answer is no.' Here she referred to studies of the development of natural number concepts between the ages of two and three-and-a-half. 'When you compare children's performance by sex, you see no hint of a superiority of males in constructing natural number concepts.'[9] She also cited studies of mental rotation ability among pre-school children, which, she said, contradicted claims of innate male superiority. In one study, four-year-old children were brought into a room, something was placed in a corner and then their eyes were closed and they were spun around. Their task was to remember the shape of the room, open their eyes and work out how best to rotate themselves back to the direction of the hidden object. The results showed no advantage for boys over girls.

Sex differences *do* emerge later in children's lives, but Spelke said these related to the ways boys and girls were raised and their preferred *strategies* in solving certain kinds of problem. If a task can be solved only through geometry, there's no difference in male and female performance. However, if it can be solved either through geometry or through identifying individual landmarks, females on average prefer the landmarks approach and males the geometrical approach. In tests where a problem can be solved either through a mathematical formula or through diagrammatical spatial reasoning, girls tend to favour the former; boys the latter. In some timed tests one way of solving the problem is quicker than the other, which is why males and females might show differing cognitive profiles. She insisted: 'This pattern of differing profiles is not well captured by the generalization, often bandied about in the popular press that women are "verbal" and men are "spatial." There doesn't seem to be any more evidence for that than there was for the idea that women are people-oriented and men are object-oriented. Rather the differences are more subtle.'

But are males better at mathematics? Spelke proposed an experiment to find the answer: take a large number of students from both genders and, over a significant period of time, present them with the kinds of tasks that real mathematicians face – new material that they haven't yet mastered. 'The good news,' she said, 'is [that] this experiment is done all the time. It's called high school and college. Here's the outcome. In high school, girls and boys now take equally many math classes, including the most advanced ones, and girls get better grades. In college, women earn almost half of the bachelor's degrees in mathematics, and men and women get equal grades... . The outcome of this large-scale experiment gives us every reason to conclude that men and women have equal talent for mathematics.'

She argued that the imbalance in the numbers of men and women majoring in mathematics, science and engineering had nothing to do with innate ability. Instead, it had everything to do with socialisation, and she specifically challenged Pinker's belief that parents treated children equally, referring to studies of parents interviewed shortly after the birth of their child. The parents of boys tended to describe them as being stronger, more robust and bigger than the parents of girls, even though the medical records showed no distinctions. She cited a study of 12-month toddlers where the parents of boys were more confident in their predictions that their child would do well on a particular crawling task whereas, in fact, no gender differences were found in this task – or in their ability to walk, crawl or clamber. She also cited a study of parents of sixth grade children on mathematical talent. Parents of boys were more likely to assume their sons had natural talent than parents of girls, even though testing showed no gender-based differences – and she referred to similar studies relating to ability in science.

Spelke also pointed to studies of infants where the researchers did not know their gender. When babies showed fear, they tended to identify them as girls. When they showed anger, they tended to identify them as boys. In one study, half the babies were randomly assigned a male name and half a female name. Those given male names were rated as strong, intelligent and active, those given female names were seen as small and soft. 'I think these perceptions matter,' she said. 'You, as a parent, may be completely committed to treating your male and female children equally. But no sane parents would treat a fearful child the same way they treat an angry child. If knowledge of a child's gender affects adults' perception of that child, then male and female children are going to elicit different reactions from the world, different patterns of encouragement.' She added that parental perceptions, from early in life, might end up deterring a girl from considering a career in science of maths.

And it's not just parents – these unconscious prejudices also affect university professors. Take, for example, a study where professors of psychology were sent the CVs of two candidates for a senior, tenured position: one a brilliantly qualified candidate and the other an average tenure-level candidate. For half of the professors the names of the candidates were male and for the other half, female. There was no distinction in their judgements on the outstanding candidates but for the average candidate 70 percent of the professors said yes when the candidate was given a male name, but only 45 percent when the candidate was given a female name. Asked to list any reservations they had on the candidates, four times as many reservations were expressed when a candidate had a female name (and these ratios applied to both male and female professors).

Pulling these examples together, Spelke concluded: 'From the moment of birth to the moment of tenure, throughout this great developmental progression, there are unintentional but pervasive and important differences in the ways that males and females are perceived and evaluated.' More men than women will put themselves forward into the academic competition, 'because men will see that they've got a better chance for success. Academic jobs will be more attractive to men because they face better odds, will get more resources, and so forth.' She also suggested there was a snowball effect. 'All of us have an easier time imagining ourselves in careers where there are other people like us'. Finally, she tackled Pinker's point about male geniuses. 'I think we want to step back and ask, why is it that almost all Nobel Prize winners are men today? The answer to that question may be the same reason why all the great scientists in Florence were Christian.'

## Male success and 'presumed brilliance'

This view has been reinforced by research at the University of Illinois in Champaign, published in the journal *Science*. An academically diverse team of researchers surveyed more than 1,800 academics from 30 disciplines, and drew the conclusion that the value placed on 'presumed brilliance' was a more reliable predictor for under-representation of women than any other consideration. The variables that their research led them to dismiss included the claim that women were less likely to choose fields demanding analytical thinking or long hours of hard work and the claim that they didn't make the grade in fields where only the top percentile of elite students were successful. Instead, they found, the issue related to perceptions of brilliance that female students internalised. In subjects where women were told, or where it was presumed, that 'unschooled genius' was required, their representation was below 50 percent. As the researchers put it: "[W]omen are underrepresented in fields whose practitioners believe that raw, innate talent is the main requirement for success, because women are stereotyped as not possessing such talent."[10] But, they found, this was not because they had less innate genius, but rather because they presumed so – and they noted that the same point applied to African American under-representation in these subjects because 'this group is subject to similar stereotypes'.[11]

This imbalance relates not just to the sciences but also to humanities where there were similar presumptions about a genius premium. In the US in 2011 only 31 percent of PhDs in philosophy went to women. However, in humanities and sciences where this presumption was weaker, women dominated or numbers were equal. In 2011 54 percent of American PhDs in molecular biology went to women while there was gender parity in neuroscience and more than 60 percent of doctorates went to women in anthropology and education and more than 70 percent in psychology.[12] This suggests the divide has nothing to do with men being better at science and women at humanities. Instead, it involves the impact of perception, relating to cultural stereotypes extolling male genius (examples mentioned included the portrayal of fictional characters from Sherlock Holmes to Dr House as innately brilliant, compared with the 'swotty' cleverness of Hermione Granger[13]). One of the lead researchers, the University of Illinois psychology professor Andrei Cimpian, explained: 'Any group that's stereotyped to lack a trait that a field values is going to be underrepresented in that field.'[14] This had nothing to do with innate ability. 'There is no convincing evidence in the literature that men and women differ intellectually in ways that would be relevant to their success in the fields we surveyed,' he said. 'According to our hypothesis, female under-representation is not the result of actual differences in intellectual ability, but rather the result of perceived or presumed differences between men and women. We found that women were indeed less likely to obtain PhDs in fields that idolise brilliance and genius.'[15]

Commenting on this study and applying it to the British experience, the University of Cambridge mathematician Dr Helen Mason noted that fewer than 20 percent of undergraduate maths students at Cambridge were women (although the proportion rose to 25 percent when it came to doctoral studies), but she said this imbalance had nothing to do with males producing more geniuses. 'Females are indeed as brilliant as males,' she said, 'but perhaps they do not realise this, and society does not recognise it either.' And she adds another variable to the equation, relating to perceptions of what is intrinsically masculine and feminine. 'Peer pressure is often strong during girls' teenage years and it is often not perceived to be very "feminine" to study maths, physics and engineering.'[16]

## Stereotype threat and female test scores

But what about the maths tests that Pinker refers to where men do, genuinely, out-perform women? Are there at least some areas where men are superior to women? If we ignore the results of the child-hood tests mentioned by Spelke (where no gender-based differences were found), and concentrate on adults, we would, indeed, find some areas where men do tend to do better than women. This applies par-ticularly to tests of mental rotation ability – about three-quarters of adults who score above average in mental rotation tests are men.[17] But given that there is no difference in childhood, we cannot assume the reason is biological. There are other possibilities, one of which relates directly to the point made in the University of Illinois study – to the way negative perceptions of potential are absorbed by women.

In one US gender-based study of mental rotation ability, one group was told they were about to take a test linked to natural abil-ity in aviation, engineering, navigation and 'undersea approach and evasion'. Men did better than women. The other group was told its purpose was to predict ability in dress design, interior decoration, crocheting, needlepoint, knitting and flower arrangement. Male performance declined significantly; female performance soared.[18] A similar experiment on mental rotation ability was conducted among students at an elite, private liberal arts college in the eastern seaboard of the United States. One group of was fed encouraging informa-tion relating to their attendance at this academically elite college; the other was fed 'gendered' information about the differences in male and female abilities in mental rotation. Women in the former group scored significantly higher than in the latter.[19] In another US study of mental rotation ability one group was given gendered information while the other was given irrelevant information about geography. Men outperformed women in the gendered group but not in the geography group.[20]

There were also several studies of mental rotation ability con-ducted in Italy, including one where high school students were divided into three groups. The first group was informed that men outperform women on this task, probably for genetic reasons; the second, that women outperform men, probably for genetic reasons; the control group was told nothing. In the 'men are better' group, and in the control group, the boys outperformed the girls – but in the 'women are better' group, the girls performed just as well as the boys.[21]

What these results suggest is that male advantage in mental rotation relates significantly to self-perception. Women who take these tests believing their innate abilities are inferior, tend to do worse than men. Women who take these tests believing they are as good or better than men tend to equal and sometimes surpass men in their results. Cordelia Fine notes that attempts to find a biological basis for the male advantage have all been unsuccessful. Explanations based on later male puberty and on an X-linked recessive gene for spatial ability have not been supported by evidence, nor have theories based on hormonal differences.[22] What we know for certain is that mental rotation ability can be improved significantly through training. For example, several studies have shown that playing computer games improves mental rotation ability, and that women improve more than men in this regard[23] (perhaps because they are, on average, less familiar with computer games and are therefore starting from a lower base).

If we combine the tests on pre-school children showing no male advantage when it comes to mental rotation with our knowledge that, by-and-large, boys are more exposed to mental rotation practice when growing up (not least through the computer games they play), and our knowledge that negative self-perceptions of female performance in mental rotation tests can have a profound negative impact on their results, then we have a feasible alternative to the perception that the male advantage in mental rotation is rooted in biology.

This phenomenon of performance being influenced by the mental state of those taking the test is not confined to mental rotation.

Similar results are found in other maths tests where male advantages are claimed. One involved more than 100 students who'd received approximately the same grades taking an advanced calculus class at the City University of New York. They were given a graduate level test (way beyond their normal level) and told they could get an extra credit based on their results. They were divided into two groups, both told the test was designed to measure innate maths ability. However, one group was also told that no gender difference had ever been found with this test. In the control group, the male and female students scored the same (they averaged 19 percent). However, in the group that received the additional information, the women significantly outperformed the men (an average of 30 percent). The researchers concluded that when women were reassured they weren't inferior, it 'unleashed their mathematics potential'.[24]

Another Italian example: two groups of female students were given an advanced, graduate-level maths test. One was told men out-performed women on logical mathematical tasks, the other that there was no such distinction. Before each task, the women were asked to record their feelings on a blank page. The group told that women did worse recorded increasingly negative remarks ('These exercises are too difficult for me' etc.) and performance declined. By the second half of the test the group told that women were inferior averaged 56% compared with 81% for women in the control group.[25] Another study found that the more women tried to suppress 'irrational-women concepts' the worse they performed.[26]

Unwanted anxiety absorbs mental capacity and detracts from the focus required to perform difficult calculations. The result is that when female students are released from what the pioneering American psychologist Claude Steele called 'stereotype threat' their performance in a variety of advanced mathematical tests improves significantly, but when negative stereotypes about female potential in these tests are reinforced, their minds shift from expecting success to avoiding failure, and clogs up their working memory.[27] Steele, who conducted similar tests among black and white students, notes that those burdened with negative stereotypes 'know that they are especially likely to be seen as having limited ability. Groups not stereotyped in this way don't experience this extra intimidation. And it is a serious intimidation, implying as it does that they may not belong in walks of life where the tested abilities are important'.[28]

### Shibley Hyde: the gender similarities hypothesis

But what of the wider point about differences in motives? As we've already seen, Pinker, like almost all evolutionary psychologists, believes that men and women have evolved substantially different mindsets – different ways of viewing the world and viewing their own roles within the world, and substantially different ways of relating to the world, and that this has a profound impact on choices made of what to study and which careers to follow and it helps explain why there are more men in engineering, mathematics and the hard sciences.

There is a great deal of research showing that these supposed mindset differences, and these substantial gaps in emotional range and in intellectual direction, have been hugely exaggerated. For the sake of brevity I will cite just one – chosen because it involved meta-analysis carried out over a 20-year spell. In 2005 the journal *American Psychologist* published a paper by Dr Janet Shibley Hyde of the University of Wisconsin, entitled 'The Gender Similarities Hypothesis', which pulled together research from 46 previous studies.[29] Meta-analysis involves the researcher collating all available research on a particular topic, extracting the relevant statistics from each paper and weighting it for size, and then analysing the data. Shibley Hyde's paper offered a synthesis of research of gender differences in studies conducted since the mid-1980s.

In a few of the abilities she assessed there were indeed substantial differences – most notably motor skills (such as throwing ability). Another area of marked difference was heightened male physical aggression (but far less so with verbal aggression, where the differences were on a minor scale, or, as in the case of relationship aggression, the results were ambiguous).[30] But in most psychological variables examined, including a range of cognitive abilities, verbal and non-verbal communication, self-esteem and leadership inclination, little or no difference emerged. Males did not interrupt more; females were not more self-revealing. In some areas it depended on whether the subjects thought they were being observed. For example, some studies showed a minor difference in terms of inclination to smile. Women smiled more – but mainly when they thought they were being observed (when subjects thought they weren't being observed the difference almost disappeared, and the smiling gap also varied considerably according to age and culture).

Shibley Hyde's meta-analysis also raised queries about the claim that males were the more variable gender. As she put it: 'Most VR [variance rate] estimates are close to 1.00, indicating similar variances for males and females.'[31] And where there were minor differences these seemed to depend on the context. For example, her meta-analysis found very small differences in mathematical abilities, but she noted that these were hard to interpret. For example, girls were slightly better than boys in computation ability at elementary and middle school level but by high school level they were equal. When it came to complex problem solving there were no differences at elementary and middle school level, but a slight difference favouring boys at high school level (although in these studies, she noted that age differences might have been relevant).[32]

Her conclusion is that males and females are 'alike on most – but not all – psychological variables'[33] – and even when the differences are substantial it is not clear where nature ends and nurture begins. Shibley Hyde notes that the unscientific popularity of the opposite, Mars and Venus view, involving over-inflated claims of gender difference, can have a negative impact on conflict and communication among heterosexual couples, on self-esteem, particularly of adolescents, and on women's opportunities in the workplace.

## Women not hard-wired for chess?

Nigel Short, English chess grandmaster from the age of 19, told a chess publication in 2015 that men were 'hardwired' to be better chess players than women. 'Why should they function in the same way?' he asked. 'I don't have the slightest problem in acknowledging that my wife possesses a much higher degree of emotional intelligence than I do. Likewise, she doesn't feel embarrassed in asking me to manoeuvre the car out of our narrow garage. One is not better than the other; we just have different skills. It would be wonderful to see more girls playing chess, and at a higher level, but rather than fretting about inequality, perhaps we should gracefully accept it as a fact.'[34] He added: 'It's a fact that men and women are hardwired differently'[35] and that, 'Men and women do have different brains. This is a biological fact.'[36] He elaborated in a television interview: 'It's quite easy to demonstrate there is a fairly substantial gap between men and women. ... I'm talking about averages here ... statistically women don't [compete] in the same numbers. The average gap is pretty large and that is down to sex differences ... Those differences exist.'

Short's attitude to women was suggested by his comments in 2012 that a particular chess tournament in Manilla was 'unsurpassed by the sheer volume of totty', and that 'there were literally hundreds of smiling and invariably polite 18–20-something-year-old [Filipina] hostesses. Not a few liaisons were struck up during the course of two weeks.'[37] But that doesn't, in itself, disqualify his view on sex differences. For example, at the time of writing 98 out the top 100 chess players in the world were men. What other causes could there be?

One explanation is offered by Judit Polgar, the now-retired 40-year-old Hungarian who entered the world's top 100 at the age of 12, broke Bobby Fischer's record by becoming the youngest-ever grandmaster at 15, once beat Gary Kasparov (and 10 other world champions) and reached number eight in the world, and whose record against Short was eight wins, three losses, five draws. Her father taught her that there was no difference between men's and women's chess-playing ability, and 'he absolutely wouldn't let me take part in female-only competitions'.[38] This, she said, contributed to her ability to beat the top men. 'I grew up in what was a male dominated sport, but my parents raised me and my sisters [to believe] that women are able to reach the same result as our male competitors if they get the right and the same possibilities.' She went on to say: 'It's not a matter of gender, it's a matter of being smart'.[39] And she added on Twitter: 'Men and women are different but there are different ways of thinking and fighting still achieving the same results'[40]

Most female players do not get the same parental boost as Polgar, and they absorb the prevailing attitude that men are naturally better at chess. Also, far more boys play chess than girls and the gap between the numbers of men than women is even greater (for example, only 5.82 percent of players on the German Chess Federation rating list were women).[41] Sue Maroroa, a British women's international master, said that one reason related to the ethos at chess clubs. 'Sometimes when I go to a new chess club, I can tell guys don't think I can play …. There is an attitude within the chess community that women are worse than men. It's just like any old boys' club which is dominated by older men who still have that attitude, "Oh, she's a girl, so she can't play." But I know my capabilities, so I just take it within my stride.'[42]

But most girls and women don't take it in the stride. Sabrina Chevannes, another British international master, said that the culture of sexist jokes and of overbearing male superiority prompted a high female dropout rate. 'Unfortunately, I do think there is a lot of sexism at every level of chess, from beginners right the way to the top. … Generally when I've gone to a tournament, they'll ask me if my child is playing because they presume I'm the mother of a player, or even ask if I'm the wife of someone playing. God forbid I would actually be there to play. And if they did find out I was a player, they'll always assume I'm in the beginners section. They assume I'm terrible because I'm female and it is completely infuriating.'[43]

Rita Atkins, another British International chess master, and now a chess teacher, said one reason for the imbalance at the top was that from early on boys are more aggressive. 'I teach a lot of chess to school kids and I think it has to do with the fact that girls shy away from aggressive competitiveness at a young age whereas young boys are very competitive. I think that is the main reason why girls don't get into it as much when they are young, and so don't get to competition level.'[44] As already seen, one reason for greater male aggression relates to higher testosterone levels, magnified by culture. This is, in part, a biological explanation, but not one related to the intellectual potential of women or to the way their brains are 'hardwired' for chess. The neuro scientist Dr Gina Rippon said there were no neurological differences in male and female brains that could explain differences in chess-playing ability, and she suspected one reason related to the lack of female role models.[45]

## Why girls out-perform boys at school and university

So let's look at another area where there are gender differences in most countries: primary and secondary school education. Wherever you look – the UK, Europe, the United States, Asia, Africa – girls or women consistently do better than boys and men and in much of the world the gap is growing. For example, at all levels of British schooling girls out-do boys and this gap continues all the way to A-levels, both in terms of performance and participation.

A 2015 report by the Sutton Trust, based on a sample of 3,000 British students who were studied from age three to 18, found that while 66 percent of girls took AS, A-levels or another qualification, only 55 percent of boys did the same. The gap was most marked among children from working class backgrounds – and particularly white working class boys – with only 29 percent of boys from homes with low family income going on to study after GCSE.[46] And contrary to the view that males out-perform females at the top percentiles, among those achieving A or A* grades in A-levels in 2014 girls outperformed boys in 23 of 29 subjects, including maths, physics and ICT.[47]

Inevitably, this has an impact on higher education. Among those applying for university courses in England in the 2014–15 academic year, 42.47 percent were men and 57.53 percent, women, and among post-grads, 58.8 percent were women. By 2016 women in England and Wales were 35 percent more likely than men to go to university, and the gap was widening, prompting the Higher Education Policy Institute to predict that if current trends continued a girl born in 2016 would be 75 percent more likely to go to university than a boy. The gap became wider the further one went down the economic scale, with only ten percent of white boys from disadvantaged families going on to university (significantly less than disadvantaged black and Asian boys from the same class background).[48] In Scotland the gap is wider-still – women were 49 percent more likely to apply to university in 2014 than men – five percent higher than two years earlier. As with A-levels, this gulf in educational achievement does not disappear in the higher percentiles. For example, the percentage of English women graduating with first class or 2:1 degrees was 63.9 in 2010 compared to 59.9 percent of men.[49]

Strangely enough the ubiquity of this female-favouring gender gap does not prompt claims that it reflects innate female intellectual superiority. Instead the debate around this issue relates to education styles – on the one hand, those suggesting the gap can be explained through the supposedly female-oriented emphasis on coursework rather than exams (a claim weakened by the fact that girls also outperform boys in exams – and in the UK the gap has grown despite a return to exam-focussed assessment); on the other hand those blaming it on the dire socialisation of boys, particularly those from working class backgrounds who are raised with an anti-learning culture. The idea that girls might just be 'hard-wired' to be smarter than boys is not considered – and quite rightly so.

## Back to sense of direction

So to return to my poor direction sense and whether this is more typically female (along with my related inability to read a map upside down). Four possibilities present themselves.

First, it could be that more women than men fall short in these areas for biological reasons.

Second, it could be that women are merely *perceived* to fall short in these areas, with each example of women lacking a sense of direction, or being unable to read a map upside down, or struggling to parallel park, seeming to confirm the initial prejudice, while male failures in these zones are either ignored or dismissed in 'drives like a woman' terms.

Third, it could be that there are, indeed, more women who struggle in these areas, but that this relates to the way they are raised (they get less practice with orienteering and computer games and cycling and driving than their brothers).

Fourth, it could be that slightly more women struggle in this regard, but that the reason relates to 'stereotype threat' – women perceive they will be bad in these respects because they are women, and this affects performance.

It could also be a combination of points two, three and four. Which illustrates a more general point relating to the conclusions of Shibley Hyde's research: that just because there is a perceived difference in the behaviour of males and females it does not imply that these perceptions are valid – and even when they are shown to be valid, the implication that they are therefore necessarily biological in origin should always be questioned.

# CHAPTER TEN

# MEN, WOMEN, WORDS

We all know girls are chatty. Women too. They gossip. They share. They emote all over the place, crying away on each other's shoulders. They spend hours on the phone to each other. They gab-gab-gab away. Chat ten-to-the-dozen. They just won't shut-up. And men? Well now, we keep to ourselves, don't we? Hold it in. We prefer the monosyllabic approach to life – men of few words, we are. We grunt. And let's face it, when we do choose to use language, we use it differently from the ladies: we talk about facts and stuff; they talk about people and emotions. Hell, sometimes it almost as if we come from different planets.

That, at least, is the view that emerged from the pages of numerous gender-obsessed pop psychology tomes that spewed out of America in the 1990s. Read these books (if you must) and you'll find several common themes, including the assumption that women are inherently more 'verbal' than men – better at using language, more linguistically dexterous and far more inclined to chat. As the Oxford University language professor, Deborah Cameron, put it (tongue deeply buried in cheek): 'It's like our consolation prize. We're not very good at anything that actually counts, but we can certainly talk.'[1]

This idea that men ration their words and speak a different language from women is at the core of John Gray's 1992 best-seller *Men Are From Mars, Women Are From Venus*, which sold more than

50-million copies, and the 1990 best-seller *You Just Don't Understand: Women and Men in Conversation*, by the Georgetown University socio-linguistics professor, Deborah Tannen, which claims that the patterns of speaking used by men and women are so different that they belong to different linguistic cultures or communities – a book that spent four years on the *New York Times* best-seller list, including eight months at number one, and was translated into 30 languages. It is also the view that emerges from the papers and books pumped out by evolutionary psychologists, and it features prominently in the writing of several pop science authors.

### Brizendine: men 7,000; women 20,000

The most prominent of these was the Californian psychiatrist Louann Brizendine, whom we met in chapter 8 with her subsequently discredited claim that the 'sex-related centres in the male brain are actually about two times larger than parallel structures in the female brain' (a reference to the hypothalamus, which actually had nothing do with sexual thought). But Brizendine's money quote is the one she made about language. In her 2006 book *The Female Brain* she made the astonishing statement, highlighted on the jacket cover, that women use 'about 20,000 words a day' compared to a mere 7,000 for men.[2] This claim, that women have almost three times as much to say about life as men, was so remarkable and seen as so inherently newsworthy that it went viral. Within days it had been reported in a range of American media outlets including CBS, CNN, National Public Radio, Newsweek, The New York Times and the Washington Post and it quickly spread to the international media through websites, web chatrooms and the like. It not only seemed to confirm conventional wisdom about chatty women, it took it significantly further.

But Brizendine was plain wrong, which she was eventually forced to admit. And not just a bit off the mark, but spectacularly so. In fact, as we shall see shortly, men and women use approximately the same number of words on average – most women are no chattier than most men. But at the same time, there is huge variation in the number of words used by women, and huge variation in the number of words used by men. You get talkative and taciturn women, and it is the same with men. But, as always, the overwhelming evidence that soon emerged against Brizendine's false statistics attracted negligible publicity compared with the original claim. Nine years after Brizendine's 20,000–7,000 figure was thoroughly debunked, I still occasionally hear it repeated at dinner parties as if it is an incontrovertible fact.

## Liberman: pop psychology and urban myths

The first savaging came from Mark Liberman, a University of Pennsylvania linguistics professor who specialties include working with recorded speech. His previous research had suggested there were no more than minor differences between the amount men and women talk. However, up until then he'd been unable to find a reliable study of total daily word usage that compared men and women, but he guessed that 'whatever the average female vs. male difference turns out to be, it will be small compared to the variation among women and among men; and there will also be big differences, for any given individual, from one social setting to another.'[3] The 20,000–7,000 figure was so out of kilter with his own experience that he delved deeper into Brizendine's research, starting with her footnotes, and published his findings in *The Boston Globe* soon after Brizendine's book hit the shelves.

It turned out Brizendine had gleaned her figures from the self-help book, *Talk Language: How to Use Conversation for Profit and Pleasure* by Allan Pease and Alan Garner. Pease's perspective on the world can be gleaned from his previous titles – *Why Men Don't Have a Clue and Women Always Need More Shoes* and *Why Men Can Only Do One Thing at a Time and Women Never Stop Talking*. Liberman found the self-help universe was entirely self-referencing, throwing around figures for the male-female daily wordcount ratio that ranged from '50,000 vs. 25,000 down to 5,000 vs. 2,500'[4]. Sometimes Pease and his fellow self-help authors would give different figures in different publications. Liberman's detective work led him to the conclusion that these figures came from, well, nowhere. They were guesswork, entirely invented – sucked out of thin air rather than being based on actual research. As Liberman put it: 'Pease and his co-authors never cite any specific studies as the source of these various numbers.'[5]

He compared the 20,000–7,000 claim to other popular social 'facts' like the claim that the Inuit have 48 words for snow, or is it 200 or seven or four? (It turns out the number is the same as in English). It took off and spread and solidified, becoming a hard-to-move urban myth like the nonsense claim that we only use 10 percent of our brains. He was not prepared to let it rest. Instead, he mounted a concerted campaign against Brizendine's figures, noting that they were drawn from the urban myth that women 'always gab, gab, gab,' containing more than a hint of misogyny.[6]

Liberman's conclusion should have made the feature, comment and news editors responsible for trumpeting Brizendine's figures hang their heads in shame. 'The authors of self-help works, as a group, don't seem to have any particular standards of accuracy,' he wrote. 'Journalists, meanwhile, generally take them at their word in reviews and interviews, and publishers are happy as long as the books sell well. It's a shame to see this approach to the facts spreading into the growing genre of books about the neuroscience of sex differences, where the facts can have real consequences.'[7]

In this case, however, his efforts drew at least some reward – a retraction from the author. When contacted by *The Guardian* on Liberman's critique of her 20,000–7,000 claim Louann Brizendine admitted that language wasn't her specialism and that she'd misfired. 'I understand Mark Liberman's point and I am grateful to him,' she was quoted as saying. 'He felt I was passing on data that was not nailed down, and thus perpetuating a myth, so it will be taken out in future editions.'[8]

## Shibley Hyde: differences 'close to zero'

If the editors had bothered to cross-check the data, or had read more widely, they would have come across Janet Shibley Hyde's meta-analysis (discussed in the previous chapter), published a year before Brizendine's book came into their review pile. Shibley Hyde, who'd analysed numerous gender-based studies over the previous 20 years, had a great deal to say about language use – all of it contradicting the claims of Brizendine and her self-help sources. She broke down the verbal realm into a number of sub-categories covered by the studies analysed. The differences between males and females in reading comprehension, vocabulary and verbal reasoning were found to be 'close to zero'. The differences in conversational interruption (where 70 studies were analysed) was found to be small, as was talkativeness (73 studies), assertive speech (75 studies), 'affiliative' speech (46 studies), speech production (12 studies) and self-disclosure (205). In fact, only in spelling, where there was a 'moderate' difference favouring women, was the gap anything other than small (and this finding is more shaky because it only involved five studies).[9]

Newspaper, radio and television editors might also have perused a 1995 textbook by J K Chambers, professor of linguistics at the University of Toronto, who noted that the amount of 'non-overlap' between males and females in terms of verbal ability was about a quarter of one percent. This suggested, he said, that 'for any array of verbal abilities found in an individual woman, there will almost certainly be a man with exactly the same array'.[10] This followed an earlier paper (1988), focussing specifically on verbal ability, by Shibley Hyde and Marcia Linn, professor of development and cognition at the University of California, Berkeley. They concluded at the time that the differences between men and women when it came to verbal ability was in the region of 'about one tenth of one standard deviation', which is the kind of language academics use for 'next to nothing'.[11]

However, in at least some of the verbal categories chosen by these researchers, the conclusions reached should come with a prominent cautionary asterisk. Take, for example, Shibley Hyde's finding that men were slightly more likely to interrupt in conversation (the margins in the studies she collated ranged from 0.15 to 0.33). The problem here is that context is everything. As Cameron, points out, interrupting someone 'may be rude or domineering behaviour – a way of silencing and belittling them – or it may be supportive behaviour, signalling enthusiasm for what they are saying'. She adds: 'If we take no account of what interruptions mean, simply counting how many men or women produce will not tell us what any difference signifies.'[12]

## Observational studies: men talk more than women

There have also been numerous gender-based observational studies (where the researcher would analyse single interactions between men and women, and then measure their contributions), and in most of these it has been found that men talk a bit more than women. A 1993 review of 56 such studies found that in 34 of them men talked more than women, in two of them women talked more than men, in 16 they talked the same amount and in four no clear pattern was discerned.[13]

However, the reason men talked more than women in these studies might relate to questions of status, with men more likely to occupy higher status positions, or to be regarded as having a higher status, and women deferring to them. As Cameron puts it: 'The basic trend, especially in formal and public contexts, is for higher-status speakers to talk more than lower status ones.'[14] She points to studies on group discussions relating to topics where female expertise is assumed (such as pregnancy and fashion). In these cases men tend to defer to women, who talk more.[15]

The problem with using observational studies to determine who talks more is that they are always context-specific, which means they cannot accurately reflect the number of words used by males and females on a particular day, which will cover numerous different contexts. To do that, we would need to find a way recording a significant sample of men and women throughout a day without them feeling they needed to perform.

## Pennebaker et al: 16,000 for men; 16,000 for women

One stab at a figure came from Liberman himself. He re-analysed tape-recorded daily conversations from 153 participants from the British National Corpus in 1997 and then, very tentatively, estimated that women use 8,805 words per average day and men 6,073 words. If this proved to true, men would be using around 70 percent of the number of words used by women, double the percentage in the Brizendine version. However, Liberman doubted this estimate because no information was available on when participants decided to turn off their manual tape recorders (which might have varied between men and women). It also covered all of those involved in any of the recorded conversations, not just the people who were recording all of their output during two days (the total number of people recorded were 561 females and 536 males).[16] The best that could be said for this study therefore is that it provided a pointer suggesting that the difference was far smaller than Brizendine had claimed, but the methodology was too flawed to be certain.

The definitive wordcount study was conducted by a five person team from three leading American universities. Their paper, published in the journal *Science*, delivered the death blow to Brizendine's claims by concluding there was no statistically significant difference between men and women in terms of the number of words used. They spent eight years developing a method for recording 'natural' language use, using a digital voice recorder called EAR that unobtrusively tracked people's moment-by-moment interactions by periodically recording snippets of their conversations as they went about their lives (30 seconds for every 12.5 minutes – meaning that four percent of their total word output was recorded). The volunteers couldn't switch it off and didn't know when it was recording.

Between 1998 and 2004 the research team transcribed the words recorded using this 1:25 method from 396 volunteers (210 women and 186 men – all of them American and Mexican students). Their results showed that both men and women used about 16,000 words during a 17-hour day. They therefore found no statistically significant gender difference in word use between men and women but that there were significant differences *within* each gender group[17] The result was unambiguous: 'We therefore conclude, on the basis of available empirical evidence, that the widespread and highly publicized stereotype about female talkativeness is unfounded.'[18] One of the researchers, the University of Texas in Austin psychology professor Jamie Pennebaker, elaborated: "Whatever people might think, the stereotype is wrong. What is interesting about this study is that we found nothing at all. It's unusual in science for a study that finds nothing to generate such interest. It overturns a notion that has become part of the cultural mainstream."[19]

### Cameron: EP's role in myth-making

As usual, the results of this study received nothing like the level of publicity received for Louann Brizendine's original 20,000–7,000 claim, even though, as we have seen, Brizendine's figure was a complete thumb-suck. One reason is that stories relating to big differences between men and women are more newsworthy than stories about no difference. But its persistence – its refusal to die – suggests something more is involved. So what is the underlying source of this view that women are chattier and why is it so resonant despite the overwhelming evidence against it?

Deborah Cameron offers what might seem like a counter-intuitive answer: it thrives precisely because of the growing *similarities* (or declining differences) between the sexes. 'People want to believe there are clear-cut differences between men and women,' she argued, 'because they are men and women. They don't want to think about the similarities, which outweigh the differences.'[20] She says that as a linguist she's more interested in the variations in language use which may be greater within each group than between them – another thing she suspects that people are reluctant to think about because they prefer the idea of gender-specific paths.

Cameron blames the spread of the mythology of loquacious women and silent men on the growth of EP, which feeds the self-help and pop psychology oeuvre. From these quarters comes the view that men are less chatty because of their Pleistocene past as hunters who had to stand silently for hours, waiting and watching game, while women are talkative because back in their prehistoric past – when they were gatherers – they would chat away to each other while picking berries.[21] For example, the American evolutionary psychologist Rhawn Joseph wrote that while humanity was evolving, 'female mothers and female gatherers were able to freely chatter with their babies or amongst themselves'.... Unlike the men, who must remain quiet for long periods of time in order to not scare off game, the women are free to chatter and talk to their hearts' delight.'[22]

Actually, the men-hunt, women-gather view of our Stone Age past is no longer accepted by anthropologists and archaeologists. It was the business of gathering berries, fruit, herbs, insects and so-on that provided most of the sustenance of hunter-gatherer bands, and gathering was engaged in by both sexes (and remains so among the few remaining hunter-gatherer groups still around today). Also, it would appear that in most hunter-gatherer communities, hunting was not an everyday thing and women were also involved in it – particularly when it involved hunting for smaller game. Furthermore, hunting for big game was undertaken in groups and involved planning and coordination and long periods of travelling to the hunt sites. The hunters would work cooperatively during the hunt and then in butchering the meat before returning home. In other words, it would have been a bonding experience involving plenty of conversation.

Another evolutionary psychology version of the women-are-more-verbal idea is that like everything else in the EP universe, it arose from sexual selection. In this version, which starts from the retrospective observation that males court and females select, women are better *listeners* than men. The reason given is that men evolved to talk about themselves when courting (a bit like peacocks flaring their colourful tails at a 'lekking' courtship ritual) and women evolved to judge the quality of their verbal displays to judge their suitability as fathers. One of the many problems with this view (quite aside from its Lamarckian evolutionary premises), is that it seems to go against the women-are-chattier view. If it were true, we'd expect that the self-advertising men would have evolved to be the chattier sex.

These fairy tale versions of the past, which are the stock-in-trade of evolutionary psychology, are usually impossible to verify or falsify. As Cameron put it, EP 'takes today's social prejudices and projects them back into prehistory, thus elevating them to the status of time-less truths about the human condition'.[23] Faced with these Flintstone claims, whether on language or any other gender-related question, I sometimes find myself tempted towards the 'absence of evidence is evidence of absence' approach, and I have to remind myself that, really, absence of evidence is no more than absence of evidence. Still, when someone makes a historical or prehistorical claim without a shred of evidence to support it, we have no reason to take their word for it. A bit like Louann Brizendine's 20,000–7,000 figure, it's just stuff they kind-of invent – uneducated guesswork. As Cameron puts it: 'There are too many different and incompatible stories that can be made to fit the supposed facts – especially if... you approach the (modern) evidence like a peahen at a lek, fastening enthusiastically on the splashiest generalisations while disregarding the more serviceable but drabber specimens.'[24]

## New Guinea and Madagascar: women
## are from Mars, men from Venus

Having dispensed with the raw figures produced by Mars and Venus writers, and the Just-So explanations from evolutionary psychologists, we are still left with a range of other claims relating to the way language is used by men and women. Even if males and females use approximately the same number of words on average, it doesn't mean they use them in the same way. Among the other claims made in this regard are that men talk about things and facts, women about relationships and feelings; that men use language in a more competitive way than women, aimed at raising their status, while women use language in a more co-operative way; that for this reason male language use is more direct and less polite; that because of these different ways of using language there is miscommunication between men and women, which causes relationship problems.[25]

None of these claims can said to be 'wrong' because no doubt there are communities and cases where each of these generalisations hold. One question is whether they are typical in all societies, or, indeed, in most societies. Another is to ask whether we are 'hard-wired' that way, or do these generalisations persist because the structures and values of society prompt these kinds of differences? Cameron suggests that the missing element when considering differences in the way men and women use language is power: that we still live in male-dominated societies. 'Rather than being treated unequally because they are different, men and women may become different because they are treated unequally,'[26] she suggests.

One way of testing this is to consider whether there are societies or communities where men and women use language in substantially different ways. An example involves the women of Gapun, a village in Papua, New Guinea where, it would seem, they have overcome the frustration famously expressed by Bathsheba Everdeen in Thomas Hardy's *Far from the Madding Crowd*: 'It is difficult for a woman to define her feelings in language which is chiefly made by men to express theirs.'[27]

The Gapun women use a speech genre known as a *kros* (angry talk) when they are upset with their husbands or anyone else. This involves a highly abusive, profanity-filled, deeply insulting monologue that often lasts longer than 45 minutes and is intended to be heard by the whole village. The accepted rule is that the male target has no right to answer back, nor can anyone else interject on their behalf. The *kros* is only available to women and is an accepted way for them to air grievances.[28]

After quoting a particularly profane and insulting example of a real-life *kros*, Cameron notes that it is not very different to the kind of obscene language one might hear from women in a British town centre on a Friday night. However, while western women who behave like this might be branded for adopting masculine traits, in Gapun, using direct, abusive language is thought to be 'doing what naturally comes to women'. On the other hand men are considered to be naturally less belligerent and more co-operative, and therefore more capable of expressing themselves indirectly and of avoiding conflict. A clear case, it would seem, of men are from Venus, women are from Mars.[29]

A similar example comes from Madagascar, based on anthropological research conducted in the 1970s. Open confrontation was taboo there, but it appeared to be only men who were considered capable of using a formal, indirect and traditional style of speaking for ritual occasions, called *kabary*. More generally, they found men admired those who use language subtly, who promoted inter-personal ease and did not express their sentiments openly. The researchers found that women, on the other hand, tended to voice criticism and expressing anger directly to people's faces, and that both men and women agreed that women had *lavalela* (a long tongue). They also found that men would use women to communicate unwelcome information, issue reprimands, request favours and ask direct questions. Women would also do most of the buying and selling in the markets.[30]

The point of these examples is not to suggest that these are matriarchal societies. In both cases it was the indirect, polite, conflict-avoiding form of speech that was admired and considered appropriate for the political sphere, and this form of speech was considered an exclusively male preserve. Women were thought to be far too direct for leadership positions. However, what they do show is that the common western assumption that genteel, conflict-avoiding, supportive, affirming speech is feminine, while direct, assertive, competitive, adversarial speech is masculine, is way off the mark. It is often said that masculinity and femininity are 'constructs' and, at least in the case of language use, it rings true. What we regard as masculine and feminine in the way people speak is culturally specific. Which is another way of saying that it is not genetic in origin.

A different illustration comes from research on the speech tones of Japanese-British women. When speaking Japanese their voice tones were found to be higher than when speaking English because femininity appears to be associated with higher voices in Japan than in the UK. In addition, when comparing contemporary British female voice tones with recordings of those of 40 years earlier, researchers found that women today speak in a lower tone than they did in the 1960s – again, probably explained by the observation that notions of what is the feminine norm have changed.[31] This illustrates that the way people speak, even their voice tones, can vary according to cultural perceptions about what is gender appropriate.

One of the many fundamental errors made by the Mars and Venus self-help authors, by the pop-science authors like Louann Brizendine, and by evolutionary psychologists, is that they assume that what they observe, or claim to observe, in the way males and females talk, is universal and genetically rooted. It is, in fact, time-based, parochial and culturally-rooted.

# CHAPTER ELEVEN

# EP AND THE PREDATORY MALE

About 20 years ago I went on a weekend away at a friend's country house, and I remember a three-year-old girl climbing up on the arm of a sofa, rubbing herself up and down on her groin area. This happened a few times until the child's mother asked her what she was doing. 'I'm rubbing my 'gina,' she replied. 'It feels nice.' The mother smiled and affirmed this point before very gently suggesting it might be better to do that on the armchair in her own bedroom. But not every girl has parents that sensitive.

From a different angle, an elderly relative had some words of advice that she would impart to my daughters: 'Remember girls, men are after only one thing!' This notion came with an implied corollary – that women are not after that thing at all and therefore have to keep men at bay. In some cultures this idea is unheard of but in others it is pervasive and is taken to extremes: women must wear Burkhas or Nikabs to protect their modesty from the leering eyes of men, who can't help it, or, worse, girls must have their genitals mutilated because female sexual desire is dirty.

Part of the problem relates to the perspective that women enjoy sex a good deal less than men. A related view is that while men relish the physical act of sex, for women enjoyment is all about emotional closeness with their lover – in other words, that their pleasure in 'making love' is all about, well, making love. But is this really true?

We know that for physiological reasons, men and women experience sex differently, and this might also be one of the reasons why their post-coital response often differs, but does this mean that there is also a difference in the *extent* of their enjoyment? According to Janet Shibley-Hyde's meta-analysis of 46 studies of gender traits taken over a 20-year period – discussed in the previous two chapters – the gender difference relating to sexual satisfaction (or at least to what men and women said about their own sexual satisfaction) was 'close to zero'. However, she did find that there were differences between men and women in some aspects of sexuality, most notably in the frequency of masturbation.[1] – but this could be mainly or partly cultural (because, unlike the sensitive mum in my opening paragraph, many cultures view male masturbation as far more acceptable than female masturbation).

## Men naturally polygamous; women naturally monogamous?

The opposite view – that men have sex on their minds all the time and that they will look for any and every opportunity to try it on while women have an inherent interest in protecting what is theirs by keeping men at pikestaff length – is one of the staples of evolutionary psychology. The story we are told, over and over, is that because of natural selection, men have a hard-wired interest in spreading their genes as widely as possible; women have a hard-wired interest in attracting men – but only with the purpose of getting the best of the batch and then keeping them as partners for life so that they can be adequate providers. We are told that the female inclination not to sleep around and not to 'give it up for nothing' is every bit as ingrained as the male inclination towards incessant promiscuity. In other words, men are naturally polygamous; women are naturally monogamous.

The University of Texas evolutionary psychologist David Buss speaks for the team when he explains supposedly different attitudes to sex held by men and women in terms of the different adaptive challenges back in the Pleistocene. Women were confronted with the challenge of surviving pregnancy, childbirth and lactation and then rearing children. Men, on the other hand, faced the challenge of paternity uncertainty, with its risk of misallocating parental resources, and therefore developed an evolved inclination to increase their potential number of offspring. Men are therefore primarily motivated to spread their genes; women, to provide for their families (and to find a man who will do this for them).[2]

But if we consider the evolutionary imperative from another angle, we might come to a different conclusion – that women also have an evolved interest in a multiplicity of partners. We might ask why it isn't just as likely that the *females* who pass on more genes would be the ones who hedged their bets, slept with more than one man and who had children with different men. You might think that no culture encourages this attitude among women, but you'd be wrong. There's a huge variance between cultures and communities regarding attitudes to female sexuality and female promiscuity specifically.

The University of California anthropologist Dr Monique Borgerhoff Mulder, studied the Pimbwe women of Tanzania for 15 years. They live in small villages, have few material possessions and survive mainly by hunting, fishing and gathering, as well as by farming, and there are few divisions of labour (with, for example, the men helping with the cooking and child care). Those women with multiple partners were most likely to prosper, while with men, the higher the nuptial count, the lower the social ranking. Incidentally marriage is not launched by a set of rituals, and it ends when one partner leaves another.

Borgerhoff Mulder found that some Pimbwe women had five or more consecutive spouses, and that those with more than two husbands had, on average, higher reproductive success (and more surviving children) than those with only one spouse. Even more significantly, she found they had greater reproductive success than the male average (no matter how many wives the men had).

One reason for this related to another of Borgerhoff Mulder's findings – the women who had the highest number of spouses were considered high-quality partners (more reliable, harder working and more sober than the one-spouse women) – the opposite of the prevailing custom in the West where women's status and income tends to decline after divorce. 'We're so wedded to the model that men will benefit from multiple marriages and women won't, that women are victims of the game, but what my data suggest is that Pimbwe women are strategically choosing men, abandoning men and remarrying men as their economic situation goes up and down,' she said. 'Throughout history and cross-culturally there has been fantastic variability in women's reproductive strategies.[3]

Commenting on the implications of this study, the American primatologist and evolutionary theorist, Sarah Blaffer Hrdy, suggested the reason the multi-spouse women did best was that they ended up with more potential caretakers. 'The women are lining up more protection, more investment, more social relationships for their children to exploit. A lot of what some people would call promiscuous I would call being assiduously maternal.'[4]

The Stanford evolutionary biologist Paul Erlich, whom we met in earlier chapters, has long despaired of the polygamous males/ monogamous females claims made by genetic determinists. 'If a male-female difference exists in the desire to have multiple mates, it does not necessarily need to have a genetic basis. Even if women enjoy sexual variety as much or more than men, for thousands of years they have not needed to be rocket scientists to understand that they make a greater potential commitment per copulation than do men. The restraint could simply be learned.'[5] 'Elsewhere, he summarised this point by simply noting: 'Women, like men, evolved to be smart.'[6]

Even if we restrict our gaze to sexual relations in the advanced industrial world, the gap between male and female attitudes and behaviours would seem to be exaggerated. Every year or so one newspaper or another will publish the results of a poll that asks men and women how many sexual partners they have had in their lives. The answers always show a significant gulf – men say they have many partners; women, rather fewer. In some of these studies I have perused men have averaged twice as many sexual partners as women. But how could that be possible?

If we assume the number of heterosexual males is roughly the same as the number of heterosexual females, then how could it be that the average man has, say, 16 sexual partners by the age of 40 and the average women, 8? Who were the men having sex with then? If a man has an affair or 'fling' or a one-night-stand it is likely to be with a woman, which should produce a tick in the box on both sides. It is possible that the male average would be raised slightly by gay male sex, and we do know that as a result of earlier death, there are slightly fewer men than women, at least in the West, but neither of these factors would explain anything close to a 2:1 ratio. We also know that some men visit prostitutes, which would skew the female 'promiscuity profile', but it wouldn't change the averages (because each encounter with a prostitute would produce a tick in both boxes). The real answer would appear to be far simpler: men over-report and women under-report.

### Men hardwired for younger women; women hardwired for older men?

David Buss argues that women are pre-programmed by their genes to seek out older, richer men because they are better providers for their children who would therefore be more likely to survive. Men on the other hand, are pre-programmed to seek out younger, more nubile women – as many as possible – because they have a higher chance of reproductive success. Drawing from an American attitude study of more than 10,000 people from 37 cultures Buss found that women placed greater emphasis on older mates whom, he said, had higher odds of social success, while men placed more emphasis on youth.[7]

It could be said that the exceptions disprove the rule because there is convincing statistical evidence that in societies where the gender gap in income and job prospects narrows, so goes the gap in couples' ages, albeit gradually. Popular images of pre-industrial Britain frequently portray fathers being significantly older than their wives – but this too is in doubt. The author Adrienne Burgess researched records from Stoke-on-Trent in 1701 and found that 29 percent of wives were older than their husbands.[8]

In late 20th century Britain there's been a steady rise in the proportion of couples where the woman is the older partner and/or prime earner. The proportion of women in England and Wales marrying younger men rose from 15% in 1963 to 19 percent in 1981 to 26 percent in 1998 (with men marrying younger women in 65 percent of cases, and women of the same age in nine percent). The proportion of women marrying men more than five years younger than themselves doubled between 1963 and 2003.[9]

Figures from the US Bureau of the Census show that the average first marriage age in 1890 was 26.1 for men and 22 for women (a gap of 4.1 years). In 2007 it was 27.7 for men and 26 for women (a gap of 1.7 years – the lowest in recorded history). In one third of US marriages men and women are the same age or within one year of the other's age and in more than 14 percent of marriages the woman is two years or more older than the man.[10] The figures for Australia were similar – in 11 percent of first marriages in 1974 the woman was older than the man; by 1995 this had risen to 14 percent.[11] In Sweden the mean age difference between Swedish-born parents fell from around 3.5 years in 1940 to less than two by 2010. One Swedish study noted that 'the age difference between parents shrunk rapidly in the sixties after it began to slowly rebound in the eighties but has, over the last two decades, shrunk to the lowest level so far.'[12]

This also applies in some traditional communities Borgerhoff Mulder's research on women in Tanzania, for example, shows that Kipsigis women no longer favour wealthy men. And according to figures released by the United Nations Department of Economic and Social Affairs ('World Marriage Patterns 2000), the country with the lowest gap between partners in a first marriage (in the 1990s) was Belize, where, on average, the woman was 0.3 years older than the man. In several other countries including Iceland, Ireland, Israel, Jamaica and Vietnam, the average male marrying age was no more than 1.6 years older than the female. Countries where the gap averaged more than seven years included Afghanistan, Congo, Burkina Faso and Gambia – no doubt a reflection of the low status of women.[13] On average, Africa has the largest age gap between spouses on first marriage of all the continents. In South Africa the difference at first civil marriage was four years in 2011. In 13.3 percent of civil marriages that year the bride was older than the groom, in 8.1 percent they were the same age and in 78.6 percent the man was older.[14] Two years later the percentage of marriages where the bride was older had risen to 15, and the percentage where the groom was older had fallen to 77 percent.[15]

Based on this data it would seem that rather than seeing men as having evolved to seek out younger women and women as having evolved to seek out older, richer men, these strategies relate to the position of women in society, particularly regarding money and economic power. Reduce the income gap between men and women and, usually, the age gap also declines. There has also been research showing a correlation between wider age gaps and lower ages of mortality (the greater the gap, the shorter the woman's life expectancy), which would hardly count as a sensible evolutionary strategy.[16]

## Men hardwired for 36–25–36?

I recently re-read *Adam Bede*, George Eliot's tale of love and labour in rural England, set at the end of the 18th century and start of the 19th. Seventeen-year-old milkmaid Hetty, with her 'spring-like beauty', is the love interest of both the working man hero, Adam, and the land-owning young patrician, Arthur. Dark-haired, dark-eyed

Hetty is described as so ravishingly, irresistibly gorgeous that men just can't keep their eyes off her. 'If ever a girl looked as she had been made of roses,' Eliot's narrator tells us, 'that girl was Hetty in her Sunday hat and frock.' And yet we are also told that 'there is such a sweet baby-like roundness about her face and figure'[17] and about her deliciously plump and dimpled arms, and so-on. In fact, so plump that no-one knew she was heavily pregnant until it was too late.

Well, that's Eliot writing in the 1850s on the rural England of more than 200 years ago but in several sub-Saharan African countries, many African men tend to favour a rounded female figure that might be described as matronly in other cultures – certainly plumper than the ideal in white or Indian African culture. While Western tastes are starting to influence these preferences, they still persist – particularly outside of the big cities.

On the other hand, many Western men and women idealise the 'slim' version of the female figure – so much so that it is sometimes assumed that dieting and watching your figure are innately feminine characteristics. But there is an obvious paradox here. In the United States, and the United Kingdom, and several other Western countries, average waistlines for both men and women are expanding as people eat more of the wrong food and exercise less. So the female ideal is increasingly at odds with the female reality, which, no doubt, contributes to many women feeling shitty about themselves. As the songwriter, Kimya Dawson, put it in her song 'I like giants', 'All girls feel too big sometimes / Regardless of their size.'[18]

Some genetic determinists insist that all men are attracted to the same standard of beauty. EO Wilson, in his sociobiology days, decided that men evolved to favour a particular kind of face. Addressing a conference in 1998, he refuted the idea that men favour the average of all faces, referring to tests he'd conducted among his students. 'Evolutionary psychology is not as simple as *that*,' he was quoted as saying. 'Oh, no, the ideal woman is *not* the exact average.' He explained: 'The real surprise of the tests is that certain characteristics of the face found to be attractive give considerably more beauty when they are exaggerated ... – high cheek bones, thin jaw, large eyes and a slightly shorter rather than longer distance between mouth and chin and between nose and chin. Few women approach this standard of facial beauty, which should be the case were it just the normal example of natural selection. ... Instead we have a *supernormal* exaggeration of those features which are signs of youth, virginity and the prospect of a long reproductive period.' Winking at the audience he referred to Bill Clinton's peccadillos. 'Ask the American president!' he said, adding: 'Look at the *second* wives of most academics!'[19] If the thin jaw, high cheek bones and small gap between nose and chin sound very much like a Marilyn Monroe type of white Western beauty rather than say an African beauty, so be it. That is how we evolved in Wilson world.

One persistent shibboleth about beauty standards is the claim that men, all over the world, favour the identical hourglass hip-waist ratio. Desmond Morris has made this claim and so have many others. The idea is that a 0.7 waist-to-hip ratio (such as 36–25-36) is ideal. The evolutionary psychologists who upheld this view used their favourite laboratories to prove their point: American college campuses. A number of research projects using US students found that when shown pictures of a number of different body types they made a beeline for 36–25-36. The neurobiologist Roger Bingham, a one-time advocate of EP who saw the errors of his ways, noted that these hip-waist claims 'led to complaints that many of these experiments seemed a little less than rigorous to be underpinning an entire new field.'[20]

Since these claims were first made, there have been several under-reported studies that came to the opposite conclusion: that ideal hip-waist ratios were culturally contingent. For example men in remote parts of Peru and Tanzania prefer 0.9 and any woman with a 0.7 figure seems unhealthy in their eyes.[21] The anthropologist Elizabeth Cashdan compiled data from 33 non-Western populations and four

European populations, and found that the average waist-to-hip ratio was 0.8. She noted that androgens (including testosterone) alter waist-to-hip ratios in women, and are also associated with greater strength and stamina, which could be desirable in places where women do manual labour. Finding and carrying food is undertaken mainly by women and it can be hard work.

Cashdan also found that in industrialised countries where women tended to be less economically independent (she mentioned Japan, Greece and Portugal) men place a higher value on a smaller waist than women in, say, Denmark and the UK, where she found greater sexual equality. In other words, men in cultures where women bring home some of the bacon (either by having jobs or by gathering food), appear to favour a lower waist-to-hip ratio than in cultures where women are seen as essentially decorative (incidentally, Cashdan said the average *Playboy* ratio was 0.68).

In other words, far from being set in stone, favoured waist-to-hip ratios differ significantly between cultures. 'Waist-to-hip ratio may indeed be a useful signal to men, then,' Cashdan noted, 'but whether men prefer a ratio associated with lower or higher androgen/estrogen ratios (or value them equally) should depend on the degree to which they want their mates to be strong, tough, economically successful and politically competitive. And from a woman's perspective, men's preferences are not the only thing that matters.'[22]

So, it would seem that far from having a fixed hip-waist mental module firmly rooted in their minds, men are influenced by their environment and their culture in their preferences. Where women are regarded mainly as objects of desire, the Barbie ratio prevails, but where women are regarded as independent earners, or as the prime gatherers of food, different ratios are preferred. And the same point would apply to EO Wilson's Caucasian notion of the perfect female face. Even though we are all influenced by the standards of beauty and sexual attractiveness that emerge from popular culture, there remain different versions and standards of beauty in different parts of the world – and these versions change over time. The small-mouthed, thin-lipped women of renaissance art are no longer seen as ravishing beauties – and Rubens' voluptuous nudes would now be considered obese.

There are also no universal standards when it comes to male appreciation of women's breasts. Breast development is viewed as a female secondary sexual characteristic because they develop during puberty, even though they have no direct role in reproduction, and their appearance has nothing to do with their prime role, producing milk for babies. What is less widely known is that the erotic fascination with breasts is confined to societies where they are normally covered (almost all societies these days). There is also no generally accepted cross-cultural standard about how they should look – their size and shape.[23]

## Have men evolved to rape?

The Texas-based EP proselytisers Randy Thornhill and Craig T Palmer take Mars-Venus perspectives significantly further, arguing in their much-publicised book *A Natural History of Rape* that rape 'arises from men's evolved machinery for obtaining a high number of mates in an environment where females choose mates'. They insist: 'There is no doubt that rape has evolutionary – and hence genetic – origins.'

They believe the inclination to rape was naturally selected because men who carried rape genes had a reproductive edge, meaning they had more children, and these children would also carry the rape gene and therefore have more children, and so-on. Part of their argument is based on the notion that rape increases the fitness of a woman's offspring.

Incidentally, they define rape narrowly: coerced vaginal penetration of women of reproductive age (excluding the many rapes of women not of reproductive age and of other men) and say that the capacity for rape is either an adaptation or a by-product of adaptive traits such as sexual desire and aggressiveness. They also argue that the view that rape is essentially a crime of violence is wrong, and that the motivation is primarily sexual (they add that the contrary view, that rape is motivated by a desire for power, makes as much sense as arguing men visit prostitutes out of charity)..[24]

As a first test of this view we might ask whether all men rape, or have the desire to rape. The answer is that most men never rape and never desire to rape. An alternative, if you believe that the tendency to rape is a naturally selected trait, would be to ask if most men who rape differ genetically from those who don't. Again, the answer is no. Do men who rape have more children (part of the evolutionary psychology argument about spreading their genes far and wide)? Again, no evidence of this.

Another problem with the argument is that it treats rape as a single, definable evolved trait. But is it really? Is the nature of the urge to rape the same for the knife-wielding serial offender who hides in a bush and attacks women, or the soldier or guerrilla fighter who rapes women as part of the largesse or conquest or as part of the process of humiliation of the conquered people, or the husband or boyfriend or father or uncle who won't take no for an answer? They all include huge doses of misogyny as part of their motivation and they all involve the use of power to force women (or other men) to have sex against their will and they all involve the rapists being sexually aroused and women being brutalised and abused. In that sense all rapes are alike. But are they all motivated *mainly* by sex, as Thornhill and Palmer claim?

They argue that female rape victims are usually sexually alluring young women, which fits in with their evolutionary psychology version that older men are innately attracted to women younger than themselves. But as Michael Kimmel points out in a book published in response to *A Natural History of Rape*, the reason why most reported victims of rape are younger women has everything to do with the fact that they aren't married, don't have children, and are therefore more likely to be out on the town, or out on dates with young men. The reason most reported victims are younger women has everything to do with opportunity.[25]

It is impossible to test the pet theories of evolutionary psychologists because we don't have time machines that can take us back 100,000 years, so the best we can do is to look at the few remaining hunter-gatherer tribes still around today and then try to apply their theories to what we know of these groups. The anthropologist Kim Hill, from Arizona State University, studied the Ache, a hunter-gatherer tribe in Paraguay, and decided to test Thornhill's rape theories against what he knew of this tribe (who, he surmised, might have lived more or less like people did 100,000 years ago – although that too is pure guesswork).

Hill and his colleagues asked what evolutionary prospects a 25-year-old Ache tribesman would have if he was a rapist. They worked with Thornhill's rape criteria (only of younger women of reproductive age) and applied a cost-benefit test (although they didn't find any rapists in their research on the Ache). On the benefits they noted the 15 percent chance the woman was fertile, the 7 percent chance she would conceive, the 90 percent chance she would not mis-carry and the 90 percent chance she would not let the baby of a rapist die. On the other hand, they noted that rape would be detrimental to the future of their genes if the victim's husband or another relative killed him. They would also lose reproductive points if the mother refused to raise a child of rape. In addition, rapists would be known within small hunter-gatherer tribes, which would make others less willing to help them find food. They put all this together and found that the cost of being a rapist exceeded the benefit by a factor of 10, when considered in terms of reproductive potential. 'That makes the likelihood that rape is an evolved adaptation extremely low,' said Hill. 'It just wouldn't have made sense for men in the Pleistocene to use rape as a reproductive strategy, so the argument that it's pre-programmed into us doesn't hold up.'[26]

Human populations are basically the same genetically (the differences relating to skin colour, nose shape, hair type and ethnic diseases are miniscule when considering the whole human genome). So if rape was an evolved trait then we might anticipate that the proportions of people who rape would be more or less the same from country to country. One way to test their thesis is to look at rape statistics in different countries. Certainly, in all societies there are men who rape, and most rapes are never reported, but the proportions clearly differ from area to area and culture to culture.

Rape figures (both official and estimated, based on surveys of people's experience) show a huge country-by-country disparity, with the Democratic Republic of Congo, South Africa and Ethiopia at the top of the pile for both adult and child rapes. For example, a 2010 survey found that 37 percent of men from South Africa's Gauteng province (which includes Johannesburg) said they had raped and 78 percent said they had committed violence against women while 25 percent of women said they'd been raped and 51 percent said they'd experienced violence from men[27] – and similar results were found in other South African provinces.[28] This compares to, say, 8 percent of Ghanaian women who said they had been raped in their lifetime (while 5 percent of Ghanaian men said they had raped), according to a 2005 United Nations survey.[29] Incidentally, based on data relative to population levels, there's a correlation between rape and murder rates in these two countries – in South Africa you are over five times more likely to get murdered than in Ghana.[30] In terms of reported rapes (which in most and perhaps all countries are a small proportion of the actual total), South Africa is at the apex with 132.4 rapes reported to the police per 100,000 people in 2010 compared with Liechtenstein with zero rapes reported in 2010, while among the G7 industrialised countries, Japan was lowest with one reported rape per 100,000 people in 2010.[31]

The reasons for these differences relate not just to law enforcement but also to sociological factors including the position of women in the society and tolerance of violence. Most men in most countries never rape, but in some countries more men rape than in others, and the reason for that is clearly cultural.

## Men have evolved to kill unfaithful wives?

Evolutionary psychologists claim that while both men and women have evolved to have the jealousy module, they feel jealousy in different ways – with men more concerned about sexual infidelity (because if another man impregnates his woman, he can't pass on his genes for at least nine months), and women more concerned with emotional infidelity (she doesn't much care if her man is sexually unfaithful but if he falls in love with another woman he may abandon her and her children).

A related view is that this innate male sexual jealousy prompts an inbuilt inclination to be violent towards their errant spouse. The argument goes that way back when in the Pleistocene era a man could never be sure whether he was the father of his wife's child. What therefore evolved was a strategy of preventing women from having sex with other men. This evolved response includes the inclination towards jealousy-induced violence. It is noted that in some countries and cultures it is viewed as socially acceptable to murder unfaithful wives.

The Canadian evolutionary psychologists Martin Daly and Margo Wilson were the first to run with this, arguing that in order to prevent cuckoldry, men evolved a range of strategies – from 'vigilance' (watching their every move) to violence, to murder. 'Spousal homicides are not primarily cold-blooded "disposals" but are the tip of the iceberg of coercive violence,' they wrote.[32] They elaborated with the point that if men can prevent infidelity, they're less likely to be violent, but if unable to offer positive benefits, they're more likely to become violently jealous towards their partners (or, alternatively, towards their rivals). And they stressed: 'Male sexual proprietariness is the dominant issue in marital violence. In studies of "motives" for spousal homicide, the leading identified substantive issue is invariably "jealousy".[33] Following from this they argued that the 'unintended killing' of wives was also an evolved response, related to the male jealousy module. However, they rowed back from seeing spousal murder or violence as simply a *reflex* evolutionary response, noting that 'the application of such an evolutionary model to the study of violence .... is neither simple nor direct', and adding that homicide was 'a rare, extreme product of motivational mechanisms whose outputs are only expected to be adaptive on average ...'[34]

In US attitude studies on this question, it's certainly true that more men than women say they'd be upset by sexual infidelity, but one of Buss's own Texan studies showed that men were evenly split on which kind of infidelity upset them more (emotional or sexual). And when we move out of Texas, the picture changes. A similar study in Holland found that only 23 percent of men said they would find sexual infidelity more worrying than emotional infidelity, and in Germany the figure was 28 percent.[35] What this suggests is that the jealousy quotient is strongly influenced by culture. In cultures with a more relaxed attitude to female sexuality, men are less threatened by their partners having a quick fling with another man, and more worried about an emotional liaison that could threaten their relationship.

It could also be pointed out that rates of violence, including violence against women, and rates of spousal murder, differ hugely from culture to culture, and country to country, depending on attitudes to violence generally and attitudes to women specifically. In societies where there is greater equality between the sexes, there is proportionately less violence against women. What this suggests is that spousal violence is deeply affected by culture, relating not to evolved male jealousy modules but to prevailing male attitudes to women. Men who murder their partners out of sexual jealousy are usually men with a deeply patriarchal attitude to women, viewing them as their possessions.

## Male victims, female perpetrators?

The idea of women as perpetrators of violence against male spouses fits less snugly within the evolutionary psychology schema. And yet there is evidence that at least in Western countries, levels of domestic violence against men have increased as a proportion of the total, which might also be a reflection of the changing position of women. The British Crime Survey, considered to be the most accurate indicator of crime rates in England and Wales, found that between 2004 and 2009 men made up between 37.7 and 45.5 percent of victims of domestic violence victims each year while slightly higher percentages relative to the total (up to 48.6 percent) said they were subjected to a single incident of severe force from their partner. The number of British women prosecuted for domestic violence rose almost three-fold from 2004/5 to 2008/9 (from 1,575 to 4,266).[36] The UK Home Office's 2009 bulletin stated: 'More than one in four women (28%) and around one in six men (16%) had experienced domestic abuse since the age of 16. These figures are equivalent to an estimated 4.5 million female victims of domestic abuse and 2.6 million male victims.'[37]

It is worth adding that this does not take into account the nature and severity of the domestic violence, nor the fact that most victims of spousal murders are women. According to the UK Office for National Statistics for 2012/13, while there were many more male murder victims than female (13.6 per million population, compared with 6.0 for women), 45 percent of all female murder victims in England and Wales were killed by a partner or ex-partner compared with just four percent of male victims (which means five times more women were killed by their partners than men). Female victims were also more likely than male victims to have been acquainted with the principal suspect (75 percent, compared with 45 percent for men). Overall though, there's been a downward trend in the number of murders committed in the UK, along with a downwards trend in assaults and, in fact, in most crimes.[38] Quite simply, men in most Western countries, are becoming less violent.

This returns us to the starting point about the approach of evolutionary psychologists. Whatever claim we examine – the nature of male and female sexual desire, the desired age of spouses, standards of beauty, male and female jealousy, the inclination to assault or kill unfaithful sexual partners, the inclination to rape – we find that the behaviour is always culturally contingent, and never universal. When the position of women in society changes, it invariably has an impact on male behaviour in each of these zones. This strongly suggests that notions of hardwired mental modules for rape, male jealousy, mate choice, hip-waist rations and the rest are without foundation. Human nature is hugely variable and not just from individual to individual, but from culture to culture.

# CHAPTER TWELVE

## BOTOX, BRAZILIANS AND BOOB JOBS

When I was an 18-year-old student in Cape Town, on my first day on campus in January 1979, my older brother, Michael, introduced me to a friend of his and we had a chat. When she left, I remarked that 'Andy seems like a really nice chick', to which Michael promptly replied: 'She's not a chick.' I thought about this for a second and said: 'OK, but what I mean is that she's a nice girl, a nice *lady*.' This time, it was my brother's girlfriend, Clare, who corrected me: 'She's not a girl – and she's not a lady either: she's a *woman*!' The following day I moved into a house with seven others. A guest, Sharon, asked me about my impressions of my first days on campus, and I imparted my instant opinions on all sorts of things, including the feminist women. 'I don't mind that they don't shave their legs,' I ventured, 'but I'm not so sure about the armpits thing.' At which point Sharon raised her arms and suggested I feel her 'lovely, soft armpit hair'. I instantly corrected myself.

Later that year I went with three friends to a conference in Johannesburg, stopping off at a student house in the university town of Grahamstown, where a first-year student welcomed us. After she went on her way, my best friend remarked to me, sotto voce: 'She's sweet but you can see she's new to it all – and not a proper feminist." I asked her how she came to this realisation after such a brief encounter. "Did you look at her toenails?" she asked. "They're *painted*!"

Anyway, I rapidly absorbed these ideas. Although we were all activists whose main concern was to fight apartheid, feminism was seen as part of the package, and we read Germaine Greer and Sheila Rowbotham and Spare Rib, herded ourselves into consciousness-raising groups, and became nearly as fervent about gender equality as we were about racial equality and 'class struggle'. In those days, equality had many implications and demands, one of which was women not shaving – because their body hair was as natural as men's and women were not hairless children. They also gave up dieting because the fetish for thin women was an example of misogyny. And it extended to not wearing makeup because why should women be objects of display? Most took this seriously – at least in the circles I moved in. Once, a few of us were invited to a bad taste party, and the women decided the ultimate in bad taste was to arrive dolled up. But they had to go to a drama student friend, and borrow her stage makeup, because, by then, none of them possessed make-up of their own.

This boycott of shaving, makeup and dieting lasted for about as long as these women remained at university or in activist-type jobs. However, those who moved on to jobs as lawyers, nurses, doctors, teachers, town planners, engineers and the like, had to compromise. And even for those who moved into activist jobs, the change came when a State of Emergency was declared and they had to blend in with the rest of the population to avoid detention without trial. One of my friends confided in me that, actually, this was a bit of a relief: 'It's so easy for you men because you don't really look any different from other guys,' she said, 'but it's really hard for us women because having hairy legs and unplucked eyebrows and no make-up makes us stand out, and people look and comment and sneer and tell you it's alienating.'

## Lipstick and the bums of apes in oestrus

I tell this little tale not because I think that all the feminist values and prescriptions of the 1970s and 1980s are worth emulating today, nor to make fun of them, but rather because it seems to say something about the very common EP nugget that women have hardwired mental modules to beautify themselves, with some going significantly further, arguing that each of the specifics of contemporary female adornment has a distinct biological basis – for example, that the inclination for women to wear lipstick is an evolutionary adaptation that arose from male apes being turned on by the inflamed bums of female apes in oestrus. I first heard this expressed in a television programme by the socio-biologist Desmond Morris whose books are full of this kind of thing, and I've since read similar views from the prominent American evolutionary psychologist Donald Symons, who argued that beauty was important in sexuality because people look for signs of reproductive fitness in potential mates, and, for this evolutionary reason, the qualities men find attractive in women include full red lips, smooth, clear skin and high, firm breasts.[1]

Soon after seeing Morris in action, I was hired to edit a special edition of *Men's Health* magazine. Along the way I came across a feature that tried to explain the specifics of modern beautification – not just lipstick but also high heels, lipstick, nail polish and smooth legs – in evolutionary terms, quoting liberally from the words of various evolutionary psychologists. Teaching a first year university course on gender and the media, I asked students what they thought of this logic. Most seemed to find it rather funny. One pointed out that unlike lipstick, the 'inflamed' sexual organs of female primates in oestrus were a universal attribute for female apes, and not a selected strategy to give added advantage in the quest to attract male apes. Another responded in a tone of sarcasm: 'That would be a very strange evolutionary change considering that humans like us have been around for tens of thousands of years but widespread lipstick wearing only kicked in during the 20th century. What took it so long?'

Her point on lipstick was essentially correct – even though there were examples of lip colouring among the elite going back to the ancient Egyptians, it only took off as a ubiquitous item of European and American 'grooming' after the first world war. Perhaps prompted by the Western ideal of beauty (pale skin, flushed cheeks, rosebud lips), lip painting began to make its appearance among a small section of the 'lower orders' early in the 19th century. Certainly in the Victorian era in Britain and its colonies, in Europe and the United States, much of what we now call make-up was mainly considered to be the province of 'cheap' women (although there were exceptions, including powder, which was widely used among the well-do-do classes for women's cheeks and men's hair and wigs).

Queen Victoria, in particular, was a vehement foe of made-up women – the actresses and prostitutes she considered vain and cheap. Another example from George Eliot's *Adam Bede,* published in 1859: the book's eponymous hero is taking a walk with the vain, beautiful milkmaid Hetty. He disapproves when she puts a rose in her hair and notes that it reminds him of the 'painted women outside the shows at Treddles'on fair.' He goes on to tell her: 'If a woman's young and pretty, I think you can see her good looks all the better for her being plain dressed.'[2]

Which is not the way Hollywood and its imitators like to portray women in their period pieces from this era. After a spell of realism in the 1970s, film and television directors returned to an earlier model: dress the women in period costume but make them up in ways that would encourage today's audiences to identify – and this goes way beyond the requirement for contemporary essentials like straight white teeth, perky breasts and six-packs. I first noticed its revival about 20 years ago when watching Jennifer Ehle playing Elizabeth Bennet in a television series on 'Pride and Prejudice'. It seemed that every time this heroine went out, her lips were freshly lipsticked. Elizabeth Bennet strode through Jane Austin's pages about a century or more before women like her would have worn lippy. Or to take a more recent adaptation, the 2016 BBC version of *War and Peace*, we see Gillian Anderson at the society hostess Anna Sherer, dressed in 1805 style and made up in 2015 style – and perhaps it's also worth mentioning the ill-fated and beautiful Princess Lise: in Tolstoy's novel possessing 'a pretty upper lip with its barely visible black moustache' – a moustache that is regularly praised and a lip that is 'too short for her teeth'.[3] Needless to say, the Lise played by Kate Phillips had none of these attributes. And when it comes to the more popular forms of faux-historical swords and sorcery fantasy, there's no pretence (the painted, plucked and waxed women of *Games of Thrones* are some of many examples). And just to show this doesn't only apply to women, who can forget Mel Gibson's 'Braveheart', which featured a clean-shaven, mullet-topped William Wallace, which was not at all how the short-haired, heavily bearded William Wallace appeared in his portraits?

The reason the industry adopts this approach is, quite obviously, because with some notable exceptions they calculate that modern audiences would be uncomfortable with lead women characters with the realism of no make-up, discoloured teeth, unshaven armpits and unplucked eyebrows, or, for that matter, until recently, with a bearded male hero's face (Braveheart was produced in 1995, well before the current fashion for bearded young hipsters emerged). It is presumed they would find it plain, unattractive and even offensive. Put differently, the studios and their directors calculate that today's audiences would struggle to identify with characters whose faces and bodies diverged significantly from contemporary standards of beauty. Perhaps it will change and there'll be a return to realism, but, for now, the calculations made by the directors are probably financially prudent even if historically inaccurate.

## Foot-binding, corsets, high heels and skinny jeans

The point of these examples is that the nature of beautification has chopped and changed over the centuries, with some of its forms anathema to us today, which can be seen most clearly from those we would now consider extreme, bizarre, cruel or distasteful.

The practice of deforming female feet through the agonising process of foot-binding that prevailed in much of China for a thousand years (starting in the royal court in the 10th century AD and eventually dying out, or being killed-off, early in the 20th century). Part of the process, which began at four-years-old, involved the toes being curled under the rest of the foot, after which they pressed with extreme force downwards. They were then squished into the sole of the foot until the toes broke. It was extremely painful for the girls and created permanent deformity. Like so many zones of female subjugation, it was probably a product of male aristocratic fetish for Cinderella-type little feet but enforced with conviction by women (who did the binding) in much the same way that female genital mutilation is enforced today. By the 19th century more than 40 percent of Chinese women had bound feet, including virtually all women from Han Chinese upper class – because the tiny feet of 'ladies', and the particular style of walking it prompted, were considered alluring. Yet this deeply-entrenched habit died out within a generation in the 20th century, partly because of concerted campaigns against it and partly because it was banned in 1912. Today I doubt that many men, including Chinese men, would regard bound feet as anything other than hideous.

An example closer to home is the corset, which first emerged in Europe in the 16th century but reached its heights of popularity in the 19th. One of its purposes was to compress women's waists, frequently to 16-inches, sometimes to as little as 13, squeezing ribs and restricting breathing so much that women were known to pass out, prompting a range of health problems, including, in some cases, damage to internal organs, and even cracked ribs. To get there, teenage girls had to 'train' in corset use, with the compression getting ever-tighter. Corsets all but disappeared after the First World War – briefly replaced by the 'girdle' – and today someone with a compressed 16-inch waist would look absurd.

One more ancient example: some women in the Victorian era and earlier, along with Japanese Geisha women, used white foundation to acquire the desired alabaster look. Unfortunately, this was usually made from lead, which, with prolonged and regular use, would kill them.

We can sigh about the bizarre habits of the past, but even today we're not beyond risking health for the sake of fashion. The revival of the stiletto heel – with contemporary versions often higher than those of our grandmothers – is associated with several temporary and long-term health problems – from bunions and ingrown toenails to permanently damaged leg tendons, nerve damage, osteoarthritis in the knee and lower back pain. The American Osteopathic Association says one third of American women who regularly wear high heels suffer permanent health problems as a result[4].

A running friend of mine who was training relentlessly to get under the 3-hour mark for the marathon complained she was being set back by lower back pain. I asked if she knew the cause and she explained it was the heels she wore to work for her high powered job in the City. 'So why don't you wear flats then?' I wondered. Her reply: 'I saw what happened to one of my colleagues when she came to work in flats and the male traders chanted: "Lezza, lezza, lezza." I didn't want that to happen to me.' In the end, she preferred back pain to the humiliation of being called a lesbian.

Perhaps killer heels will go the way of foot binding and corsets, but I wouldn't count on it any time soon. Too many people view them as a feminine essential. And again, the film industry can take a bow: at the 2015 Cannes film festival women wearing flats rather than heels were banned from the red carpet. And one more example: in 2016 a receptionist working as a temp at the London branch of the services multi-national PricewaterhouseCoopers was sent home on her first day at work after arriving at work in flats rather than heels – and laughed at when she complained to her temp agency supervisor. She was also told she had to wear make-up and was supplied with

a colour chart of 'acceptable shades'. This prompted an online peti-
tion, signed by more than 100,000 people within 24 hours of being
publicised, and a welter of stories from other women who were given
similar high heel ultimatums.

And just one more: a recent article in an American medical journal reported on the dangers of skinny jeans that include
'Compartment Syndrome' – a potentially serious and painful condition caused by swelling or bleeding within a tightly-enclosed set
of muscles (the calves).[5] This followed a case where a 35-year-old
Australian woman had to be cut out of her skinny jeans after spending several hours squatting to empty cupboards. By the end of the
day her feet were numb, she was struggling to walk and her calves
had ballooned to twice their normal size. Soon she couldn't get up
and when she reached Royal Adelaide Hospital her legs were severely
swollen, the muscles and nerves weakened and damaged and she'd
lost some feeling. It took four days before she could walk unaided.
The article noted that previous skinny jean studies reported 'lesions
of the lateral cutaneous nerve of the thigh, likely caused by compression of the nerve of the inguinal ligament'.[6]

Skinny jeans, heels, corsets, lead-painted faces and bound feet are
not evolved habits. Evolution doesn't work that way. They're transitory cultural preferences. The same applies to the use of (and attraction for) lipstick and the rest. They're no more evolved than fishnet
stockings and lingerie.

## Feminism and adornment

The subject of female adornment can be a tricky one for feminists.
On the one hand, most feminists want to support the choices women
make and if these choices involve what previous generations might
have considered the vanity of excessive primping and preening, then
so be it. On the other hand choices taken on how we present ourselves
to the world say rather more than we might suspect about our status
in the world – how we fit into a gendered universe. Ignoring the

subject means ignoring a significant part of the identities of women and men.

As I illustrated with my tales of student life at the start of this chapter, in the 1970s and early 1980s some feminists (mainly of radical or socialist bent) made an issue out of adornment. It was common in these circles in those days for women to stop shaving their legs and armpits because, it was argued, women's body hair was no less natural than men's and was therefore part of their adult femininity – and also because the demand for depilated women was part of a male desire to infantilise them. There was also a tendency to eschew diets, make-up, heels and revealing clothes – in part as a statement against the notion that women were essentially decorative and that their role was to please men in the way they looked.

But by the 1990s feminism no longer resembled a coherent movement. The solidarity fostered through rallies, protests and consciousness raising groups was no more. For many young women, feminism had become a dirty word – seen as synonymous with being anti-men and with dressing in a dowdy or masculine way. Meanwhile, it was becoming apparent that women were spending more and more of their disposable income on clothes, heels, make-up and beauty treatments. Those vocally rowing against this tide risked being cast as frumpy, out-of-time blue stocking puritans or dismissed as dungaree-wearing lesbian earth mothers. It was to put themselves in the same box as nuns or the female victims of extreme Islamist rule.

In this changed milieu vocal feminists (mainly in the media and academia) retreated from the body hair and no make-up days. The watchword became choice-choice-choice, and the subject of adornment was largely ignored. There were exceptions, however. Naomi Woolf created waves in 1991 with her book, *The Beauty Myth* by telling us that ' "Femininity" was a code for femaleness plus whatever a society happens to be selling'.[7] One of Wolf's points was that versions of femininity and masculinity vary from time-to-time and place-to-place. In this sense she wrote in the tradition of Simone de Beauvoir

who argued that ideas of femininity were socially constructed, usually by men. As De Beauvoir put it in her 1949 book *The Second Sex*:
'One is not born a woman, one becomes a woman.'[8]

To take a personal example of De Beauvoir's point: not long ago
I was running with a friend, who spat in the bushes along the way,
as most runners are inclined to do. 'Ooh, I'm so sorry,' she said. 'That
wasn't very lady-like of me!' Lady-like is a version of femininity, a
version of womanhood, and in this version things like spitting, farting and burping fall short of the feminine ideal. But when we think
about if for a single second, spitting, farting and burping are as natural to women as to men. The point is that ideas of what is 'lady-like'
or legitimately feminine are culturally moulded – social constructs,
in other words. According to Wolf (and De Beauvoir), a significant
part of this socialised construct relates to transient standards of beautification (and perhaps to illustrate the point Wolf followed her pioneering book with a magazine cover portrait in which she appeared
in full, glossy make-up).

From a different angle, in another fine book, *the new feminism*,
published in 1999, the British feminist journalist Natasha Walter
included a chapter on cosmetics entitled 'let boys wear pink' in which
she noted examples of women wearing make-up to show resilience
and resistance – for instance, women in Afghanistan demonstrating
against the Taliban by making a point of wearing lipstick, rouge, nail
polish and high heels as an act of defiance.[9] She ended the chapter by
saying that when women and men are more equal in terms of pay,
childcare and opportunities, '[t]he catwalk will then cease to be a
symbol of our subordination, and become a path to simple delight'.[10]
Walter followed this with a Guardian Saturday magazine story in
which she extolled the joys of painting nails.

For all its merits, this kind of show-and-tell about individual
choice has its limitations – and Walter herself seemed to row back
from this kind of emphasis. 'Since the idea has taken hold that
women and men are now equal throughout society, it is seen as

unproblematic that women should be relentlessly encouraged to prioritise their sexual attractiveness,' she wrote in a follow-up book, 11 years later. 'The assumption is that this is a free choice by women who are in all other ways equal to men.'[11] And she ends her chapter on 'Choices' on a note of despair: 'In the hypersexual culture the woman who has won is the woman who foregrounds her physical perfection and silences any discomfort she may feel. This objectified woman ... is the living doll who has replaced the liberated woman who should be making her way into the twenty-first century.'[12]

One of the problems with the emphasis on choice when it comes to self-decoration is that it begs the question of why women – and men – make the choices they do. Another problem is that choice often doesn't exist. As Wolf put it: *The real problem is our lack of choice.'* (her italics). And where choice does exist, it's invariably constrained. For men it is different. A young man who decides not to hone his pecs or pump-up his guns and says no to a number one haircut, and shows a preference for being clean-shaven and an avoidance of the tattoo artist, would not find himself socially isolated or the subject of ridicule on Twitter.

For a young woman, and even more so for an older woman, it's a different game. One example. Two students of mine, in previous lives, had been air stewards. The one from a Middle Eastern airline said a condition of the job was to arrive at work with painted nails. The student who'd worked for an Oriental airline rolled her eyes. 'That's nothing. With us it was a firing offence if we didn't wear the *approved shades* of lipstick and nail polish, and when we applied for the job we had to jump and out of a swimming pool wearing a bikini.'

So, clearly, in some zones of life women have no choice at all – and this covers more than airline stewards (for example, would a woman newsreader be permitted to go television 'bare-faced'?) For every woman who chooses to wear full make-up as a symbol of rebellion against the Taliban, or as a sign of life-goes-on defiance while facing sniper fire in Sarajevo, there are millions who don't have the right to refuse. But more commonly, choice for women regarding adornment is constrained by the intensity of social pressure. What would happen if, for example, an aspirant political candidate was pictured with a make-up-free face? Or if, say, a film star raised her arms and displayed her unshaven pits?

Well, in both cases, we know the answer. Hillary Clinton was the offending politician (and she went further by admitting she was tired of having to wear make-up), prompting a predictable Twitter storm. The *Daily Mail* columnist Jan Moir, picked on this by accusing her of wanting to roam the globe 'looking like a lightly boiled bag lady'. She added: 'For giving up caring how you look is not an expression of emancipation, it is one of resignation and defeat.' After further condemnation of Hillary and her 'hairy-legged basket-weaver' tendency (i.e. wearing glasses and no slap on a tour of Bangladesh), Moir informed her readers: 'I do think those in high office should be as groomed as possible.'[12] For Moir female grooming meant not leaving the house without a face full of make-up.

The other case involved the actor Julia Roberts who casually raised a sleeveless arm revealing her unshaven armpits back in 1999 (a 'stand' – perhaps the first of its kind from an American celebrity since the days of Janis Joplin a generation earlier – that prompted several others, including Madonna, to follow suit, again setting off a social media storm, as well as the obligatory condemnation from the Daily Mail and many others). The story that caught my attention at the time was by the *Sunday Times* columnist India Knight, who is a feminist. She told readers of her time at university when some feminists took to dressing frumpily and flashing their hairy armpits. This was a bad idea, she suggested, because it put young women off feminism. Which struck me as an odd way of looking at things – confusing a word with an approach to life and a set of ideas. It is possibly true that some women might be put off the word 'feminism' by the sight of unshaven pits, but it's rather less likely that this image, by itself, would put them off the whole idea of gender equality.

Anyway, after these social experiments Hillary reverted to full make-up and Julia duly shaved her pits. Perhaps their earlier decisions were taken on no more than a whim, but perhaps too they found the level of abuse directed their way too much to cope with.

A further example of cost came in a pair of programmes the BBC ran at the turn of the millennium. One group of women volunteered to go without make-up for a while; another to stop shaving. Most found it hard to last a full week. As Wolf expressed it: 'The problem with cosmetics exists only when women feel invisible or inadequate without them.'[13] The incident that struck me most forcibly at the time involved one of the no make-up women who went clubbing. She was confronted by an irate younger man who insulted her aggressively and obscenely, seeming to believe that it was personal affront to him to have to rest his eyes on a make-up-free face. The point here is that choice for women on how to present themselves is seldom free choice.

## Is female adornment hard-wired?

Back to the question of why men and women make their particular adornment choices. Anyone with a sprinkling of common sense would laugh at the absurd evolutionary adaptations dreamt up by socio-biologists and evolutionary psychologists on the specifics of hip-waist ratios or lipstick wearing or leg-shaving or whatever, but there is a trickier question of whether women, in general, are more 'hard-wired' than men to decorate themselves according the fashions of the day. Here, I have to admit, it's easy to argue both ways.

Those punting the evolutionary position, including some feminists, point to the fact that in most societies we know of, throughout recorded history, women have been more inclined than men to spend time and effort on their looks. More than that, most women in most societies consider the way they present themselves to the mirror and the world a far more important part of their essence than do most men, and society endorses this behaviour. When I or my friends proudly display pictures of our daughters' achievements on Facebook, the comments made often relate to how 'gorgeous' and 'stunning' they look. When their mums post their own selfies, they too tend to receive a brace of compliments – usually about how they haven't changed since their youths and so-on. Similar comments are seldom made about pictures of fathers and sons.

As I illustrated in the opening chapter, for many young women this focus on their looks reaches its apex on their wedding day, when all eyes are on the dress, hair and makeup worn for their 'big day'. The groom is an afterthought. Another example is awards ceremonies where the dress, shoes and nails of the female stars garner most of the column lines while the men, in their virtually identical dress suits, tend to be ignored.

Twenty years ago *Esquire* magazine asked me to interview the women's world welterweight boxing champion Jane Couch who'd just won a long fight for the right of women to fight professionally in the UK. They even asked me to spar a round with her (which I did, and was relieved when the three-minute bell finally sounded). One thing I noticed about Crouch, who ended up having 40 professional fights, was that she wore no make-up and didn't seem to give a toss about how she looked, perhaps because she didn't seem to give a toss for whether she was regarded as masculine or feminine. Instead she told me she was a 'wild child from a normal nine-to-five working class family' and that she could easily beat 'half the geezers out there.'[15] But Crouch was an exception among elite female sports stars. Soon after, I read an interview with Sally Gunnell, Olympic, World, European and Commonwealth 400-meter hurdles gold medallist and world record holder. She said she gave extra attention to her hair and makeup because what she did for a living was not exactly feminine. Later she acknowledged that she felt under pressure to wear lots of make-up for this reason. I have since seen several other interviews with female sports achievers, making a similar point: because they and others see that what they do as kind-of butch, they want to bend the stick in the opposite direction when it comes to adornment. In each case they had in their minds the idea that running fast or jumping high or throwing far were inherently masculine, whereas giving attention to hair, face and nails was inherently feminine.

This level of physical self-inspection, self-criticism, anxiety and guilt that is normal for women would be considered obsessive or vain or camp for men. When I leave the house, how I look is not a significant consideration. I splash water on my face, brush my teeth and hair, perhaps have a shave, put on some deodorant and it's done – two minutes, maximum and another two to get dressed, and that's it for the whole day and I won't look in a mirror until I brush my teeth at night. With my two daughters and my female friends, it is very different.

In some cultures that gap is even wider. A great deal has been written, for example, on the cultural significance of black women's hairstyles in the West. Following a brief interlude when the 'Afro' was popular came a return to the earlier demand for 'relaxed' or at least hanging hair – an apparently laborious process that some have interpreted as an accommodation to the dominant (white) culture whose beauty ideal has long included straight hair. The recent shift to more 'natural' hairstyles (i.e. less 'relaxed') among black American and British women might suggest a greater cultural self-confidence – or perhaps no more than another temporary fashion shift. Anyway, what is less often observed is that there was no such requirement for 'relaxed' hair among black males, who were therefore free to do things like diving into chlorinated swimming pools without worrying too much about the effect on their locks or looks.

I'm aware that men a generation younger than me are considerably less lackadaisical about their looks, to put it mildly, and it's sometimes pointed out that there have been, and are still, concomitant obligations on men for various forms of adornment in some cultures (from Indian men wearing kohl for eyeliner to shaven armpits for men in several parts of the world and the clear nail varnish worn by some Latino men; from gentlemen of the past with their powdered wigs and rouged cheeks to today's fashion for creative facial hair, tattoos and hair dye), but there are few cultures where the requirements are steeper for men than for women.

With such profound behavioural differences between men and women, and such cultural ubiquity for these differences, surely there must be a biological component – perhaps having arisen out of the need for women to show good health, fecundity and youth in order to attract the most desirable men? As one of my friends, a feminist novelist, put it: 'I agree with you on everything else – that the differences have more to do with culture than biology – but with adornment, I'm not so sure. It seems to me that women have always been far more concerned about their looks than men, and that must have something to do with biology.'

Those questioning biological explanations for female patterns of adornment sometimes start with the observation that throughout pre-history *both* women and men have been adorning themselves, as well as their cave walls – from the earliest beads and body paint going back 70,000 years or more. So it would seem that self-decoration is an extension of human nature. We have no idea whether any of these forms of adornment was gender-specific, but if we look at the few remaining hunter-gatherer groups today, we might conclude that both men and women were interested in adornment and although distinctions certainly existed, they were relatively minor.

And it is not true that there are no cultures where the beautification demands on men are higher than for women. One example involves the men of the Wodaabe, a 100,000-strong, loosely Islamic nomadic people who specialise in cattle herding and trading in Niger. In addition to being liberal regarding the sex lives of unmarried women and of married women (who are allowed to take on lovers), they also break the mould by allowing women to wield economic power. But perhaps their most notable departure from international norms comes from their admiration for male beauty, typified by the

Yaake, a beauty contest-cum-courtship ritual which is part of a week-long festival known as the Guerewol. Marriageable young women judge the young men who spend many hours dressing up, painting their faces and donning feathers and beads, after which they will sing and dance by swaying their hips seductively in their bid to entice the women.[16]

However, the Wodaabe are hardly typical of nomadic cultures, or of most other cultures for that matter. Once agriculture emerged (about 10,000 years ago) followed by the rise of villages, towns and cities and social classes, women came to be regarded as property and prizes, and in different ways in different cultures this was reflected in marriage gifts, either from the husband's family, or from the wife's.

In some cultures the women's family paid a dowry on marriage. This probably started as a means of wealth transfer in early agricultural society in ancient India, parts of China and in Babylon (the earliest references come from the Babylonian Code of Hammurabi from nearly 4,000 years ago, although its origins probably pre-dated writing). It survived in the UK until the late Victorian era, in other parts of Europe well into the 20th century and still exists in large chunks of Asia, the Balkans and North Africa. The supposed intention was to set aside money or goods to provide for the bride's upkeep – a form of female inheritance – but the reality was that it helped establish the marital household and added to the husband's wealth (and in some cases part of this dowry went directly to the groom's family). So a man with power and status might seek out a young woman from a wealthy family who could afford a larger dowry, and would negotiate with her family about its nature and amount. It would follow that the family of a bride viewed as particularly alluring might have to pay less than if their daughter was considered plain.

In other cultures, it has worked the opposite way around: the man (or his family) gives a bride price gift to the *bride's* family and the beauty and desirability of this young woman is likely to raise her price. In effect, the bride is being 'purchased' by the groom or his family. There are references to this in ancient Babylonian writing and in the Old Testament and it became part of Islamic culture through the mahr system prescribed in the Qur'an (in this case, a payment directly to the bride). One example is the southern African lobolo system in which the two families reach agreement on the price to be paid by the man. The bride is then accepted by the man's family and, they believe, by his ancestors (who then take care of the woman while the wife's ancestors are released from this obligation).

It could be said that there are residues of this in contemporary Western culture. For example, when marriage is proposed, a man might buy his fiancé an engagement ring, which is a sign to the world that she is 'taken'. There is no reciprocal obligation. And in most marriages, the woman still takes the man's surname (or, in a contemporary variant, she hyphenates the two surnames while he doesn't) – a tradition rooted in the idea of the wife as the property of the husband, having previously been the property of the father.

The dowry and bride price might be seen as opposites but with both systems the bride-to-be has a pecuniary value, which be influenced by her perceived beauty (with the dowry, the bride's family might be required to pay less if they have a more alluring daughter whereas with the bride price the groom and his family might pay more for a woman seen as physically attractive). So with both, it encouraged a culture that put pressure on young women to try to look as desirable as possible according to the ever-shifting standards of the day.

Naomi Wolf argued that 'beauty' as an objective and universal entity did not exist. 'Beauty is a currency system like the gold standard,' she wrote. 'Like any economy it is determined by politics, and in the modern age in the West it is the last, best belief system that keeps male dominance intact.' She added that 'beauty' was not universal or changeless, 'though the West pretends that all ideals of female beauty stem from one Platonic Ideal Women; the Maori admire a fat vulva, and the Padung, droopy breasts.'[17] She specifically disputed the idea that beauty was a function of evolution, noting that 'its ideals change at a pace far more rapid than that of evolution of species'.[18]

An example of the ever-changing mores of beauty could be drawn from the different attitudes to female body hair. Some evolutionary psychologists like Donald Symons have argued that the desire for smooth female skin is an evolutionary adaptation[19], but a quick cultural survey suggests otherwise. It is thought that at least some aristocratic women in Ancient Egypt and India shaved and this preference also seems to have prevailed among some upper class women in ancient Greece and Rome, and, more recently in much of the Islamic world, including Turkey (and this applied to men too) as well as in parts of Renaissance Europe. But the habit of aristocratic depilating began to wane in the 16th century and, at least in Britain, it virtually died out during the Victorian era. And we should not assume that it was anything like a universal standard, even in the places where it was practiced. Through much of history only the rich had time to consider such things, and the rich made up a very small proportion of the population (and one of the reasons we tend to exaggerate the depilation and cosmetic use of past centuries and millennia is that it is the pictures and possessions of the rich that survive).

At least until the 20th century in most of the world, most women have not removed their body hair. For example, an exhibition of Japanese erotic ('Shunga') art from the 17th to the early 20th centuries, held at the British Museum, showed pictures of Japanese women with underarm hair having fun in various love-making poses. In the United States it was only in the first quarter of the 20th century when women began baring legs and armpits, that shaving came into fashion. In 1915, Harper's Bazaar showed a picture of a model in a sleeveless dress with hairless armpits. Later, the razor manufacturers Wilkinson Sword ran a campaign claiming that underarm hair for women was 'unhygienic and unfeminine'. This was so successful that by the end of the 1920s underarm hair for American women was, by and large, a thing of the past. But in Germany and other parts of Western Europe, unshaven armpits remained the norm at least until late in the 20th century.

Even today there are parts of the world where Western norms have yet to dominate. In Ghana, for example, female leg and chest hair is still considered desirable, although underarm hair, for both men and women, is not. The Observer columnist Afua Hirsch cited a Ghanaian wedding she attended a few years ago. The well-to-do bride was made up to the nines. 'It was as if the bride's whole outfit was designed to give maximum impact to one central feature: her chest hair. The bride had chest hair – lots of it. ... I looked around, wondering if anyone else was as stunned as I. No-one battered an eyelid.' After spending time in Ghana, she said this kind of image became her expectation 'It's getting to the point where if I see a pencil-skirt suit and stilettos without a generous layer of leg hair, it feels as if something is missing.'[20] She also noted, however, that among the younger generation, Western standards were taking over.

So, cultural change prompts change in the desired *forms* of female beautification. But, still, the requirement persists, starting in early childhood, through observation of mothers, sisters, aunts, cousins and friends and carrying on until old age. Over thousands of years this requirement has become so deeply rooted in human consciousness that it is tempting to think it is innate. This was explained to me by one feminist friend (working in an environment where she's not required to put effort into 'grooming'): 'I sometimes put on makeup even though I won't see anyone during the day, and I do this because I find the ritual calming and relaxing. I don't think this is evolutionary at all. It stems from the culture I grew up in. For example, wearing makeup/using products etc. is talked about in terms of "looking after yourself" and "pampering". This creates a very positive association that I find hard to break out of."

As an aside, until fairly recently I held what might be called a traditional feminist view on women who did the opposite – covered their heads with a veil or sheitel and even more so with the hijab. It seemed to be a clear expression of a deeply misogynistic culture based on the idea that men are naturally voracious so women have to cover-up and that women aren't so men don't have to cover up. I shifted my perspective after speaking to one of my students, a Muslim feminist who chose to wear a headscarf. 'It allows me to be valued for what I am – for what's in my head and my character rather than for my looks,' she said, adding that she lived in a patriarchal culture where men learnt to be predatory. 'It also means that when I argue for women's rights, more conservative women and men take me more seriously.' It struck me that her argument was similar to that used by feminist women I knew in the 1980s who sometimes felt obliged to explain why they chose to wear make-up or shave their body hair – a desire not to be an outcast in a patriarchal society and a desire to be taken seriously.

Anyway, there is one conundrum in the 'all culture' explanation for female 'beautification': in today's more equal society, women, on average, spend higher proportions of their disposable income on adornment than in the more gender-divided past. One report, covering the years 2002 to 2014, showed that the amount spent on cosmetics each year in the United States increased steadily, with $62-billion predicted for 2016). The largest chunk of spending (33.8 percent) was on skin care.[21]

If it's all rooted in patriarchy, why do modern women, living in a less patriarchal milieu, put ever more effort and money into a particular version of femininity (the current fashion for 'Hollywood' and 'Brazilian' waxes is one example; another would be the rise and rise of cosmetic plastic surgery and Botox injections)? And it is the women who came of age at a time of feminism's rise who seem to spend most (although that could also be explained by the fact that they have more money).[22] What is clear is that the amounts spent each year on female adornment are increasing relative to income rather than decreasing, and there remains a large gulf in terms of the amount of money and time spent on appearance between women and men. For example, a survey conducted for the BBC Radio 4 programme, *Women's Hour*, found that women spent eight hours more than men per week on appearance – and a lot more money too (£93 a week).[23]

But here too there is an alternative cultural explanation. As we shall see in the next chapter, the gaps between men and women in contemporary Western society have narrowed in a number of important areas (income, career prospects, the range of jobs available, the amount of time spent on child care and household chores). Males and females also rub along together in a way that is markedly different from cross-gender interaction of earlier generations. The old image of the men smoking cigars and telling lewd jokes in the den while the women chattered away in the kitchen has passed – these days the women join the men in the telling of lewd jokes and the smoking of cigars, and the men join the women in the kitchen. The distinctions between males and females are more blurred than ever.

And yet, we all emerged from versions of masculinity and femininity that cast them as opposites – versions that carry a deep impact on sense of self. The result is that many feel an undertow of unease with this new androgyny and want reassurance that despite it all, they're still real men and real women. Gender similarity prompts the desire for gender difference. They therefore seek new ways of emphasising the last unambiguous area of distinction: appearance.

I'm aware that correlation doesn't equate to causation, but it is perhaps worth recalling that in the 1960s before the new wave of feminism had much of an impact on wider culture, a kind of androgyny was part of mainstream youth fashion all over the West – not least in the flowing locks and floral shirts worn by many men (my father, from an earlier generation, dismissively called the first batch of long-haired sixties men, 'shims' – his little joke based on the idea of 'she/hims') – and, a bit later, the 'glam rock' fashions of the early 1970s with the make-up and platform heels of their pop icons. By the

1980s, however, when gender equality kicked in, fashions changed. For men, there was a return to short hair, and, later, shaved heads or number one haircuts, along with tattoos and muscles, and, over the last decade in particular, there has been the widespread and rapidly growing use of anabolic steroids to achieve the lean body-big arms look. Another development has been the revived fashion for beards among young men – the fuller the growth, the more manly the grower. There's even an emerging market for beard transplants.

Meanwhile, for women, nail bars sprung up on every corner along with salons advertising intimate waxing, and there was a return to the fashion of stiletto heels. We have also seen a renewed emphasis on perpetual female youthfulness (at a time when the average population in the West is growing older) and the stubborn persistence of the cult of thinness (at a time when most women in the West are getting bigger). Within the space of a decade or two it became increasingly unusual to see a woman of any age with grey hair – just eight percent of UK women coloured their hair in the 1950s whereas today the figure is 75 percent[24] (and the colour of choice is, of course, blonde – a colour that seems only to exist for women: some women *are* blondes; men are not). The amount spent on wrinkle-reducing techniques (including Botox and cosmetic surgery) and on nose jobs, lip jobs, liposuction, breast 'enhancement' and even vagina 'enhancement', has also risen rapidly. For example, in 2014 there were 45,406 cosmetic surgical procedures recorded in Britain by the British Association of Aesthetic Plastic Surgeons. By 2015 this figure had risen by 13 percent to 51,140, with breast 'augmentation', eyelid surgery and face and neck lifts the most popular procedures.[25]

But there is a further paradox here. Precisely because men and women in most advanced industrial societies, and particularly younger men and women, rub along together so intimately in their couplings and friendship groups, without many of the culturally-policed separations of the past, they tend to pick up on each other's habits and standards despite their subliminal desire for distinction. So it is that by the 1990s growing numbers of women were getting their bodies tattooed and were developing their 'guns' and working on their six-packs in the gym – while in some Western sub-cultures more androgynous fashion trends emerged (for example, goth, grunge and heroin chic). Meanwhile, men too are spending more of their disposable income on self-decoration – they have become more inclined to colour and highlight and gel their hair, to wear multiple earrings, to wax their 'backs, cracks and sacks', use concealer and a wide range of skin products, and to spend money on cosmetic surgery. For example, the 2016 UK figures on cosmetic surgery show 12.5 percent year-on-year increase in procedures for women compared with an 89 percent increase for men, albeit from a far lower base (still only 9 percent of the total).[26]

A complementary (or alternative) explanation is that all this increased spending on adornment relates mainly to advertising and the priorities of the media, as well as the increased selfie-obsessed narcissism encouraged by social media – that ultimately it relates more to the marketing systems of post-industrial capitalism than anything else. Many people have more disposable income than in previous generations and companies trying to sell cosmetics or beauty treatments or plastic surgery are able to entice these consumers in all sorts of ways not available in the past. Aside from the beauty pages of newspapers, and magazines, billboards and bus stop advertisements, television advertisements and cinematic portrayals, there is the Web, particularly through its social media platforms, with their ever-more targeted forms of personalised advertising, along with YouTube films demonstrating how to do this or that in the cosmetics line. There are other influences as well. It is hard to avoid the impression that the fashion for Hollywood waxes has much to do with the ubiquity of web pornography (encouraged by demands for the 'right' camera angles). The impact on all this, among both women and men, is to create insecurities, desires and obsessions that didn't previously exist.

Where does that leave us on the question of why women give more attention to adornment? As I've illustrated, an entirely cultural explanation makes sense. But it could also be *mainly* cultural, with a biological nudge. It goes without saying that there is nothing approaching scientific proof of this. No extra 'adornment' genes have been found in women but that does not eliminate the possibility of a less direct genetic link. The question remains open.

# CHAPTER THIRTEEN

## SUPER MUMS AND
## NOT–SO–NEW DADS

My father, Bruce Evans, was indisputably the head of our family. He said so himself, and sat at the 'head' of the table, and he worked long hours, six days a week. My mother, Joan Evans (or, occasionally, Mrs Bruce Evans), didn't have a job of her own. That would have been unthinkable. Her role was to support my father's work and raise their three children. This didn't mean that my loving dad played no role in child-rearing and housework. He could change a nappy, helped in washing dishes, dispensed advice to us and listened to us, and he was the last word in discipline, which very occasionally took on physical dimensions. That then was the model of fatherhood I grew up with – the benign pater familias provider.

My own experience of fatherhood was different. For a start, I wasn't married when my first daughter was born in 1990. And my wife didn't become Mrs Gavin Evans after we married – in fact, there was no question of her taking my surname. We were both providers and played equal roles (worked out in meticulous detail) in childrearing and housework – and our two children saw their mother working full-time throughout their lives. I was not, and never wanted to be, the pater familias, and my children grew up to learn that their dad was a better nurturer and playmate than bread-winner. Discipline never took on physical dimensions, and my children certainly regarded me as fallible in all sorts of ways.

No family can be described as typical without an asterisk – they all have their quirks. But it could be said that the nuclear family I grew up in was the norm in many middleclass families in the 1960s and 70s, not just in white South Africa, but all over the world. Viable alternatives were seldom seen. In contrast, the way I raised my children was a-typical even within my own peer group. Most of my friends, in four continents, did not end up with equal parenting arrangements. Instead, one parent, usually the dad, worked more and the other, usually the mum, did more child care, although in each case the mother had a job and the father spent more time on nurturing than was normal when I was a child (and if they were divorced – more common than a generation earlier – the children saw their dad rather more than one Saturday per week). So from my own very limited experience the roles played by at least some dads and mums appear to have changed markedly even if they haven't been reversed or reached equality.

The limit to my experience meant that I assumed it was only those from the educated, cosmopolitan, urban middle classes who turned their backs on traditional parenting, at least in the UK, where I was living by then. So I pricked up my ears in 1998 when the Labour Party's chief whip Clive Soley announced that 'close to 50 percent of main carers for children at home in South Wales are men' – the result of the closure of coal mines. No doubt this was an exaggeration, but it prompted a newspaper quest to find these men, which led me to Penrhiwceiber in South Wales to meet with a 16-stone former mineworker, former army squaddie, former rugby prop called Brian Hick who wasn't the sort you'd have in mind when words like 'househusband' were thrown about. He was the product of a culture of rugged machismo and when the local pit closed in 1988 he was 'shocked and devastated', but eventually had to accept that his wife was the prime breadwinner after she got a job. 'There was hardly anything for us men but there were lots of jobs for women – they have more nimble fingers for things like typing,' he explained.[1]

Brian realised he should play a greater role in raising his four children. 'On the mines, I hardly saw them,' he said, 'but when the pit closed I began taking them to and from school. I've always enjoyed spending time with my children so I took an interest and found I wanted to get more involved.' Soon he was helping with other people's kids – managing a junior rugby team, running youth events and babysitting for parents on his housing estate, until one day, after taking a neighbour's toddler to a drop-in group, he had a kind-of epiphany, gave up his periodic work as a caterer and became a full-time childworker. 'I suddenly decided this was what I wanted to do with my life. Most of these women were single mums who needed help. Their children needed a father figure and I got a lot of pleasure seeing them grow up.' Along the way, Brian dropped his prejudice about this being women's work. 'It took me a while, but now it's like riding a bike – second nature. You've got to be able to understand children, get down to their level, to being a two and a half-year-old again, because it's no good trying to bring them up to yours. It's hard but you get used to it.'

So how much does this esoteric case study, and my own, reflect broader societal trends? The answer changes depending on whether you're taking a snapshot or allowing the film to run over a generation. The snapshot shows that women spend more time on childcare and housework than men, and that men work longer hours and earn more. The cross generation film shows something different: in much of the world men are spending more time on childcare and housework than they did in the 20th century, and women are spending more time on paid work.

## Same old, same old?

Let's start with the snapshot. In 2011 British men in paid employment spent an average of 38.4 hours a week on the job compared with 33.3 hours for women in paid employment[2] but the gap widened when all adults were taken into account, including those not in paid employment, with men doing 61.7 percent of the work. In contrast, women spent an average of 4 hours 40 minutes a day on childcare and housework, compared with 2 hours 28 minutes for men.[3] More specifically, British women spent more time caring for children and older adults (63.9 percent of the total).[4] The data on housework is also telling, with women devoting more time to chores – washing up and cooking (66.6 percent), washing clothes (82 percent), cleaning and tidying (78 percent), shopping (59 percent) and pet care (53.8 percent). Only on repairs and gardening did men have the lead (59 percent).

When total hours are computed (paid work plus child care plus chores), British men spent an average of 18 minutes per day longer at the grindstone than women.[5] But when it came to pay, the gap was larger in the other direction. In 2014 British men earned an average of £558 per week compared with £462 for women. This 19.1 percent gap was the sixth highest in Europe. The EU average in 2012 was 16.4 percent with Slovenia the lowest at 2.5 percent. Other countries with gender pay gaps of 10 percent or lower included Belgium, Italy, Luxemburg, Malta, Romania and Poland.[6]

Three other interesting British nuggets:

- 13.5 percent of single parent families were headed by men in 2011.[7]
- 14 percent (1.4-million) of primary carers in two parent families were men.[8]
- In step families with dependent children, 18 percent were from the man's previous relationship, 78 percent from the woman's and 4 percent with shared residence.[9]

The gaps are narrower in the US and several European countries, but, still, it's tempting to reach a conclusion of 'same old, same old' – tempting, but wrong.

## All has changed, changed utterly

What about when we let the cross-generational film run? What we see when we look at the changes since the 1960s is a steady decrease in the gender pay gap – and that men are spending more time on childcare and housework. Nearly 20 years ago I had a chat with Dr Jonathan Gershuny who'd just directed a pioneering study by the Economic and Social Research Council, which analysed data from three long-term surveys of British life involving interviews with 9,000 people over a 20-year period. Nothing like this had been done before and the results suggested something new was percolating in family life: both mothers and fathers were spending more time with their children but the change was most dramatic with fathers – from an average of 10 minutes a day in 1975 to 54 minutes two decades later. 'There is no doubt about it,' Gershuny said. 'There's a considerable increase in the time spent by men interacting with children and with housework, albeit from a low base.'[10] I began to look for evidence of a trend and it was easy to find. By the year 2000 fathers were spending an average of an hour a day with their children, while between 1961 and 2009 men doubled the time spent on daily household chores to 146 minutes (and with women it fell from 303 minutes in 1961 to 277 minutes in 2009.[11])

Significant shifts emerged in other areas. Figures cited on the number of single fathers in the UK in the 1980s and 1990s hovered around the 9 percent mark. By 2011 it had risen to 13.5 percent (almost 1-million children).[12] And the proportion of UK families with children under 18 where childcare was shared equally between parents rose to 25 percent in 2011 from 18 percent a year earlier (although the speed of this rise suggests considerable margin for error[13])

Similar trends can be seen the US. Time commitment to household chores from American men rose from four hours a week in 1965 to 10 hours in 2011.[14] Time spent by American fathers with their children rose from 2.5 hours a week in 1965 to seven hours in 2011.

Meanwhile, time spent by American mothers on childcare rose from 10 to 14 hours a week in this period, but time spent on housework fell from 32 hours per week to 18. Put these figures together and the relative proportion of time American men spent on *both* childcare and housework rose from 13.4 percent in 1965 to 34.7 percent of the 2011.

Also, the number of American men heading single parent households has grown dramatically. In 1960, one percent of *all* American households had a single father, representing 4 percent of the single parent total. By 2011 eight percent had single fathers, representing nearly 25 percent of the single parent total.[15]

The most significant change in American family life has involved the proportion of income earned by women. Those earning more than their husbands rose from 28 percent in 2005 to 35 percent five years later – and one demographic study suggested that women would earn more than men in careers like law, medicine and academia by 2024.[16] In some US cities the average woman in her twenties is already earning more than the average man (for example, 20 percent more in Dallas and 17 percent in New York City).[17]

Meanwhile in Britain, according to a survey of data conducted by an insurance company, the percentage of women in full-time paid employment earning more than their partners rose from 26 percent in 1993 to 41 percent in 2013.[18] Government data shows that the overall gender pay gap fell from 27.5 percent in 1997 to 19.1 percent in 2013 (and 17.5 percent in the private sector).[19] By 2011 British women aged 22 to 29 were earning more than men for the first time.[20]

Finally, a change of a different kind: in the behaviour of fathers on the birth of their children. Today around 93 percent of British fathers attend the births of their children, up from one or two percent in the 1950s, and not much more until the 1970s. Similar patterns are seen in other European countries and in Canada. In the US around 15 percent of fathers attended the births of their children in 1960. Forty years later, the figure had risen to between 75 and 80 percent.[21] This might seem a trivial change but being involved in the birth of a child can be significant in establishing an emotional link.

## What is fuelling these changes?

The changes in the home and workplace are directly related. If women spend more time in paid work, they'll want to spend less on housework (aided by dishwashers, driers and microwaves) and if men do more around the house and with the children, women have more options for paid work. This is also prompted by the fact that women workers are more in demand. The decline in mining and manufacturing in the advanced industrial world, the rise of service industries and the increasing demand for employees with IT skills has all made better educated, 'nimble-fingered' workers more desirable to employers. In Britain, the closure of coal mines, steel foundries and other industries in the 1980s meant that many men like Brian Hick were put out to pasture, lacking the skills and inclination needed for the new economic order. Women stepped into the breach to take up the new opportunities.

A key consideration is education. As we have saw in chapter 9, girls out-perform boys at all levels of schooling in the UK (and in most countries around the world). They are also significantly more motivated to go on to tackle A-levels, matric or equivalent secondary school qualifications, and to go on to university – and this gap is growing. Again, these trends are even more marked in the US where 60 percent of American university graduates are women. In New York City in 2010 53 percent of women employees in their twenties were graduates, compared with 38 percent of men).[22]

There is another, related, factor behind the shifting balance of work and home life: changing attitudes. Most women, and many men too, have become used to greater equality and have learnt to embrace it. Opinion polls in the US suggest that while Americans may be becoming more conservative about marriage and divorce, they have become more liberal about gender equality – for example, by a margin of nearly three-to-one they agree that the main purpose of marriage is the 'mutual happiness and fulfilment' of *both* adults.[23] The author and demographer Maddy Dychtwald, highlighted these changed perceptions. 'There are economic changes, but also shifts in cultural attitudes showing up in many polls. Women are more ambitious, going for the top jobs, and younger women would find disparity with their male peers a joke. While older men find this threatening, the majority of men under 40 have little problem with their wives earning more than they do. It takes the burden off their shoulders and they can move into jobs previously unthinkable, such as teaching.'[24]

A study of 5,199 single people in the United States, conducted by researchers at Rutgers University, found that changing attitudes also related to the prospect of having children – 51 percent of single men aged 21 to 34 wanted children, compared to 46 percent of single women. And contrary to popular perceptions, there was a similar gap when it came to romance – 54 percent of American men surveyed said they'd experienced love at first sight, compared with 44 percent of women. The anthropologist Helen Fisher, who headed the study, commented that men's attitudes were closer to the female archetype than before. 'They are becoming the broody ones – they are more likely to want to settle down sooner,' she said. 'Complicating matters is the change in women's attitudes towards life and relationships, mostly driven by the huge numbers flooding into the workforce.'[25]

## Unmarried fathers

The proportion of unmarried parents has increased throughout the advanced industrial world and in much of the developing world. Less than two-thirds of British families consist of married couples. The number of unmarried, co-habiting opposite sex couples rose from 2.2 million in 2003 to 2.9 million in 2013 and the number of children in these couplings rose from 1.4 million to 1.9 million.[26] When you look at figures for newborns, the trend is more remarkable. In 2012,

47.5 percent had unmarried parents (346,595 babies) and the government estimated that by 2016 the majority of babies would be born to unmarried parents.[27] A similar pattern is seen in the US where 40.6 percent of all births in 2013 were to unmarried women[28] and only 46 percent of American children under the age of 18 were living at home with two married, heterosexual parents in their first marriage (compared with 73 percent in 1960 and 61 percent in 1980).[29]

The law in the US, UK and many other countries gradually changed to reflect this shifting reality, particularly regarding the position of unmarried fathers.

In the US the issue went to the Supreme Court, which affirmed constitutional protection for unmarried fathers to parental rights (under the 14th Amendment), finding that the biological parental link between the child and the unmarried father allowed him to maintain an *existing* relationship with the child. Also, half of the 50 states have provision for an unmarried father voluntarily to register paternity, which gives him rights to receive notice of court proceedings, petitions for adoption and actions to end parental rights. It also gives him the right to apply for visitation with the child, and the obligation to provide financial support.[30]

Until December 1 2003, unmarried British fathers could be frozen out of the lives of their children, who could be taken to another country or put up for adoption without them being informed. The mother had the exclusive right to decide on their upbringing while the father had no legal rights – not even to give consent to medical treatment. Unmarried dads could only acquire legal rights if the mother agreed through signing a parental responsibility order or through a court order, but these were rarely granted. The result could be devastating with fathers cut off from all contact with the children they helped raise. In 1996 there were 232,663 British births outside of wedlock, yet only 5,500 parental responsibility orders for fathers.[31] The law finally changed giving unmarried dads who signed the birth register an automatic right to parental responsibility (putting him in the same position as a divorced dad). However, in the 20 percent of cases where the father hadn't signed the birth certificate, they were in the same position as before.

Until recently UK courts routinely granted residency (custody) to the mother, with the father only having a contact order. But in 2013 the government shifted the balance with a law giving a statutory right to children from broken homes to see both parents (unless their welfare was threatened). In recent years it appears that in applying divorce law the courts have been less fixed on giving mothers sole custody. A rising proportion of fathers are being granted residency orders, and there has also been a steady rise from a low base in the number shared residence orders, which were more common in other parts of Europe and in the US. Along with the changed situation for unmarried fathers, this has helped prompt the increasing role played by fathers in nurturing their children.

## Parental leave

In most marriages in the past, the mother would take maternity leave while the father might take a week off, then return to the grindstone, establishing a pattern where mum was regarded as the main nurturer and dad the main provider. In the UK the possibility of substantial change was introduced in 2015, allowing parents to share parental leave following the birth or adoption of their child. Fathers are still entitled to two weeks of paid paternity leave (introduced in 2011), but mothers can now exchange maternity leave for shared parental leave. So, if the mother decides to end maternity leave 10 weeks after the child's birth, she still has 42 weeks left, which she can exchange for parental leave, allowing the father to take part or all of it – and it will not have to be taken continuously.

However, there are two catches. First, not all parents are eligible – only those who've worked at least 26 weeks for that employer. According to the Trades Union Congress, 40 percent of fathers will not be eligible. Second, there's the money. Shared parental leave guarantees parents a mere £139.58 a week, or 90 percent of an employee's weekly wage, whichever is *lower* and it lasts for just 37 weeks. This amount is the same as for Statutory Maternity Pay although in the first six weeks of maternity leave, the mother is paid at 90 percent of her salary or wages.[32]

This system appears to put a dampener on the proportion of British fathers who take parental leave beyond the initial two weeks – although how much of a dampener, we don't yet know. A survey of 200 employers, their employees and their partners by the UK firm My Family Care found that an average of one percent of fathers took parental leave. Half of the men surveyed said they assumed taking additional parental leave would be looked on unfavourably by their managers, while more than half of the mothers interviewed said they did not want to share their parental leave. Sixty percent of employees said there was no encouragement from their employers to consider this option.[33]

This research – and particularly the one percent figure – prompted a spate of media reports asking what was wrong with British men. In fact, this was merely yet another example of the media not looking beyond the press releases, and not subjecting the data to serious review. It turned out that this one percent figure applied to *all* men in these firms, 95 percent of whom did not have children in the year after the new law came into effect. So one percent of the total would amount to 20 percent of the men who'd been eligible for parental leave. The BBC radio programme, *More or Less*, which subjects statistical claims to scrutiny, did its own instant survey (admittedly of only 30 fathers) and came up with a figure of 30 percent. However, they made no claims about this figure, and, as they noted, there was no reason to question the government's prediction of a UK take-up rate of between two and eight percent of fathers (itself allowing for a massive margin of error).[34]

A different system operates in Sweden and much of the rest of Western Europe, with very different results. Swedish parents are entitled to share 480 days of paid parental leave, which can be taken by the month, week, day or hour at any time up to the child's eighth birthday. For 21 years after parental leave was introduced in 1974, fathers took an average of just six percent of the leave available. To encourage change, the government amended the law, reserving 60 days for the father, known as 'daddy leave' (extended to 90 days in 2016). The family loses all three months of subsidies if he declines it.

But the most significant difference between the Swedish and British systems relates to money. For 390 days, the parental allowance since 2013 has been 80 percent of pay or £2,900 per month, whichever is lower. For the remaining 60 days, this falls to around £13.50 per day.[35] Today Swedish fathers take about 25 percent of parental leave, a substantial increase (in its first year, 1974, they took 0.5 percent) – and 80 percent of all Swedish fathers take at least four months. The impact on women's earning power has been considerable – on average, a mother's earnings increased by seven percent for each month the father took leave in 2010[36].

Several other European countries followed suit. In Iceland three months is reserved for the father, three for the mother and three shared, while in Germany two out of 14 months of paid leave was reserved for fathers in 2007, prompting a surge in uptake (from 2 percent to more than 20 percent).

The European experience suggests that the combination of generous parental leave pay and months set aside specifically for the father has a profound impact on the relation between fathers and their children – perhaps more than any other single factor.

## The 'new dad' phenomenon

But is this a good idea? In the 1990s, when I first wrote on this subject, the most prominent British naysayer was the right-wing columnist Melanie Phillips, who fulminated against the changes taking place in family relations. First she wrote a Social Market Foundation pamphlet, *The Sex-Change State* followed two years later by a book on the same theme, *The Sex-Change Society,* which explained the simultaneous arrival of large numbers of hands-on dads and the larger numbers of no-show dads and single mums as two sides of a coin – the result of a single pernicious cause: American-led 'female supremacist' feminism (an ideology that pushed mums into work and dads into 'surrogate motherhood' or irrelevance). She castigated 'androgynous' dads who spent too much time with their children, as well as those who spent none, adding that 'societies which work most successfully give men a role as principal family provider and protector'. Parental roles were based on 'hormonal and genetic impulses', which we ignored at our peril. Her solution was to buck up masculine identity, block attempts to 'emasculate' men and oppose policies that displaced working men with women (women other than the hard-driven Melanie Phillips, that is).[37]

We'll return to 'hormonal and genetic impulses' in chapter 14, but what about the argument that it leads to bad things? The research data takes us in the opposite direction: the more dads are involved in nurturing, the better their children do in school, IQ tests and socially.

A 12-year Yale University project involved children being monitored from birth to early teens. It found that across the board children raised primarily by their father scored higher than the rest of their peers from the same social class on IQ tests.[38] A British study of 11,000 men and women born in 1958 drew its data from the National Child Development Study which asked mothers about the level of their partners' involvement. It came to the same conclusion: children who spent large amounts of time with fathers had higher IQs at the age of 11 than others from their same class cohort, and this paternal investment also had a positive effect on social mobility. Both sons and daughters benefited – but particularly sons.

They also found that fathers of higher socio-economic status had more impact on IQ than those of lower socio-economic status.[39] The psychologist leading this study, Daniel Nettle, explained: 'It's not

[just] having dad around; it's about the kind of dad he is.'[40] He added: 'What was surprising about this research was the real, sizeable difference in the progress of children who benefited from paternal interest, and how, thirty years later, people whose dads were involved are more upwardly mobile. The data suggest that having a second adult involved during childhood produces benefits in terms of skills and abilities that endure throughout adult life.'[41]

## The fathers that time forgot

Opponents of the 'sex-change society' often portray the hands-on dad as something dangerously new under the sun, going against nature itself. The patriarchal father-provider is seen as the natural, timeless model. But when you peruse the history of fatherhood from before the industrial era, a very different picture emerges: of a variety of forms, many involving far more father-child contact than the contemporary norm.

The author Adrienne Burgess included a history of British fathers in her ground-breaking book *Fatherhood Reclaimed*,[42] noting that the first half of the 20th century, and the second half of the 19th, were marked by a hardening of the 'separate spheres' for men and women – partly as a result of rapid industrialisation which led to the separation of work and home, and partly because of two world wars. This, however, was far from being a continuation of pre-industrial parenting where the available evidence suggests that, by and large, fathers were more emotionally and physically engaged with their children than in the industrial era.

Burgess drew from pre-20th century diaries, letters, reports and parish records and found that those fathers who recorded their thoughts treasured their children for the joy they brought. Child mortality rates were far higher than in the 20th century, but there's no suggestion of fathers keeping their distance in case their children died. Thomas More wrote of his grief at the death of his daughter in 1517: 'It is not so strange that I love you with my whole heart, for being a father is not a tie which can be ignored. Nature in her wisdom has attached the parent to the child and bound them together with a Herculean knot.'[43]

It is sometimes said that pre-20th century fathers were remote because of the size of families – too many children to know them individually. In fact for several centuries in pre-industrial Britain the average couple had five children and the odds were high that one or two would die before reaching 15. When children were ill, fathers as well as mothers would watch over them. One reason for this close bond is that they tended to work alongside each other, and in most houses there was no clear separation between adult and child space, and work was frequently interrupted by children who had to be minded constantly because of the danger from open fires and tools. There are several accounts of pre-industrial fathers minding children or doing household chores while their wives were spinning yarn.

When mothers died or were ill, fathers often had to take over the childcare, perhaps with the help of older siblings (widowers frequently stayed single). One in three pre-industrial British marriages ended prematurely, sometimes through death when giving birth, frequently through illness and in about ten percent ended through formal separation – which usually led to the father continuing to 'head' the household (until 1839 married fathers were routinely given custody). Between 1599 and 1811 almost a quarter of children under 16 were living in single parent households. One in three British lone fathers in pre-industrial Britain had no 'live-in' support of other adults.[44]

*Silas Marner*, George Eliot's allegorical novel on the all-that-glitters-is-not-gold theme (published in 1861 but dealing with village life earlier in the century), provides English literature with its most memorable single father. Silas loses his gold but finds new gold in Eppie, an orphaned child. My favourite passage sees him taking advice from his genial neighbour, Dolly:

' "Thank you … kindly," said Silas, hesitating a little. "I'll be glad if you'll tell me things. But," he added, uneasily, leaning forward to look at Baby with some jealousy, as she was resting her head backward against Dolly's arm, and eyeing him contentedly from a distance – "But I want to do things for it myself, else it may get fond o' somebody else, and not fond o' me. I've been used to fending for myself in the house – I can learn, I can learn."

' "Eh, to be sure," said Dolly, gently. "I've seen men are wonderful handy wi' children. The men are awk'ard and contrary mostly, God help 'em – but when the drink's out of 'em, they aren't unsensible, though they're bad for leeching and bandaging – so fiery and unpatient. You see this goes first, next to the skin," proceeded Dolly, taking up the little shirt and putting it on.

' "Yes," said Marner, docilely, bringing his eyes very close, that they might be initiated in the mysteries; whereupon Baby seized his head with both her small arms, and put her lips against his face with purring noises.'[45]

Another myth about pre-industrial fathers is that they were tyrannical, dishing out beatings, disinheriting errant sons, forcing daughters into unwanted marriages. No doubt some behaved this way. But by 1750 arranged marriages were dying out[46] and the fact that, on average, three out of four children left home in early adolescence (often to be apprenticed), and were therefore not around to be controlled by father, makes the image of the looming presence of the disciplinarian paterfamilias unrealistic. And not all fathers beat their children. There was perpetual debate about whether to use corporal punishment from at least the 17th century – and where it happened it was as likely to be from the mother as from the father (and there are records of fathers protecting their children against harsh mothers).

Again, Silas and Dolly offer a glimpse. Silas needs to get on with his weaving, but Eppie, is full of mischief. Dolly suggests he puts her in the coal-hole as punishment. ' "That was what I did wi' Aaron; for I was that silly wi' the youngest lad, as I could never bear to smack him. Not that it was in my heart to let him stay I' the coal-hole for more than a minute ..." She goes on to propose that he uses 'ayther smacking or the coal-hole'. Silas can't bear the idea of smacking

Eppie, so, when she next misbehaves, he tries the coal-hole but as soon as she cries, 'Opy, opy!' he lets her out. He gives up this method of discipline while refusing to try smacking because 'I can't do that'. In the end, he decides: 'If she makes a bit o' trouble, I can bear it. And she's got no tricks but what she'll grow out of.'[47]

The harshness of factory work was one factor prompting harsher treatment of children in the home. However, while the changes brought on by the industrial revolution were momentous, their impact on families took a while to percolate. In 1850 factory workers made up just five percent of the population and few workplaces employed more than 20 people. Most sons (three quarters) followed the same trade or profession as their fathers. Accounts of middle class families from before 1850 involved relaxed and approachable fathers, but this changed later in the century, when well-to-do fathers became more remote (although the traditional image of the invariably harsh Victorian paterfamilias is certainly not reflected in most of the writing of Dickens, Eliot, Hardy and other novelists of the time). For working class families, the workplace was separated from home, meaning the father had to go out to work while the home became then terrain of the mother, backed up by grannies, aunts and older daughters. Working fathers in the late Victorian era spent very little time at home, beyond the evening meal and sleeping.[48]

So it appears that the impact of industrialisation was the prime factor behind the more remote fatherhood of the 20th century, with the often-absent dad as provider, protector and disciplinarian and the ever-present mum as nurturer and housewife. Before the 20th century, fathers were more engaged with their children. The notion advanced by the likes of Melanie Phillips that child-raising is the inherent preserve of mothers and providing the inherent preserve of fathers is a relatively recent invention and it is worth noting that we're entering a post-industrial era that in some respects resembles pre-industrial times. More people were self-employed, working from home, and most households have two working parents. This raises fresh possibilities for parenting – including increased contact between fathers and children.

## Aka Pygmy fathers

If the natural model for parenting was indeed the paterfamilias-housewife combination then we'd expect it to be close-to universal. After all, no rule can co-exist with an exception. But when we dip into anthropological studies on people cut off from industrialisation, we find many exceptions. Among the most interesting emerged from a study by an American anthropologist Barry Hewlett, which led to his book *Intimate Fathers: the nature and content of AKA Pygmy paternal infant care*[49]. His focus was on a 20,000-strong nomadic, Mbenga pygmy hunter-gatherer tribe in a tropical forest region in the western Congo basin. He studied them for 15 years when they were relatively untouched by Western influence.

Hewlett found that Aka dads played a greater role in nurturing babies than those in other societies whose parenting had been documented (spending around five times as much time with their infants than average.[50]) They held or remained within arm's length of their babies 47 percent of the time, and frequently hugged their infants close to their bodies for an hour or more, and they'd often take their children with them when they went to drink palm wine with friends. Aka fathers regularly comforted their crying babies at night and would clean them, wipe their bottoms and offer their own nipples for a suck. 'It was not uncommon to wake up in the night and hear a father signing softly to his fussing infant,' said Hewlett.[51] He noticed Aka children would frequently call for their dads – crawling to them and demanding to be picked up. Even when the mothers weren't working, fathers often took charge.

Hewlett elaborated: 'One thing that's crucial in the raising of the young is the importance placed on physical closeness: at around three months, a baby is in almost constant physical contact with either one of her parents or with another person. There's no such thing as a cot ... because it's unheard of for a couple to ever leave their baby lying unattended – babies are held all the time.'[52] He seldom heard parents telling children not to touch things or children getting told off when they interfered in adult business. 'When an infant hits another child a parent will get up and move the infant to another area; the infant is not told *no, no!* Violence or corporal punishment for an infant that misbehaves seldom occurs. In fact, if one parent hits an infant, this is reason enough for the other parent to ask for a divorce.'[53]

Aka parents interchanged roles within their small camps (25 to 35 people) – whether hunting, cooking or nurturing. One reason related to their main subsistence activity, the net hunt (for small animals), which was a co-operative venture. Aka women played a significant role – during one visit Hewlett observed an eight-month pregnant woman hunting with nets and spears and she returned to the hunt a month after giving birth. He also noticed women hunting duikers with babies strapped to their sides in side slings. Sometimes this placed them in danger. 'If a woman chases a game animal into the net, she will place the infant on the ground to run after the game and kill it. The infant is left there crying until the mother or someone else comes back.'[54]

This did not mean that that Aka women played a secondary child raising role. Overall, they had more physical contact than their husbands. For one thing, they nursed their babies on demand and outside of camp, when the group was on the move, mothers usually held the babies. But as Hewlett explained, these roles weren't fixed: '[T]here's a level of flexibility that's virtually unknown in our society. Aka fathers will slip into roles usually occupied by mothers without a second thought and without, more importantly, any loss of status – there's no stigma involved in the different jobs.'[55]

There are, however, significant differences between the nurturing of the Aka parents and the aspirations of Western equal parenting couples. Hewlett noted that Aka fathers tended not to play with children – this role was largely reserved for other children and aunts.

And theirs was not a child-centred culture in the Western sense. Mothers and fathers usually wouldn't stop doing their thing to focus on their children (rather they'd pick up the child, and get on with it). Also, fathers did not attend the births of their babies, although in one case mentioned by Hewlett a father did attend (because his wife gave birth while they were walking in the forest), he was not teased or stigmatised.[56] And although on a day-to-day basis their roles were often interchangeable, the tribes were led by men, who were also the healers.

## India's Khasi women

One final example where gender relations do not conform to the traditional Western mould: the matrilineal society of the Khasi in India. Theirs is not an example of fathers playing a major role in raising their children. The differences lie in other areas of home life.

Three criteria are used to decide if a society is matrilineal: descent through the mother (including family name); a residence system where the husband lives in the wife's home; inheritance of parental property by daughters.[57] The Khasi are not unique in this respect. The Garo and Jaintia tribes in Meghalaya also fulfil the criteria, as do small pockets in other parts of India, and there are parts of Africa, as well as the Maldives and South-East Asia where matrilineal communities exist. The largest is the Minangkabau of West Sumatra.[58]

Among the one million Khasi, who live in the north-eastern state of Meghalaya, the youngest daughter inherits property and wealth and children take their mother's surname. Many Khasi women prefer to remain single, but if they get married, their husbands live with them in their mother-in-law's home. It would appear that significant numbers of Khasi women, particularly in urban areas, prefer having daughters to sons, perhaps because they provide more long-term security (although the most desired combination is two daughters and a son)[59] The husband does most of the housework, taking orders from the mother-in-law. He's also not permitted to take part in family gatherings and is regarded as a member of the weaker sex. Women take most of the important domestic and commercial decisions, although these are supposed to be approved by a maternal uncle. There also appears to be less domestic violence than in the rest of India.[60] However, this matrilineal system is not a matriarchy because the power of the women in this predominantly Christian community does not extend to the political arena – village councils comprise mainly men.[61]

The value in using the examples of the Aka and the Khasi is not to hold them up as an ideal but rather to illustrate a point made throughout this book: that the way men and women relate to each other and their children is moulded mainly by culture. It is tempting to observe norms in gender and parental relations and assume this is the natural way of doing it – the way *I* do things (or my parents did things) is all too easily seen as the universal. But really, that's the solipsism of the known. When you take a cross-cultural view you see that what seems natural to one tribe, community or society, seems unnatural to another. Culture can be an extremely powerful and resilient force – sometimes so powerful that we are tempted to conflate it with biology, as we shall see in the next chapter.

# CHAPTER FOURTEEN

# MATERNAL INSTINCT, COUSIN LOVE AND THE CINDERELLA EFFECT.

When I became a father for the first time in Johannesburg and for the second in London, I would regularly take my daughters to playgroups, library sing-alongs, romps in the park and the like. Sometimes I would get sideways glances from mums who seemed to resent a male presence. Other times I would bristle when mothers tried to take over with my own children, or tried to tell me what to do, assuming that I must be an inadequate nurturer because I was a man. Once a mum told me it was 'so nice that you take a turn in babysitting'. Behind all this was a view that looking after toddlers was a mother's business and that fathers were out of place there – inherently lacking in the required skills and mindset.

This attitude to fathers dovetails with one of the most persistent claims made by those pushing a biological agenda on parenting: that mothers have a huge nurturing advantage because of 'maternal instinct'. The strongest claims around this 'instinct' relate to a hormone called oxytocin, and the most vociferous campaigner for its recognition as the big thing that causes mums to adore their children is the Canadian psychologist Susan Pinker.

## Susan Pinker: maternal and paternal instincts

Pinker parks herself squarely in the *viva la difference* camp. Reading her and reading her brother, Steven Pinker, you notice they're echoing the same script, including 'males are the more variable gender' and 'males do better in business and academia because they are that way' views – citing the same surveys. She insists differences between male and female brains are profound and that this explains why women lack career ambition but long for babies. Her book *The Sexual Paradox*[1] asks why girls lead boys at school and university and fall behind in the workplace. Discrimination? The way our gendered society is structured? Entrenched attitudes? Not a bit of it. It's all down to genes. Women have 'biological networks that evolved to promote the survival of infants', prompting their 'longing for their infants and their drive to nurture them'.[2] They have a wider range of interests than men and are more concerned with intrinsic reward, more service-oriented, better at assessing their impact on others, 'wired for empathy'. The paradox of the title is this: many women with the same career opportunities as men choose not to aim for high status positions and the 'plain vanilla' male model of life. 'If you were to predict the future on the basis of school achievement alone, the world would be a matriarchy,'[3] she says.

Men are exposed to higher levels of testosterone, making them more competitive, assertive, daring and vengeful, but women get regular doses of oxytocin, 'helping them to discern the emotions of others – the truest social enabler'. Pinker tells us that the maternal neural pathway is 'exquisitely sensitive' to stimulation by oxytocin, which surges during pregnancy and again through childbirth, breastfeeding and through nurturing more generally as well as through orgasm and 'at critical moments in women's relationships and menstrual cycles, damping down stress responses' by providing 'sedative and analgesic effects'. It also helps women 'reach out to others when they are in trouble', 'read emotions in other's faces' and 'increases their trust'[4]. It operates in the opposite way to testosterone, which 'may alter some neural connections related to reading others' emotional states'. Oxytocin, along with another pregnancy-boosted hormone, prolactin, produces 'the elixir of contentment' – the 'high' that prompts mother rats to choose their newborn pups over cocaine.

She adds that other female hormones increase connections to other regions of the brain, 'linking motherhood to problem solving rewards'. With humans, these make most women want to limit time at work and find 'inherent meaning' in family rather than pursuing domination, and they make women more empathetic than men. Like most evolutionary psychologists, she goes back in time to explain how natural selection made this happen. 'There's a heavy cost to becoming a mother in pure energy and freedom to move around. The neurochemically induced feeling of being rewarded by nurturing might have evolved to counteract those costs,' she said, reflecting a purpose-rich view of natural selection.[5]

Much of what Pinker says has been disputed by other scientists and psychologists. One example: she refers to research by Sandra Witelson that involved looking at brain activity while men and women performed emotion-related tasks. In the easier task volunteers had to decide which of two faces matched the emotion of a third. The harder task involved deciding which of two emotions matched that expressed in a recorded voice. Pinker summarised the results: 'When women looked at pictures of people's facial expressions, both cerebral hemispheres were activated and there was greater activity in the amygdala, the almond-shaped seat of emotion buried deep in the brain.' However in men, 'perception of emotion was usually localised in one hemisphere.' She added that women have a thicker corpus callosum, which allows for quicker inter-hemispheric transmission of information.

In fact, as shown in chapter 7, women do *not* have a thicker corpus callosum. But the more interesting gap is that the researchers found no differences in how quickly men and women performed the tasks.[6] Summarising the brain hemisphere research, and drawing the opposite conclusion from Pinker's, the cognitive psychologist Cordelia Fine writes that 'researchers didn't find any regions in the hemisphere that were activated more in men than in women'.[7] She adds an additional warning about interpreting brain images: 'Even though a part of the brain might light up during a task, it may not be especially or crucially involved'.[8]

Another example: Pinker swallows Simon Baron-Cohen's views whole, including his dubious claim, discussed in chapter 8, that Asperger's syndrome and attention deficit disorder are examples of the 'the extreme male brain' – which helps males progress as adults when they can focus single-mindedly on their careers. This, she claims, is the reason why boys might lag behind at school but leap ahead at work. As we saw, Asperger's and attention deficit disorder do affect more males than females (although female prevalence has, in the past, been significantly underestimated). But they are examples of neurological disorders rather than epitomising 'the extreme male brain' and tell us nothing about the typical male brain.

She also embraces Baron-Cohen's most disputed study[9], the one showing that newborn boys preferred looking at mobiles and newborn girls at human faces, which was not replicated elsewhere. The key flaw in the Baron-Cohen study was that the researcher knew which babies were boys and which were girls. When that knowledge was eliminated in another study, no differences were found between girl and boy babies.[10]

And her claims about boys struggling at school but excelling at work might have a different explanation, partly relating to development. Girls mature earlier, both physically and emotionally, but boys start to catch up in their teens. By the time they're ready to work, they are (potentially) intellectually equal to women, after which discrimination and socialisation hold women back and push men forward. As one reviewer asked: 'Why would girls' hard-wired predilection against competition stay on ice while they blithely sweep all the academic honours and then kick in only at work?'[11]

Susan Pinker downplays discrimination faced by women at work, instead claiming that barriers have been 'stripped away'[12] and her book is full of examples of those rather unusual working women who say they've never faced sexism or had to struggle against male-slanted odds. She views occupational sex discrimination in much of the West as natural reflections of women's innate preferences.

What Pinker misses is that discrimination relates not just to opportunities but also to working patterns modelled on the lifestyle of a man with a housewife at home (which applies to only six percent of US households). Discrimination also relates to a work culture that subtly hints to women that they don't belong at the top. Reviewing Pinker's book, the psychiatrist, Anna Fels, concluded: 'To say women are less career-oriented than men on the basis of our current workplace is suspect. Pinker has fallen into the old and hoary tradition of assuming that what is, is "natural".'[13]

But the key flaw involves Pinker's claims about oxytocin and her wider claims of significant genetic differences profoundly affecting parenting abilities. Oxytocin is implicated in triggering childbirth and milk production, and is recognised as playing some role in bonding process between mothers and babies. But does it have a profound effect, in itself, on making mothers *better* nurturers than fathers? The answer is no.

Contrary to the thrust of Pinker's book, oxytocin is not a mum-only or female-only 'love hormone'. The neuroscientist, Lise Eliot, notes that all available research suggests 'there are no significant differences' between girls and boys in terms of oxytocin levels'.[14] One study[15] compared levels of oxytocin and vasopressin (a hormone influencing ability to recognise familiar individuals and to form social bonds) between children who'd suffered severe neglect before being adopted and a control group raised in more typical home environments. In both groups hormone levels in boys and girls were equivalent (vasopressin was slightly higher in boys; oxytocin slightly higher in girls) but those in the control group had higher levels of baseline vasopressin and also had higher levels of oxytocin after physical contact with their mothers and with unfamiliar adults. The researchers concluded that 'a failure to receive species-typical care disrupts the normal development of the oxytocin and vasopressin systems in young children. Perturbations in this system may interfere with the calming and comforting effects that typically emerge between young children and familiar adults who provide care and protection'[16]

When it comes to adult males there's a similar variation in oxytocin levels, strongly influenced by the nature of their contact with children. Recent research shows that when fathers interact intimately with their children, there's a significant rise in their oxytocin levels (similar to that found in mothers) as well as a rise in oxytocin levels found in their babies. One study of 112 mothers and fathers measured their oxytocin levels after they had engaged in 15 minutes of play with their four-to-six month-old infants. The results showed that the baseline oxytocin levels in both mothers and fathers were similar, and among both there was a rise in oxytocin levels detected in those who had 'high levels' of stimulatory contact with their babies'. The researchers concluded that this underscored the need to 'provide opportunities for paternal care to trigger the biological basis of fatherhood'.[17]

It doesn't stop with oxytocin. Men also experience a rise in levels of vasopressin and prolactin (a lust-reducing, milk-producing hormone that seems to make them more sensitive to their babies' crying) after becoming dads – and male testosterone levels tend to decline with fatherhood.[18] With each of these hormones, the level varies according to the time and intensity of the contact. The more the father responds to his baby's cries and the more he plays with his children, the more these hormonal differences will be triggered (or, in the case of testosterone, supressed). 'There seems to be some kind of fundamental social-neurobiological framework that comes into play when fathers interact with their kids,' said Lee Gettler, one of the Notre Dame researchers behind the prolactin study.[19]

This is not to say there are no biological differences between mothers and fathers when it comes to bonding with babies. Mothers have a head-start during pregnancy, both because of hormone release and because of the emotional experience of carrying a baby – and it's reinforced during childbirth and breast-feeding. But this does not guarantee that a mother will dote on her baby. I've had friends and acquaintances who experienced post-natal depression, and others who admitted that they didn't bond one child or another. Still, most mothers have an early lead over most fathers when it comes to bonding. The father's increased production of oxytocin, prolactin and vasopressin only kicks in when he puts in time and focus on his babies. But once that happens, he can bond just as closely with his baby as his partner or wife can, and sometimes more so. In other words, there's no reason why a father can't be just as accomplished as a mother at nurturing – particularly once his baby is weaned.

## David Buss and maternal cousin love

As seen in chapter 4 one of EP's shibboleths is kin-based altruism – the disputed idea that for biological reasons we favour genetic kin over others. Some evolutionary psychologists have taken kin selection theories further, including the EP pioneer David Buss who was described in The Guardian by William Leith as 'the world's foremost authority on human evolutionary biology'[20] even though he's not a biologist. Buss, along with his University of Texas colleague Joonghwan Jeon, tried to 'prove' their version of kin selection theory through a study of 56 undergraduate students[21] who were asked whether they preferred cousins on their mothers' side or their fathers'. The rationale was that while we can always be sure of who our mums are, we can't be sure about our dads – some fathers, throughout history, have been raising other men's children without realising it. The authors elaborate: 'We develop a formal mathematical model that predicts that individuals should be most willing to act altruistically towards their mother's sister's children and least willing to act altruistically towards their father's brother's children. Altruism towards father's sister's and mother's brother's children are predicted to fall in between.'[22]

Students were asked to select cousins of their age from each of the four cousin categories and on a scale of 1 to 7 say how close they felt to each of them. Next, on a 1–10 scale, they were asked how often they communicated with these cousins. They were then presented with a scenario of a burning building containing their cousins, and asked: 'How likely would you enter the burning building and attempt to save your cousin's life, despite the considerable harm to you?'[23] Finally, they were asked about emotional closeness, empathic concern and the willingness to help cousins.

Joonghwan and Buss analysed the data and found that in most categories their hypothesis was borne out: students rated their maternal cousins higher although, contrary to expectations, there was no difference in levels of altruism expressed for fathers' brothers' children and fathers' sisters' children. Still, they concluded that their results 'support the hypothesis that humans have evolved psychological adaptations regulating discriminative altruism towards cousins that are sensitive to varying numbers of paternity uncertainty links, which characterize the distinct cousin categories.'[24] In other words, for evolutionary reasons people are closer to cousins on their mothers' side (because mothers are more likely than fathers to be their blood parents). People have therefore evolved to mistrust paternity.

This prompted much media excitement, with most reports taking it all at face value. 'Why we are closer to our cousins from our mothers' side' was the headline in the Daily Telegraph[25] while The Guardian had: 'Maternal cousins more likely to find favour, says study'.[26] None of the newspapers asked whether there might be independent variables that caused these cousin preferences. Yet there are obvious candidates unrelated to kin selection theory. As seen in chapter 4, one reason we may be more drawn to blood relations is because we spend more time with them. Another is that we're conditioned to invest more in them.

It's likely that most students in Texas grew up spending more time with maternal cousins for the simple reason that they spent more time with their mums – which is why they prefer these cousins and would take altruistic action on their behalf. But even if we eliminate this variable by finding volunteers who spent equal time with all four cousin categories, it is still likely there would be maternal cousin preference for non-biological reasons. The mother might spend more time talking about her siblings and show more interest in her own nephews and nieces. And when the children meet up with these cousins, the mother might lavish more attention on them, further reinforcing the positive perceptions.

The authors don't completely ignore possible environmental prompts for cousin preference but they don't treat them as alternative explanations. Instead, they claim that 'evolved decision rules for cousin-directed altruism may have been designed to convert important environmental inputs, such as the quality of sibling relationships in the parental generation, into the cognitive or behavioural outputs for discriminative altruism towards cousins'.[27] This implies that the factors they acknowledge, such as 'the quality of adult sibling relationship linking two families in the parental generation' are themselves prompted by the same genes behind the maternal cousins' results. But a different way of viewing it would be to conclude that the fact that Texan undergraduates spent more time with mom than pop was a product of the culture in which they were raised. We could also conclude that the quality of the relationship between adult siblings was the result of them growing up together – and the quality of the relationship between the maternal cousins a result of both of these two considerations. These are not just adjuncts to some unlikely kin preference genes for maternal cousin preference; it is highly likely they are the sole explanation.

## EP and the Cinderella problem

I'll start with a memoir I read. In *Not My Father's Son*,[28] the Scottish actor Alan Cumming, tells of being beaten, abused and despised by his controlling father. Later in life his father tells him the reason they 'never bonded' was that they were not of the same blood (the father claimed Alan was the product of his mother sleeping with another man). Alan, however, is used to his father's lies and so gets a DNA test showing he *is*, indeed, his father's biological son. In their final conversation, Alan tells his father that on the sole basis of an error (the mother did not, in fact, sleep with the other man), his entire upbringing was a living hell. What this implies is that a cultural prejudice held by his father, based on a false perception, was far more powerful than a real genetic link. Which seems to contradict the EP view that we favour our kin even if we are not aware they are our kin.

But evolutionary psychology has taken Alan's father's misplaced prejudice further, arguing that humans, men in particular, have evolved to be mean to their stepchildren – a process dubbed 'the Cinderella effect' by the most fervent proponents of this view, Martin Daly and Margo Wilson. This is dangerous territory in all sorts of ways, not least because it reinforces the idea that stepfathers are inherently dangerous to their children, so I will deal with it in more detail.

As seen in chapter 4, EP draws from the animal kingdom as part of their bid to show that this behaviour is hard-wired. A lion, when he assumes leadership of the pride, might kill the cubs of other males, an act that brings the lionesses to oestrus, giving the lion the opportunity to pass on his genes. Similar behaviour has been observed with langur monkeys and gorillas, among others.

Daly and Wilson base their human version of the Lion King on their interpretation of evolutionary theory, offering the following formula: 'An offspring's expected contribution to parental fitness is the product of its reproductive value and its relatedness to the putative parent.'[29] In other words, A's love for B will be the result of multiplying B's reproductive value (the number of offspring B can produce) and the genetic connection between B and A.[30] 'A' can ensure the survival of his genes by having more offspring and he can promote the survival of his genes by ensuring the survival of his children.

Kin selection theory anticipates we'll discriminate in favour of those who share our genes in descending order, and this is where reproductive value comes in. The genetic 'relatedness' of my parents to me is the same as between me and my children, but the reproductive value of my children is higher than that of my parents; therefore I'll invest more love and care in my children than my parents. Daly and Wilson note that raising a human child takes so long, at such a cost, 'that a parental psychology shaped by natural selection is unlikely to be indiscriminate'.[31] And they add that research concerning animal social behaviour provides 'a rationale for expecting parents to be discriminative in their care and affection, and more specifically, to discriminate in favour of their own young.'

From this evolutionary angle, they build a theory that stepfathers are more likely to commit infanticide and child abuse than genetic parents. But unlike some evolutionary psychologists, they don't claim a *direct* genetic link between stepfathers and infanticide, noting that 'human beings are not like langurs or lions' because they don't 'routinely, efficiently dispose of their predecessors' young'. They conclude that child abuse is a by-product of the evolved psyche's functional organisation 'rather than an adaptation in its own right'.[32] What *clearly* evolved, they say, is 'discriminative parental solicitude'. This means parents have evolved to feel deep love for children who are their genetic offspring and have high reproductive value (greater love for these children than for others who are not their genetic kin).

They offer a theory of biologically-induced parental attachment, which comes in three stages: first, assessment (in the immediate aftermath of birth) when mothers feel indifferent towards their baby. This allows the mother to assess the reproductive value of the child; second, the establishment of individual love for the child; third, a gradual deepening of parental love over many years. The first stage involves only maternal love; the second and third also includes paternal love. This deep love prompts a 'parental inhibition against the use of dangerous tactics in conflict with the child,'[33] which, they say, is particularly remarkable regarding teenagers because of their tempestuous conflicts with their parents. However, stepparents lack the evolved trigger of 'discriminative parental solicitude' and therefore lack the inhibition to restrain violent reactions to children annoying them. What this suggests is that maltreatment of children is the default adult state of mind (but is inhibited by the depth of love shown by genetic parents). We shall return to this point later.

Daly and Wilson tested their theory by joining the psychologist Suzanne Weghorst in analysing 87,789 cases of child abuse and neglect reported in 1976. As predicted, the proportion of child abuse and neglect victims living with their natural parents was lower than those living with a genetic parent and a stepparent. The maltreatment rate for children under three who were living in a stepfamily was 4.6 times higher than with genetic parents (although for children aged 14 to 17 the gap narrowed to 1.6).

They weren't satisfied with these results, however, because they believed the rate of stepfamily abuse was higher. So they conducted another study of maltreatment cases in a one year period in 1982/3 in Hamilton-Wentworh in Ontario, Canada – their most celebrated research. This time their sample was just 99 cases. They found that children under four living with a genetic parent and a stepparent were 40 times more likely to be victims of abuse than children living with both natural parents. But there was a gremlin in the works: children living with unrelated substitute parents (adoptees and foster children) were approximately 13 times *less* likely to abuse their children under the age of four than children living with a genetic parent and a stepparent.[34]

Next they devoured a report on child abuse in England and Wales between 1983 and 1987 and found that children living with a stepparent were 19 times more likely to be recorded as victims of physical injury than those living with both genetic parents.[35] When they focused on infanticide the picture became bleaker-still. They used a study of 147 cases of child killing in Canada between 1974 and 1983 and found that children under three were 70 times more likely to be killed by a stepparent than by a genetic parent (with teenagers the ratio declined to a still staggering 15:1).[36] The reason for the higher rate of infanticide from stepparents was that these parents 'don't want to do what they feel obliged to so, namely to make a substantial investment of "paternal" effort without receiving the usual emotional rewards'.[37]

The world of evolutionary psychology was thrilled with this data because it seemed to prove one of their pet theories (kin selection) – so thrilled that they over-reached, making claims out-of-step with the research. Steven Pinker said this confirmed 'the empirical prediction that the love of biological offspring is not the same as love for non-biological offspring',[38] adding that Daly and Wilson had 'documented that stepparents are more likely to abuse a child than are biological parents'.[39] In fact, all the research suggested was that children living in families with a stepparent were more likely to abuse, which is not the same thing (because, as we shall see, a high proportion of the abuse is carried out by the biological mother, or by the biological father when he has custody, and also by both parents acting in concert). Buss went further, writing in an undergraduate textbook that 'children living with one genetic parent and one stepparent are 40 times more likely to be physically abused than children living with both parents'.[40] In fact, this figure applied only to children under five. With children between five and 10 this fell to 19.4 and for children aged 11 to 17, it fell to 8.3.

There were other studies that reached different conclusions about stepparents and abuse. One by the psychologists Catherine Malkin and Michael Lamb examined cases of abuse reported to the American Humane Society in 1984. They found that non-biological parents were proportionately more likely to engage in minor physical abuse than biological parents, but that a higher proportion of *biological* parents committed *major* physical abuse. They therefore concluded that genetic parents were more likely than non-genetic parents 'to abuse severely and to kill...'[41] The limitation of this study, however, was that it was only analysing proportions of abused children per family type relative to the population of abused children (rather than relative to the population as a whole).[42]

Another involved a team of Swedish biologists who analysed child homicide cases in Sweden between 1975 and 1995. The rate for children living with both genetic parents was 3.0 per one million and with one genetic parent and one stepparent it was 3.4 per million but the rate living with just one genetic parent was 12.6 per million. They concluded that their results 'do not support the conclusion that step-parenthood is the most important risk for child homicide in families' and added that the different rates in Sweden and Canada 'suggest that cultural factors influence patterns of child homicide'.[43] The limitation here was that the study calculated homicide rates for all children under 16 and did not divide them into age categories. When Daly and Wilson examined the Swedish data for children under four they found that the homicide rate within stepfamilies was more than eight times that from two biological parent families[44] – still far lower than their own 70–1 rate claim.

A third study by sociologist Richard Gelles and psychiatrist John Harrop analysed data gathered in the Second National Family Violence Survey, involving telephone conversations with 6,002 US households in 1985, 3,232 of them including at least one child under 18. The householders, who remained anonymous, were asked questions about 'physical abuse or violence' and 'severe violence'. The overall rate of severe violence reported in this study was 1.2 higher from *genetic* parents (109 cases per one thousand compared to 93 per thousand for stepparents).[45] Here the obvious weakness was that it was based on self-reporting, making the results unreliable because people lie.[46] However, one might assume that stepfamilies are no more likely to lie than biological families, whereas Daly and Wilson's dismissal of these results would imply that stepfamilies lied about abuse far more than biological families.[47]

There were also critiques of Daly and Wilson that did not explicitly question their use of data but instead took them to task for their interpretation. The British sociologist Hilary Rose pointed out that 'an adequate theory must be able to explain both why a small minority kills and/or abuses and also why the majority do not'.[48] She accused Daly and Wilson of homogenising different household structures while avoiding powerful evidence that contradicted their case, adding: 'Even where a couple are attempting to build a second family, this is typically associated with psychological strain between the first family and the second, compounded by financial pressures. Rather obvious matters of context explain better why some men ill-treat their partners' children.'[49]

Rose said Daly and Wilson had 'serious difficulties' with the lower levels of abuse, violence and infanticide from adoptive parents (something all the studies confirmed) and asked: 'What price a Darwinian explanation for the greater love of adoptive parents?' Incidentally, in Daly and Wilson's Canadian study just one of the 99 cases involved maltreatment of an adopted child, compared to, say, three involving a single biological relative. They deal with this by saying that most adoptions come from carefully screened parents, highly motivated to simulate a natural family experience. There are two problems with this answer. First, it would imply that high motivation trumps genetics, which is hardly 'Darwinian'. Second, similar conclusions could be drawn about natural parents. A woman who doesn't want children can use contraception. If that fails there's the morning-after pill and abortion and the option of having her baby adopted. The result is that most children who come into the world in two genetic parent families are wanted. Addressing the adoption problem, Rose concludes that as an explanation for stepfamily abuse 'natural selection is self-evidently a non-explainer'.[50]

Finally, she notes that their parental love thesis would have 'tremendous difficulties' if they considered two episodes of mass genetic parental cruelty that 'throw into question their biological explanation of protective love'. First she mentions the institutionalised rape of African female slaves by their male owners and overseers, which, the historical record shows, was associated with 'brutal indifference to the fate of their offspring'; second, the high levels of foetal sexual selection, abortion and female infanticide in India 'because of the insistence of genetic fathers on male children'. She asks: 'If parental love is genetic and so compelling, how come racism and patriarchy can overcome it on such a scale.'[51]

The most trenchant critique came from MIT philosophy of science professor David Buller who wrote a 550 page book ripping to shreds the premises, research and conclusions of evolutionary psychologists. He devoted 70 pages to the stepparent theory, castigating Daly and Wilson's use of data, explaining why their conclusions about genetically inspired parental love didn't hold up, and using alternative data to arrive at different conclusions.

He started with their most famous study – the Canadian one involving 99 abuse cases. First, he pointed out that although Daly and Wilson's focus was physical abuse, 28 of these cases involved sexual abuse, and 'sexual abuse and physical abuse appear to be different phenomena with different underlying causes'.[52] These 28 cases skewed the results because stepfathers were 'over-represented' among child sexual abusers. One study he cites found that stepfathers were seven times more likely than genetic fathers to sexually abuse one of their children but that this sexual abuse was 'generally not accompanied by physical abuse'.[53]

Incidentally, this study also found that fathers who lived with their daughters during the first three years of life, and who participated in nurturing them, were significantly less likely than other fathers to abuse their daughters, and they suggested the reason was that the process of caring for a young child inhibits subsequent sexual desire for that child.[54] Anyway, if you remove sexual abuse figures from the sample, you're left with just 71 cases, which is 'not large or representative enough to allow for confident extrapolation of abuse rates to the population at large'.[55] Buller examines these 71, showing that the definition of non-sexual maltreatment in the data was not restricted to physical abuse. It covered neglect, including omissions such as failing to put a child in a car seat or to fasten the safety belt for the child, which does not stem from the same motivational base as hitting or kicking a child.

He also drew from substantial research showing that abuse by a stepfather is more likely to be reported than from a biological father, and this includes homicide, skewing the figures to the point that there was significant *under-representation* of biological family abuse.[56] One American study suggested that fatalities at the hands of legally married stepfathers were 1.37 times more likely to be recorded this way on death certificates.[57] One reason for this is that child welfare officers and other professionals routinely take the presence of a stepfather into account when assessing the cause of an injury.

Buller goes on to show that abuse by stepfamilies is not the same as abuse by stepfathers because biological mothers play a significant role as do biological fathers when they are granted custody. Daly and Wilson's data hints at this, showing that unmarried mothers accounted for 60 percent of all infanticides. This danger can be enhanced within stepfamilies – and Buller notes that children under three have a 'dramatically elevated risk' of being abused by their genetic mother if she lives with a stepfather. The younger the child, the greater the danger – children under one are slightly more likely to be abused by their genetic mother than their stepfather, and victims are often abused by both parents together. For example, children between one and two were more likely to be abused by both parents acting in concert than by a stepfather acting alone.[59] The data also shows that the odds of a single genetic father abusing his child are 1.7 times higher than a stepfather.[60]

Buller went further, working with a child abuse statistician Elliot Smith in analysing child maltreatment data compiled in 1993 by the US government's Third National Incidence Study of Child Abuse and

Neglect (NIS-3). The researchers used two standards for maltreatment in 43 US counties – the Harm Standard (including fatal maltreatment) and the Endangerment Standard (including unintentional omissions). Buller and Smith used only the Harm Standard data, marrying it with census figures to work out rates of abuse.[61] The risk of abuse to children living within a stepfamily was far lower than Daly and Wilson suggested. For children between 0 and 17 living with two genetic parents it was 0.27 percent but rose to 4.8 percent with a single genetic parent. With one genetic parent and one stepparent it was 1.07 percent (less than a quarter of single genetic parent figure and less than four times that involving two genetic parents). For children under four the risk was 8.2 times that for children living with two genetic parents (compared with Daly and Wilson's estimate of 40 times).

Notably, children living with just one non-genetic parent (including single stepparents) had a 0.39 percent risk and children living with two adoptive parents had a 0,08 percent risk (one case for every 1,250 children), meaning that the children living in adoptive homes had by far the lowest risk of sustaining abuse.[62] Of the 144,820 children under five who lived with two adoptive parents, the researchers found no cases of physical abuse[63]. Their figures also showed the rate of abuse for children under 10 living with just one genetic parent was 20 times higher than the rate for those living with two non-genetic parents,[64] which also seems to fly in the face of Daly and Wilson's premises. Incidentally, Buller felt his own results were skewed for the same reasons as Daly and Wilson's: under-reporting of cases of abuse involving two genetic parents.[65]

Daly and Wilson's 'most obvious prediction' implies that children living with non-genetic parents face greater danger than those living with genetic parents. But as we have seen this is not the case. Even if we take their data at face value, it is still clear that adopted children are at significantly less risk than those living with two genetic parents, perhaps because, as Schiller put it back in 1781, 'It is not flesh and blood, but heart which makes us fathers and sons.'[66]

It's also clear that children living with a single unmarried mother or a single genetic father are at more risk than those living with stepfamilies. This too goes against Daly and Wilson's theory, which implies that maltreatment of children is the default state of mind of adults (but is switched off with genetic parents because of the biologically-induced process of bonding). Stepparents lack this switch and so would be *likely* to abuse children in their care. But the vast majority of stepparents never abuse children under their care. If we use the NIS-3 data we find that just over one percent of all children who live with a stepparent are victims of abuse and only 0.6 percent are abused by the stepparent acting alone.[67]

Still, let's assume that children are more likely to face abuse within stepfamilies than with two genetic parents. Daly and Wilson's explanation relates to a biologically-prompted process of attachment that occurs between genetic parents and their children, which suppresses the natural urge to be violent towards annoying children. They concede this could also be simulated in early adoptions (which would suggest its basis is non-genetic). Presumably, therefore, it could also be simulated in stepfamilies if the family was formed early in the child's life. Conversely, the older the child at the time the family is formed, the greater the risk because there's no chance to trigger the genetically encoded mechanisms of parental love. We'd therefore anticipate that rates of abuse would be *lower* with younger children and *higher* with older children but the data from all sources shows the opposite – that the risk is far higher with younger children.[68]

Buller concludes that Daly and Wilson have failed to provide good evidence for their theories and that they 'have brought us no closer to understanding ... the mechanisms that ... produce sometimes fatal maltreatment of a child'.[69] He specifically rejects the idea that stepfathers somehow lack a genetically-inspired trigger to hold back their natural urges to abuse children and suggests that physical violence against children 'could, instead, be the result of some atypical condition in the engine of the mind'.[70] If this is true it is also worth stressing that there is no evidence that this condition is genetically-inspired.

There are alternative explanations for higher rates of child abuse within stepfamilies. As Hilary Rose pointed out, stepfamilies tend to be less secure than two genetic parent families. There is often more financial strain because the father has alimony obligations, so the relationship is less likely to be stable (and a higher proportion of such couples are unmarried), and there's evidence that stepfamilies tend to be lower on the economic rung. Add to this the possibility that the father will enter the family with a strong attraction to the mother but without a strong commitment to her children. There might also be conflict between children from her previous relationship and her new children, or between the parents over this issue. Put all of this together, and it would appear that, on average, stepfamilies are less stable than two genetic parent families, and there's certainly a link between instability and domestic violence, including against children. And yet, as we've seen, 99 percent of stepchildren never experience recorded abuse from their step parents. I've cited plenty of figures in this chapter, but that's the most important.

# CHAPTER FIFTEEN

## GENES, GENDER AND MEDIA MYTHOLOGY

Let's recap quickly. You might have missed it, but along the way I've acknowledged that there are indeed real physical differences between men and women that have an impact on their brains and minds. Examples I touched upon included greater testosterone production for men, women's menstrual cycles (and pre-menstrual tension) and menopause, the boost in oxytocin levels for women during pregnancy, certain sexual responses, the prevalence of autism and the prevalence of enhanced or defective colour perception. In that sense the topic of this book differs profoundly from that of my previous book, *Black Brain, White Brain*, because there are *no* innate differences in the brain power potential and innate mindset of different population groups – in every relevant respect their brains are the same when different populations are compared – whereas there are indeed *some* differences in the brains of men and women. But, the main thrust of this book is the argument that the differences between male and female brains have been hugely distorted, exaggerated and, in many cases, invented.

This exaggeration, distortion and invention has come mainly from the laptops of evolutionary psychologists who are responsible for most of the false claims I have highlighted along the way: that men are slightly more intelligent than women; that males produce more geniuses and more idiots; that male and female mathematical abilities and spatial perceptions differ profoundly; that women have evolved to wear lipstick and favour smooth legs and men to favour a Barbie hip-waist ratio for women; that women have a huge inbuilt advantage over men when it comes to nurturing potential; that women talk more than men and are better with words; that women are more naturally empathetic than men; that both genders have evolved to favour maternal cousins over paternal; that men are hardwired to rape, to be mean to stepchildren and to kill unfaithful wives; that women are hardwired to seek out older, richer men and men to seek out as many younger women as possible; and, to return to the more trivial end of the EP range, that women have evolved to favour pink and men, blue, and that women have a biological inclination to pop off to the shopping mall. As I have shown along the way, there is no convincing evidence for any of these claims – and there is compelling evidence against them.

Evolutionary psychologists have been the main culprits, but not the only ones. The distortions have also come from a few of those dipping their toes in neurology (but usually not neurologists). For example, because men and women sometimes use different neural pathways it is assumed that this explains supposed behavioural differences between men and women. But as we've seen, left and right handed people and big and small brained people also tend to use different neural pathways, but no differences in thought or behaviour patterns are read off from this. The most fervent neurological claim in this zone is that the female corpus callosum is thicker than the male version, allowing women to think with both brain hemispheres while men only think with one. This has been used to bolster the idea that women are better at multi-tasking, but as we saw from the research, there is no evidence for this – the male corpus callosum is just as thick as the female, and, on the multi-tasking question, different studies have produced different results – a British one found that women were slightly better at doing more than one thing at a time while the Swedish one found that men were slightly better.

However, if your reading on questions of sex and gender extended no further than the frequent media reports on male and female behaviour, bolstered by the steady stream of self-help books in this direction, you might assume that pink-brain-blue-brain idea was close-to universally accepted by scientists (except perhaps for a handful of politically correct die-hards). In fact, most of those making these claims are psychologists and self-help authors, not scientists, and almost all of their research has been strongly and convincingly disputed by genuine scientists as well as by other psychologists less wedded to the EP tag.

Throughout the preceding pages I've highlighted claims that drew considerable international media coverage. These included all of those I have just mentioned and in each case I've shown that these conclusions were very widely publicised, some of them settling into the realm of a kind of urban mythology (the women-talk-more-than-men one is a good example), before being shredded by serious academic critiques. Problem is, these critiques seldom, if ever, receive anything close to the publicity garnered for the original paper or book. The obvious question is, 'Why?'

One possible reason relates to slanted media interest in gendered explanations for behaviour – a conservative worldview that tends to place men and women in more traditional roles, prompting a wariness about the shrinking gender gap. Certainly, it would be hard to dispute the claim that right-wing newspapers and media outlets tend to be more inclined than liberal ones to feature stories explaining the world in pink-brain-blue-brain terms, with the *Daily Mail* being the most obvious example – both because of how often its editors use such stories and because of the prominence they are given along with their often-gloating tone, presenting them as another nail in the politically correct coffin ...

But if this is a reason, it hardly qualifies as the most significant. For one thing, in all of the major newspapers, including the *Daily Mail,* there are also regular stories on topics like the narrowing income gap between men and women, and on the growing gap between female and male academic performance. Also, as I have illustrated throughout this book, more liberal newspapers like *The New York Times, The Guardian, The Observer* and *The Independent* have also run Mars and Venus-type stories along these lines, frequently without considering alternative explanations for the gendered behaviours described, and invariably without reporting the critiques of these views when they arrive.

The main reasons for this media focus on gender differences therefore must lie elsewhere – and the places to look are the news agendas of contemporary media, the increasing reliance of newspapers on packaged PR, partly because fewer journalists have to write more stories, and the relation between university press offices and newspaper news desks. I shall look at each of these in turn.

First, news editors like to balance hard news with soft, particularly within British newspapers. If all the stories they run on their news pages concern death, destruction, catastrophe, war, crime, death and politics, readers will be put off. At a time of declining print circulation, editors sense their readers have to be enticed to stay loyal to the paper and its website. This demands more attention being paid to design and layout than ever before and it also demands large doses of sex, celebrity, fashion, lifestyle, food, travel and humour. This applies almost as much to the quality and mid-market papers as to redtop tabloids. Even on the hard news pages the leavening impact of softer news is often desired by editors.

There is a particular demand for stories that tend to confirm readers' views about themselves and to explain their behaviour in gendered terms. Stories that tell female readers that their inclination to shop is a cavewoman thing, or that their preference for pink is something that evolved hundreds of thousands of years ago, and that these inclinations are universal to womankind, tend to be reassuring, and the same could be said for stories relating to, say, male single-mindedness or preference for 36–25-36 or for promiscuity.

The undercurrent of such reporting is the message that our little peccadillos should not concern us because, after all, they are as natural today as they were to our antediluvian ancestors. Such stories have proved popular with readers partly because of that usually sub-liminal urge for definition about masculinity and femininity that is widely felt at a time when culture is becoming more androgynous. For instance, I have a friend who calls herself a feminist and yet insists that the gendered advice in *Men are from Mars, Women are from Venus* really is marvellous stuff. Perhaps it is not surprising that those with half-changed minds sometimes latch onto stories that give ballast to inherited male-female distinctions. Put differently, the media tends to echo back to people their prejudices by choosing stories that reflect the stuff they want to read, see and hear.

There is an additional element: the requirement for a viable news angle. If you are going to dress up a lifestyle story as news, you need an intro that suggests fresh facts, which is where science and, in particular, genetics come into play. Stories asserting unbridgeable gender differences that are based on academic papers, citing surveyed research, and coming with professorial comment, fit the bill because they have a clear news angle ('the latest research reveals that ...'). It helps if they come with the gloss of science and, in particular, of genetics (because of the popular, but false, perception that genes explain everything), and yet are lifestyle-ish enough to fit the require-ment for softer news. The fact that the researchers are not real scien-tists and that their research usually goes no further than a survey of their own students, is invariably underplayed and often ignored.

A further significant consideration relates to the ethos within Western universities. Especially within psychology departments – and most notably within the self-contained world of evolutionary psy-chology – lecturers and professors get ahead by competing with each other to find novel ways of 'proving' EP's number one obsession (that the brains and minds of men and women have followed very different evolutionary trajectories) and their number two obsession (that we have evolved to favour our genetic kin). As a result, there is a regular, reliable stream of papers and books along these lines, emanating from the lecture halls and professorial offices of psychology departments. The continuous supply is guaranteed.

An added consideration relates to the nature of academic research, whether in the sciences or the humanities. As we have seen, perhaps one in 20 research projects will throw up a rogue result and this is even more likely when the population sample chosen is small (as in the case with most social research). So these one-in-20-or-less research projects will produce a gendered result, which will be considered inherently newsworthy. The other 19 will be ignored because research showing no gender differences is viewed as boring. The result is that an unrepresentative sample of research gets fed to the media. In the case of evolutionary psychology, the sample is often tiny and the questions are sometimes slanted to ensure that a gendered result is virtually guaranteed.

This is where the university press offices enter the picture, and it works like this: an ambitious, publicity-hungry evolutionary psychology lecturer or professor conducts a survey among his or her students on some gender-related topic and writes up a paper based on this research. This paper is published in a tame and undemanding evolutionary psychology house journal and is then delivered to the university press office with a strong personal punt from the professor or lecturer. The press office then cherry picks from the paper, choosing the juiciest bits, with a few quotes thrown in, for a one page press release. This is e-mailed to the newsdesks of a wide range of newspapers, news websites, magazines, radio stations and television channels.

What happens next relates, in part, to the insecurity of the contemporary newsroom, with layoffs (prompted by declining print circulation) stretching the remaining staff to breaking point, making it more difficult for them to conduct real research for all but the biggest stories. So when the university press release email arrives, this is what tends to happen: the news editor skim-reads it, decides it might well fit the bill for a softer, lifestyle-related news story, and passes it on to one of the reporters, often the science correspondent, who's already likely to be over-worked because in recent years the newsroom has been short-staffed. This reporter may have three or more stories to write that day, and so will be hard-pressed to offer much more than a rewritten version of the press release, perhaps with a quote or two from the professor thrown in if there's time to make a phone call.

If the claims being made by the evolutionary psychology professor are sensational enough, then the original story will invariably be published in varying degrees of prominence in a wide selection of media outlets, partly because they are all feeding from the same trough, but also because missing a story that a rival newspaper or news website uses prominently might just upset the editor. Sometimes an overworked news editor will inadvertently bypass one of these tales, only to find that the rival has flagged it up, prompting a rapid-fire recovery job, in which case the only quotes may be those drawn from the press release itself.

Either way, the story is then published and it might well invite considerable comment on the newspaper's website and some of the readers will retweet it or share it on Facebook or other social media sites and it will reverberate in ever-more vituperative feedback loops. So it grows and grows in terms of impact and reaches further and further into public consciousness. This frenzied discussion and debate might well last for several days, but it will soon fade, perhaps to be replaced by yet another story along these lines. There is often a wait of well over one month, and sometimes several months, before other academics from outside the evolutionary psychology nest publish their excoriating critiques, ripping to pieces the premises, research and conclusions of the original paper, but, by then, the story is long dead and it is unlikely that the newspaper will bother to cover these critiques. The world will have moved on while retaining a lingering memory of the original claims.

So, in trying to understand why these stories are covered so prominently and uncritically in newspapers, websites, radio stations and television throughout the advanced industrial world and much of the developing world too, the place to look is less at the sexist agendas of editors and reporters, and more at the media milieu of the moment, which offers a happy place to the punters of evolutionary psychology because it meets the reader demand for reassuring stories that confirm gender role prejudices. What all this strongly suggests is that regardless of scientific evidence, the flow of pink brain-blue brain malarkey will continue unabated.

# CHAPTER SIXTEEN

# GENES, GENDER AND FEMINISM

It has certainly taken a while, but the next wave of feminism has finally arrived with vim and vigour. There's a buzz about the word and all that it represents. It's no longer the 'f-word' – and has become more open and publicly acceptable. You can see this from the proliferation and popularity of online feminist sites and the use of social media to tackle sexism, from the creation or revival of feminist societies on university campuses and the number of students signing up for gender studies courses, from the range of creative, feminist public actions and from the number of public figures openly declaring their feminist credentials, something that would have been unlikely in the 1990s – Beyoncé dancing in front of a massive 'FEMINIST' sign, for example, or Taylor Swift and Emma Watson punting feminism at every opportunity, backed by Tom Hanks with Malala Yousafzai joining the party, and politicians ranging from Canada's Justin Trudeau to Scotland's Nicola Sturgeon pitching in, having no hesitation in declaring their feminist credentials...

This new feminism is certainly not a carbon copy of earlier waves. Unlike the 1970s and early-80s version, it no longer has the feel of a 'movement' and in most cases it has not embraced the dimension of women-exclusive consciousness-raising groups or of women-only campaigns. All-in-all, it feels less exclusive, less judgmental (despite the fury and bile of some Twitter exchanges), more open to diversity and, significantly, far more open to men – and to persuading men.

It is also less exclusively white. Over the last decade or two we've seen the rise of black feminism, particularly in the United Sates, focusing on the 'double oppression' of being born black and female. Part of their argument is that black women face discrimination, hostility and suspicion as black people, including from white women, and that they also face abuse, disregard and other forms sexism as women, including from black men. Furthermore, while some white men might regard women as the inferior sex, they might also regard black women as inferior women.

It is also less exclusively western – the rise of Islamic feminism is an example, both in the West and in countries like Egypt, Indonesia, Turkey, Malaysia and Pakistan, and feminist thought and action is certainly flourishing in the big cities of China and India. And it has become more tolerant when considered in the round. A generation ago you sometimes heard feminist journalists asking questions like: 'Can you be a feminist and wear high heels?' More recently, you'd be more likely to hear, 'Can you be a feminist and wear a hijab?' I suspect that most of the current generation of feminists would regard both questions as intrinsically silly (and the obvious answer to both is yes). The new wave of feminists have also, by and large, embraced trans-gender people with more enthusiasm than in the past (sometimes to the unfortunate extent of 'no-platforming' those with less enthusiasm). These days, you can dress how you want, think how you want, say what you want: welcome aboard.

I don't, however, want to over-stress its departures. For example, 1970s feminism was far more diverse than often portrayed in today's media. It included radical feminists, socialist feminists, liberal feminists and lesbian feminists (with some overlap between these). Its broad thrust was one of confronting sexism wherever it was found by opposing patriarchy and misogyny, raising feminist consciousness and advancing gender equality, but within this goal there was a diversity of views. For example, while much of its emphasis was on campaigning to reduce the gap between men and women, it also embraced those like Andrea Dworkin who believed that patriarchy was innate and that the differences between men and women were profound and often unbridgeable. And it was not uncommon to find feminists on opposite sides of big debates (such as on pornography, prostitution and transgender identity).

However, the 21st century feminist wave appears significantly more diverse and wide-ranging, which is mainly a good thing. Today, writers like the Pinkers (Susan and Steven) happily describe themselves as feminists, even though they believe that men produce more geniuses, that men are inherently better at spatial skills and that the gap in career achievement and parenting behaviour is explained almost entirely by biology. Even Sarah Palin has joined the throng, calling herself a feminist and, later, using an anti-abortion meeting to call on conservative women to 'rise up' like 'mama grizzlies' and seize the cause of feminism as their own, while talking about 'the emerging conservative feminist identity'.

The views of Palin and the Pinkers no doubt form legitimate edges of the debates around gender issues, and if they choose to call themselves feminists, who cares? If it helps to detoxify the word, then why ever not? But, while saying this, I retain a niggling worry about the same words being used for contradictory purposes. Including the likes of Palin under the feminist umbrella, doesn't just detoxify the word; it also has the effect of stripping it of some of its power. If feminism is so broad and amorphous that it can embrace even those who argue in favour of profoundly anti-feminist ideas, then there is a danger that it follows the trajectory of another fine word, democracy, used to mean just about anything that you choose (remember 'people's democracies' and 'democratic centralism' in the Soviet era?)

So, if the Pinkers choose to call themselves feminists on the basis that they believe in equality of opportunity, fine. But let's be clear: the views that they (and Palin and Dworkin) have so fervently proposed about innate gender difference are the antithesis of feminism. And I am not just saying this because I believe that they are wrong or because they rub me up the wrong way. Rather, it's my concern about the implications of those views.

If you succeed in convincing women that they are less likely to be geniuses, that they are more likely to struggle with geometry and parallel parking, that their under-representation among the ranks of university professors and company executives and prime ministers is a product of their biology, that their brains are wired fundamentally differently from male brains, and that their destiny is to nurture children, pick touchy-feely career paths, adorn themselves to the hilt, totter around in stiletto heels and shop-until-they-drop, then you are succeeding in diminishing their options, thereby reducing their potential as human beings. Instead of equipping women with much-needed weaponry to counter sexism, you are tying lead weights to their feet.

And if you succeed in convincing men that they are innately poorer nurturers, that they lack the ability to multi-task, that they have evolved to favour women with hourglass figures, that they have a shortfall when it comes to language use and vocabulary, that they are hardwired for meanness towards stepchildren and biologically programmed for single-minded career ambition and that to be manly they have to be 'hard', dominant, 'A-type' blokes without much empathy, you are diminishing their options in life and cutting them off from a huge chunk of human experience. Again, you are reducing their potential as people.

The views on gender promoted by EP-punters like David Buss, Steven Pinker, Susan Pinker, Helena Cronin, Randy Thornhill, Craig Palmer, Martin Daly, Margo Wilson, Donald Symons, Robert Wright and the rest, by socio-biologists like Desmond Morris and E O Wilson, by pop science authors like Louann Brizendine and self-help salesmen like John Gray, have an anti-feminist impact, one that can have the effect of curtailing the career or academic ambitions of women, and of curtailing the nurturing ambitions of men – no matter how they try to dress them up.

What I have tried to do with this book is to debunk much of the pseudo-scientific mythology that stands in the way of female and male progress. The ideas punted by evolutionary psychologists, sociobiologists and their journalist praise singers – that, for evolutionary reasons, the minds of males and females belong in different metaphorical planets – are simply wrong. There are indeed real differences between the brains of men and women, but these are overshadowed by the similarities. In other words, the innate gap between men and women has been hugely exaggerated to the detriment of both.

I am occasionally asked – usually by people who missed out on feminism's previous wave, and have yet to be caught up in the next – what the hell am I doing writing a feminist book. 'Well,' I say, 'I am a feminist ...' after which the line of questioning sometimes goes like this: 'But how can you be a *fem*inist when you're a *man?*' The suggested implication is that the word itself, derived from 'feminine', precludes the masculine. And I have to admit, that in this, rather limited sense alone, a word derived from 'feminine' can be slightly awkward for feminist men. But it's the word we've got and if occasionally a bit of explanation is required, that's no bad thing.

It should be clear from the preceding chapters that issues and questions relating to the future of men are an integral part of the feminist oeuvre. Male horizons will be expanded if men are unshackled from the idea that they are inherently rubbish at looking after children, that their capacity for reading other people's emotions and for expressing their own is innately limited, and that they are so single-minded that they can't do the multitasking necessary to run a household. And their range of options will also be extended if they move beyond the idea that their primary role in life is to provide for their wives and families and their only viable career path is to compete with colleagues on a cut-throat's ladder. They will also be helped in their relationships with women if they can get past the notion that their evolved role in life is to spread their genes as far and wide as possible, and that their female partner's role in life is to cross her legs and raise the children. And if they can learn to get past the notion that their destiny is to 'wear the trousers in the relationship' and that their masculinity is tied up with the idea that they need to dominate, they will do rather better in coping with the changing demands of the modern world.

So, while feminism is *mainly* about the progress of women, it clearly has plenty to offer in terms of the progress of men, which is why it is wholly appropriate that the latest feminist wave welcomes and encourages male participation. What feminism offers both men and women is a significantly more expansive notion of their humanity, which is why the word belongs alongside another, humanism.

Finally, a more personal note. I was raised in a nuclear family, mainly by a mother who did not have a job of her own. I was also raised in a religion that stressed male leadership under a male saviour and a male god. I was sent to all-boys state schools where I learnt to keep a stiff upper lip after being caned. Like everyone else, I played what were then boys-only summer and winter sports and, once a week, marched around in a khaki uniform in cadet parades and learnt to handle guns. Out of school I became obsessed with what was then another male-only sport, boxing, both as a participant and as a fan (and my maiden career ambition was to become heavyweight champion of the world). And I didn't have any really close, intimate female friends until I was 17.

So, by the standards of my generation, I had a fairly typically gendered upbringing, and this is obviously well dug into my psyche because the impact of the first 17 years of life is more deeply implanted than the impact of what follows. Occasionally, I can spot the signs. For example, the only time I cry is vicariously, in movies or when reading novels. But no doubt the subterranean ripples are even more significant and less easily challenged. For example, I would like to be more emotionally engaged, I would like to move beyond the culturally imprinted standards of female beauty I inherited and I would like to divest myself from notions of success limited to career achievement, sporting prowess and academic honours. But somehow these things linger. Desire is not quite enough.

I am not, however, suggesting that in important areas we cannot move beyond the sexism of our upbringings. In my student years I was first confronted with feminism which challenged me to change many of my ideas and to accept female equality. But the more profound change came a few years later, when I had my first and then my second child. They were both daughters and I longed for them to excel in life and not to be held back by the backwash of the sexist culture surrounding them. I also found, a bit to my surprise, that I was quite good with children and that I wanted to play at least an equal role in nurturing them, and so I arranged my life and work accordingly. In addition, I found myself exasperated by the casual prejudices that came my way in playgroups and the like – that as a father, I was bound to be incompetent as a nurturer, and therefore needed interventions from mums who knew better. It was this exasperation that prompted me to read and write on parenting, which in turn exposed me to the writings on gender differences by evolutionary psychologists and socio-biologists. So I began to write on this stuff too, which is what eventually prompted this book.

The more I read and wrote in this area, the more I realised that human potential is not limited by biology alone. It is also limited by ideas that restrain people. My hope for this book – its purpose, really – is to encourage all of us to spread our wings.

# NOTES

## Chapter 1: An introduction in pink and blue

1. Steven Pinker, *How the Mind Works*, W.W.Norton & Company, 1999
2. Niel Barnard, *Secret Revolution: Memoirs of a Spy Boss'*, Tafelberg, 2015
3. Paul Ehrlich, quoted in USA Today magazine, published by the Society for the Advancement of Education, April 2001.
4. This example, based on a study by evolutionary psychologists at the University of Texas, is discussed in detail in chapter 14.
5. Published in *Current Biology*, vol 17, issue 16, 21 August 2007.
6. Quoted in The Times, August 21 2007.
7. 'Girls prefer pink – or at least a redder shade of blue', Newcastle University press release, August 20 2007.
8. Study: Why Girls Like Pink', *Time Magazine*, August 20 2007
9. The Times, op cit.
10. Ben Goldacre, 'Out of the Blue', *The Guardian*, August 25 2007
11. *Sunday Sentinal*, March 29, 1914
12. *Ladies Home Journal*, June 1918.
13. Daniel Kruger & Dreyson Byker, 'Evolved Foraging Psychology Underlies Sex Differences in Shopping Experiences and Behaviours.' *Journal of Social, Evolutionary, and Cultural Psychology,* I3 (4) December 2009, p 328.
14. Ibid, p 331.
15. Ibid, p 323.
16. Daniel Kruger quoted in Laura Bailey, 'Genes account for male, female shopping styles,' *The University Record Online*, University of Michigan, December 7 2009.
17. Sally Augustin, 'Shopping Brings Out Our Inner Hunter/Gatherer,' *Psychology Today,* December 24 2010.
18. Lee Dye, 'Why Women Love to Shop', *abc NEWS*, December 9 2009.

19. IANS, 'Genes dictate shopping styles,' *The Hindu*, December 4 2009.

20. Andrew Hanon, 'What else can you expect from a caveman?' *Toronto Sun* December 13 2009.

21. Leo Tolstoy, *Resurrection*, Nekhludoff's Third Interview with Maslova in Prison, Penguin Classics, 2009.

22. Paul Ehrlich, *Human Natures: Genes, Culture and the Human Prospect*, Penguin, 2003, p 5.

23. Quoted in 'Men, Women Really Do Have Big Personality Differences', MSNBC, January 4 2012 and in 'Men and Women Are Sooo Different, according to Sketchy Research',

24. This is discussed in chapter 8.

25. Tamara Cohen, 'Surprise! Men and women really ARE different: Sexes share just 10 per cent of their personality traits. Psychologists reach verdict after probing 10,000 people', Daily Mail, January 4 2012

26. 'Sex and personality differences underestimated: divide between male and female characteristics great, researchers say', CBS News, January 5 2012

27. Nick Collins, 'Men and women have distinct personalities', Daily Telegraph, January 4 2012.

28. Tentative because we need to be hesitant in drawing too much from the very small number of such cases. Also, there are several elements that are variable and difficult to factor into the conclusions. For example, parents of 'girls' who are really boys might be inclined to treat them differently from how they would treat real girls.

## Chapter 2: Darwin's Latter Day Pitbulls

1. 'Richard Dawkins on Charles Darwin', *BBC News*, February 14, 2009.

2. Daniel C. Dennett, *Darwin's Dangerous Idea: Evolution and the Meanings of Life*, Simon & Schuster, 1995, p21.

3. Robert Wright, 'Feminists Meet Mr Darwin', *New Republic*, November 28 1994, pp 34–46.

4. James Gleick, *Isaac Newton*, Fourth Estate, 2003, p 3.

5. Erasmus Darwin. *Zoonomia; or the Laws of Organic Life*, (4th American ed.). Philadelphia: Edward Earle. p. 397.

6. A view unequivocally rejected by Darwin's successors, although, in a sense, it has recently been revised, albeit in a different form, through discoveries in epigenetics.

7. One evolutionary thinker of the time was the palaeontologist Richard Owen, today best-known for coming up with the word 'dinosaur' and for his debates

on Darwin's theories. Owen demonstrated evolutionary sequences through fossil evidence, which impressed Darwin. He was also influenced by some of his close friends and collaborators including the botanists Joseph Hooker and Asa Gray, the geologist Charles Lyell and his premier 'bulldog', the biologist, Thomas Huxley.

8. Charles Darwin, *On the Origin of Species,* Murray, London, 1859, pp 80–81.

9. 'On the Tendency of Varieties to Depart Indefinitely From the Original Type'.

10. He also questioned Darwin's reliance on domestic animals in developing his ideas.

11. It could be said that Wallace contributed to this personification. For example, in 1889 he published a book called *Darwinism*, in which he mounted a strong defence of natural selection.

12. The word 'mutation' refers to the changes in a DNA sequence of the genome of a cell. It is 'random' partly because it can be prompted by a range of unpredictable factors

13. *The Guardian*, January 15 2009.

14. John A Johnson, Joseph Carroll, Jonathan Gottschall and Daniel Kruger, 'Hierarchy in the Library: Egalitarian Dynamics in Victorian Novels, *Evolutionary Psychology*, vol, no 4, 2008, pp715–738.

15. Ibid.

16. Joseph Carroll, quoted in 'Victorian novels like Pride and Prejudice teach us how to behave', *Daily Telegraph*, January 14 2009.

17. *The Guardian*, January 15 2009.

18. Although in Spencer hands, evolutionary theory also incorporated Lamarckian ideas and, unlike Darwin, his version had an endpoint of 'equilibrium'.

19. 'I am not conscious of having profited in my work from Spencer's writings,' he wrote. 'His deductive manner of treating every subject is wholly opposed to my frame of mind. His conclusions never convince me…. They partake more of the nature of definitions than of laws of nature.' Nora Barrow (ed), *The Autobiography of Charles Darwin, 1809–1882, with Original Omissions Restored,* Harcourt, Brace, 1958, p 109.

20. Literary studies through the prism of 'Darwinian' natural selection, with predictably absurd results.

21. See in particular Matt Ridley, *The Rational Optimist: How Prosperity Evolves,* HarperCollins, 2010

22. Emile Zola, *Germinal,* Penguin Books, 2004, pp 529–532.

23. Charles Darwin, *The Descent of Man, and Selection in Relation to Sex,* 2nd edition, John Murray, 1874, pp 563–4.

24. It could also be argued that his views on race were more ambiguous. The quotes cited (and several others revealing a deep-seated racism that became more fervent with age) should be balanced against his belief that all human 'races' belonged to a single species that emerged from Africa, his complimentary comments about individual black and indigenous people he encountered, as well as his opposition to slavery and to the ill-treatment of indigenous people.

25. For example, writing five years before *The Descent of Man*, of his experiences with indigenous peoples in south-east Asia and the Amazon, he praised their respect for each other's rights, their sense of equality and of free expression, which approached a 'near perfect state'.

26. Alfred Russel Wallace, *Social Environment and Moral Progress*, Cassel, London, 1913, pp 147–8.

27. Alfred Russel Wallace, 'Human Selection', *Fortnightly* Review, Volume 48, September 1890.

28. Galton wrote in his 1869 book, *Heredity Genius* about the superiority of Europeans over the 'lower races'. He described 'Negroes' as being 'so childish, stupid, and simpleton-like, as frequently to make me ashamed of my own species' and predicted that colonisation would lead to their decline and replacement by their betters, because they would fail to submit to the needs of a 'superior civilisation'.

29. Winston Churchill and Woodrow Wilson were enthusiasts, as was, of course, Hitler.

30. Konrad Lorenz, *On Aggression*, Methuen, London, 1966, p5.

31. This was billed as a sequel to his 1961 book, *African Genesis*, Dell Publishers, 1963.

32. Robert Ardrey, *The Territorial Imperative*, Dell Publishers, 1966, p165.

33. Desmond Morris, *The Human Zoo,* Vintage, 1994.

34. Desmond Morris, *The Naked Ape*, McGraw-Hill, 1967.

35. Desmond Morris, *The Naked Woman*, Macmillan, 2007, p 199.

36. Desmond Morris, *The Naked Ape*, Vintage Books, London, 2005, p 5.

37. Several of his claims are dissected in chapter 13 – including those about women having evolved to wear lipstick and men to favour a particular hip-waste ratio in women.

38. *Sociobiology: The New Synthesis*, Harvard University Press, 1975.

39. For example, making it to the cover of *Time* magazine and the front page of *New York Times*.

40. It is now on its 25th edition.

41. *On Human Nature*, Harvard University Press, 1979, *Genes, Mind and Culture: The coevolutionary process*, Harvard University Press, 1981, *Promethean fire: reflections on the origin of mind*, Harvard University Press, 1983.

42. Discussed in, for example, in Steven Pinker, *The Blank Slate: The Modern Denial of Human Nature*. Viking, New York, 2002.

43. He was raised a Southern Baptist.

44. EO Wilson, *Consilience: the Unity of Knowledge*, Alfred Knopf, New York, 1998, p225.

45. Ibid, pp 168–173.

46. Ibid, pp 127–128.

47. These included Debroah Tannen's, *You Just Don't Understand: Men and Women in Conversation,* Morrow, New York, 1999; John Gray's, *Men Are From Mars, Women Are From Venus*, HarperCollins, New York, 1992, Anne Moir and David Jessel's, *Brain Sex: The Real Difference between Men and Women*, Delta Books, New York, 1991 and Anne Moir and Bill Moir's, *Why Men Don't Iron: The Fascinating and Unalterable Differences between Men and Women*, Citadel, New York, 1999.

48. EO Wilson, *On Human Nature*, Harvard University Press, Cambridge, Massachusetts, 1978.

49. Quoted in Charles Jencks, 'EP, Phone Home', in Hilary and Steven Rose (eds), *Alas Poor Darwin: Arguments Against Evolutionary Psychology*, Vintage, 2001, p 40.

50. The accusation of sexism came from his perception of huge innate differences between the minds of males and females, of ethnocentrism from his limited choice of examples of 'universal' human behaviour; of racism, mainly from the potential implications of his views – that his arguments could be used to promote notions of racial superiority. However, on two occasions he could be accused of toying with scientific racism – when he was quoted backing the work of overtly racist psychologist J Philippe Rushton, who'd written a book arguing that blacks were inherently less intelligent and, in 2014, when endorsing a book by the popular science author Nicholas Wade, who explained just about every cultural stereotype, including Jews being good capitalists and Africans being tribalists, in terms of natural selection. Wilson called it 'truth without fear'.

## Chapter 3: Gay genes and mythological memes

1. The leading lights of EP, which emerged in full-blown form in the 1990s, distinguished themselves from sociobiologists partly because their focus was on people's psyches as well as their behaviour, and partly because of some of their specific concerns, such as the idea of the modular brain. However, these differences are sometimes overstated because when it came to genetic determinism they shared the same hymn book, and their attitudes to gender issues were identical, right down to the specifics.

2. As I show in my book, *Black Brain, White Brain* (Jonathan Ball and Thistle, 2015), some of the establishment figures of evolutionary psychology like Stephen Pinker, Randy Thornhill and Corey Fincher, along with fringe figures like Satoshi Kanazawa and Richard Lynn, later entered this terrain, advancing the view that some population groups may have evolved to be more intelligent than others.

3. As a pupil at a private boarding school he had 'a fairly active fantasy life about a relationship with God', imagining 'creeping down to the chapel in the middle of the night and having a sort of blinding vision'.[quoted in Stephen S Hall, 'Darwin's Rottweiler', *Discover* magazine, 9 September 2005] Later, after hearing Elvis Presley was a born-again Christian, he said, 'I felt Elvis calling me to be a messenger from God'. Entering his late teens he still had a sense of a creator along the lines of 'There must be SOME sort of designer, some sort of spirit, which designed the universe and designed life'.[Richard Dawkins interviewed on 'Midweek', *BBC Radio 4*, 11 December 2013].

4. Darwin was a theist for most of his life, gradually moving towards agnosticism, but never to atheism.

5. Stephen S Hall, 'Darwin's Rottweiler', *Discover* magazine, 9 September 2005.

6. Richard Dawkins, *The Selfish Gene*, Oxford University Press, 1976.

7. Its 30th anniversary edition, in 2006, carried the tagline, "The Million Copy International Bestseller" (*The Selfish Gene*, 30th anniversary edition), Oxford University Press, 2006.

8. These are discussed in chapter 4. However, Dawkins steered clear of Hamilton's eugenics and Hamilton's endorsement of the views of the racist evolutionary psychologist Richard Lynn. For example, in an enthusiastic review of Lynn's pro-eugenics book *Dysgenics*, published in 2000 (after Hamilton's death), Hamilton praised Lynn for showing that 'almost all of the worries of the early eugenicists were well-founded' (WD Hamilton, 'A review of *Dysgenics: Genetic Deterioration in Modern Populations*', *Annals of Human Genetics*, 64 (4), 2000, pp 363–74).

9. Richard Dawkins, *The Selfish Gene*, op cit, pp 2–3.

10. Argued in the final sentences of *The Selfish Gene*, Ibid, p 215..

11. Steven Pinker, *How the Mind Works*, Allen Lane, 1997, p 52.

12. Paul Ehrlich, *Human Natures: Genes, Cultures, and the Human Prospect*, Penguin, London, 2002, p 23.

13. Ibid, p 23.

14. Ibid.

15. Two examples include the theory of symbiogenesis first emerged in the Soviet Union in 1924, while a key development in the theory of genetic drift – the

neutral theory of molecular evolution – came from the Japanese geneticist Motoo Kimura, in 1978.

16. Niles Eldredge, *Time Frames*, Simon & Schuster, 1985, p 95

17. Charles Darwin, *The Origin of Species By Means of Natural Selection*, Adegi Graphics LLC, 2000, p 421.

18. Stephen Jay Gould, op cit, p 89.

19. The reason genetic drift is more likely in a smaller, isolated population can be illustrated by a coin tossing analogy – the more you toss it, the less chance there is of it always landing on heads. Likewise, the more people or animals in the population, the less chance there is of a particular allele taking root.

20. Motoo Kimura, *The neutral theory of molecular evolution*. Cambridge University Press, Cambridge, 1968.

21. See, for example, the contribution by Werner Kalow and Harold Kalant from the Department of Pharmacology at the University of Toronto on selection at species level – "Evolutionary Psychology: An Exchange", *The New York Review of Books*, vol 44, no 15, October 1997, *www.nybooks.com/articles/1070* , pp 3–4.

22. See for example, DS Wilson and EO Wilson, "Survival of the Selfless", *New Scientist,* November 3, 2007, pp 42–46, and Dawkins's response and EO Wilson's rebuttal in their December 15 issue.

23. EO Wilson, interviewed on *BBC Newsnight*, November 6 2014.

24. An architectural spandrel is a curved area of masonry between the arches supporting a dome. Gould invented this term when admiring San Marco Cathedral. The spandrels were not spaces planned by the architect. Instead they arose as architectural by-products. (See Stephen Jay Gould and Richard Lewontin, "The Spandrels of San Marco and the Panglossian paradigm: a critique of the adaptationist programme," *Proceedings of the Royal Society of London*, Series B, Vol 205, No 1161 1979, pp 581–589.

25. Stephen Jay Gould, "More Things in Heaven and Earth," in H Rose and S Rose, op cit, p 95.

26. Donald Symons, *The Evolution of Human Sexuality*, Oxford University Press, 1979.

27. Stephen Jay Gould, "Evolutionary Psychology: An Exchange," p 5.

28. For example, the cognitive psychologist, Dr Geoff Bunn, put it like this. 'It seems the cerebral cortex is hard-wired to be culturally constructed.' And he added: 'If there is one organ of the body that demonstrates that biology is not destiny, it is the sentient brain.' [Geoff Bunn, 'A history of the brain', Episode 10, *BBC Radio 4*, 18 November 2011].

29. Aside from the low (and falling) level of religious belief in several countries (in Scotland, for example, a recent survey found that 52 percent of adults called themselves atheists), there is at least one example of a hunter-gatherer tribe that has no belief system that we could call a religion. According to the anthropologist Daniel Everett, the Amazonian rain forest tribe, the Piraha, have no concept of a supreme spirit or god, no belief in the after-life, no belief in ancestral spirits and none of the other features commonly associated with religion (although they do believe in good and bad spirits). (See Daniel L Everett, *Don't Sleep, There Are Snakes: Life and Language in the Amazonian Jungle*, Pantheon, 2008).

30. Steven Jay Gould, "More Things in Heaven and Earth", op cit, p104.

31. For example, Daniel Kosman, editor of *Science*, boldly declared that the nature-nurture debate was over and that nature had won. [Quoted in Val Dusek, Sociology Sanitized: The Evolutionary Psychology and Genetic Selectionism Debates', *Science as Culture, p1, http://human-nature.com/science-as-culture/dusek.html* ]

32. Craig Venter, quoted in 'Nature or nurture', *BBC News*, February 11 2001.

33. Craig Venter, quoted in 'GE Fantasy shattered by human genome project', February 13, 2001, *http://www.btinternet.com/~nlpwessex/Documents/GEfantasy.htm*

34. Ehrlich, op cit, p 4.

35. bid.

36. Robert Plomin and Oliver S P Davis, 'The future of genetics in psychology and psychiatry: mircroarrays, genome-side association, and non-coding RNA', in *The Journal of Child Psychology and Psychiatry*, vol 50, issue 1–2, 2009, pp 63–71.

37. The word 'epigenetics' refers to anything that can alter the impact of a gene without having an impact on the DNA sequence.

38. For a summary of recent findings on epigenetics, see Gavin Evans, *Black Brain, White Brain: is intelligence skin deep?* Thistle, London, 2015, pp 175–183.

39. Nikas Langstrom, Kelly M Babchisin, Seen Fazel & Paul Frisell, 'Sexual offending runs in families: A 37-year nationwide study' , *International Journal of Epidemiology*, April 9 2015

40. The team, from the Karolinska Institute in Sweden and Oxford University, surveyed 21,566 men convicted of rape and other sexual crimes in Sweden between 1973 and 2009.

41. Quoted in 'Sex crimes more common in certain familes,' *Phys Org*, April 8 2015.

42. Quoted in Steve Connor, 'Men up to five times more likely to commit sex crimes than the average male if they have brother or father convicted of a sex offence,' *The Independent,* April 8 2015.

43. Quoted in 'Sex crimes more common in certain families,' *Phys Org*, April 8 2015.

44. Sarah Knapton, 'Sex offending is written in DNA of some men, Oxford University finds', *Daily Telegraph*, April 9 2015.

45. *Phys Org*, op cit.

46. A study by psychologists at Georgia State University of 5,000 Vietnam War veterans found that anti-social, sensation-seeking behaviour was more common in men who had both high testosterone levels *and* low education levels combined with low-income jobs, while those with more education and money tended to finder other outlets for these impulses. (J Dabbs, D De la Rue and PM Williams, 'Testosterone and occupational choice: Actors, ministers and other men', *Journal of Personality and Social Psychology* 1990; 59, 1261–5). Referring to the high-testosterone men who were better-off, the head researcher, Professor James Dabbs, said: 'They can do things that are both exciting and socially acceptable – driving fast cars rather than stealing them, and arguing instead of fighting,' (quoted in Malcolm Carruthers, *The Testosterone Revolution*, Thorsons, 2001).

47. Cordelia Fine, *Delusions of Gender: The Real Science Behind Sex Differences*, Icon, London, pp 37.

48. B B Sherwin, 'A comparative analysis of the role of androgens in human male and female behaviour: Behavioural specificity, critical thresholds, and sensitivity, *Psychology* 16(4), 1988, 416–425. See also, Fine, ibid, pp 36–38.

49. The United Nations Office on Drugs and Crime conducted a Global Study on Homicide, which produced tables for murder rates per 100,000 inhabitants for 2012. Of the countries cited, Malawi's rate (1.8), Sierra Leone (1.9), Senegal (2.8) and Liberia's (3.1) were significantly below those at the top of the African pile – Lesotho (38), Swaziland (33.8) South Africa (31) and the Democratic Republic of the Congo (28.3). The murder rate per 100,000 in Honduras was 90.4, Venezuela was 53.7 and El Salvador 41.2, while that in Algeria was 0.7, Indonesia 0.6 and Kuwait 0.4. The two countries with the lowest rates were Monaco and Liechtenstein with no murders, followed by Singapore (0.2) and Japan and Iceland (both 0.3). The American rate was 3.8 compared to the British rate of 1.0. In 2015, El Salvador took over from Honduras as the murder capital of the world, with gang violence pushing its rate up to 104 per 100,000. (El Salvador police data, published in Joshua Partlow 'People flee as warring street gangs drive up murder rate', *Washington Post* report published in *The Independent*, January 7 2016).

50. UN Office on Drugs and Crime, ibid.

51. Richard Dawkins, *The Selfish Gene,* op cit, p252.

52. Richard Dawkins, *The Selfish Gene* (2nd ed), Oxford University Press, 1989, p 192.

53. Richard Dawkins, *The Selfish Gene,* 1976, op cit, pp 207–209.

54. For example, the psychologist Susan Blackmore wrote a book, *The Meme Machine,* Oxford University Press, 1999.

55. Stephen Jay Gould, "Darwinian Fundamentalism", *New York Review of Books,* June 12 1997.

56. Daniel Dennett, *Darwin's Dangerous Idea,* op cit.

57. This is the approach of the philosopher, Mary Midgley, who, in her critique of Dawkins, compared thought and culture to traffic flow patterns and ocean currents. She asked rhetorically what these 'mythical' cultural units were if they are neither physical objects nor thoughts. 'They seem to be occult causes of these thoughts,' she playfully suggested. (Mary Midgley, "Why Memes", in *Alas Poor Darwin,* op cit, p 68).

58. Richard Dawkins interviewed about 'gay genes' on YouTube – April 2010 – *http://www.youtube.com/watch?v=MHDCAllQgS0*

59. Ibid.

60. Ibid.

61. Ibid

62. It has been observed in a wide variety of mammals from dogs and cats, via bonobos to elephants and also in birds such as seagulls and in insects such as fruit flies.

63. The study, based on a sample of all the adult twins in Sweden, found that the twins' unique environment accounted for 61–66 percent of male homosexuality (including their experience in utero and during childbirth, physical and psychological trauma, peer group influences and sexual experiences); their shared environment (including attitudes of society and family) accounted for 0–17 percent and that genetic factors accounted for 18–39 percent. With lesbians, there was a stronger environmental influence, which the researchers placed in the 80 to 83 percent range, with genetic factors at 18–19 percent. (N Långström, Q Rahman, E Carlström, P Lichtenstein. "Genetic and environmental effects on same-sex sexual behavior: a population study of twins in Sweden". *Arch Sex Behav* 39 (1) February 2010, pp 75–80).

64. This is discussed in chapter 8.

65. Some studies found differences between gay and straight men regarding the size of the suprachiasmatic nucleus and one found a difference in the size of the anterior commisure.

66. Meta analysis of these studies suggests a shared genetic marker on the X chromosome, but that additional genes must be present to account for homosexual orientation.

67. Hamer claimed that a marker on the X chromosome predisposed men towards homosexuality. He suggested gay men have more gay uncles and cousins on the mother's side than the father's. These results were not replicated in several other studies, including a 2010 study comparing the X chromosomes of 894 heterosexual men and 694 homosexual men (G Schwartz, R Kim, A Kolundzija, G Rieger, A Sanders, "Biodemographic and physical correlates of sexual orientation in men", in *Archives of sexual behaviour* 39 (1), 2010, pp 93–109). Another study drew links to responses to smells, showing that the hypothalamus of gay men was activated when they were exposed to a testosterone odour found in male sweat, while heterosexual men had a similar response to an oestrogen-based odour found in women's urine (Nicholas Wade, "Gay Men Are Found to Have Different Scent of Attraction", *New York Times*, May 9 2005). And there has been research suggesting that birth order has implications for sexuality (the more older brothers you have, the more likely you'll be gay). This has been explained in biological terms (boy babies stimulate an immune reaction in the mother, which becomes stronger with each boy born, and these antibodies act against the masculinisation of the brain), but it could relate to factors in the upbringing of boys with several older brothers.

68. One study found a link between the "switching off" of one of the mother's X chromosomes and the sexuality of her sons – 23 percent of mothers with two gay sons showed this "extreme X chromosome skewing" compared to 4 percent of mothers without gay sons. (S Bocklandt, S Horvath, E Vilain, D.H. Hameer, "Extreme skewing of X chromosome inactivation in mothers of homosexual men", *Human Genetics* 118 (6), February 2006, pp 691–694). This view was reinforced by a 2015 study that has yet to be published or peer reviewed, at the University of California at Los Angeles, which compared the sexual orientation of 37 pairs of twins where one twin was gay and the other not, and 10 pairs where both were gay. The team examined molecular data from nine genome sites with helped them to predict which twins were homosexual or heterosexual. The data showed how environmental factors altered the activity of genes – ie. their epigenetic impact. Lead author Dr Tuck Ngun, commented: 'The next steps are to explore how genetics and environmental factors interact to produce variations in sexual orientations over the life course.' (Haroon Siddique, 'Algorithm predicts sexual orientation of men with up to 70% accuracy, say researchers' *The Guardian*, October 8 2015).

## Chapter 4: Men, women and monkeys

1. It is usually considered to have started through the work of the Austrian biologists Konrad Lorenz and Karl von Frisch and the Dutch biologist, Nikolaas Tinbergen (who, together won the Nobel Prize in Physiology and Medicine in 1973).

2. JBS Haldane quoted in Keven Connolly and Margaret Martlew (eds), 'altruism, *Psychologically Speaking: A Book of Quotations,* BPS Books, 1999, p 10.

3. W D Hamilton 'The Genetical Evolution of Social Behaviour'. *Journal of Theoretical Biology* 7 (1), 1964, pp 1–16. For a fuller explanation of Hamilton's theory, see David J Buller, *Adapting Minds: Evolutionary Psychology and the Persistent Quest for Human Nature,* MIT press, 2006, pp 352–355.

4. Richard Dawkins, *The God Delusion,* Bantam Press, 2006, pp 218–220.

5. Richard Dawkins, letter to Donald Cameron in 'A correspondence with Richard Dawkins' – *http://www.cameronphilosophy.com/dawkins.htm*

6. One critique came from the US epidemiologist Wladimir Alonso and the Oxford evolutionary biologist Cynthia Schuck Paim, who argued that the behaviours that kin selection theory explains are not altruistic in the Darwinian evolutionary sense. This is because, first, they may favour the performer directly to increase his progeny (a case of ordinary individual selection); second, these behaviours might benefit the whole group (a case of group selection) and third, they may be by-products of a developmental system of a number of individuals carrying out a range of tasks (such as a hive of bees). W J Alonso & C Schuck-Paim 'Sex-ratio conflicts, kin selection, and the evolution of altruism' *PNAS* 99 (10), pp 6843–6847.

7. See for example, Martin Nowak, Corina Tarnita & E O Wilson (2010). 'The evolution of eusociality' *Nature* 466, pp 1057–1062.

8. EO Wilson, quoted in 'E.O. Wilson shifts his position on altruism in nature', *The Boston Globe,* November 10 2008.

9. Ibid.

10. Paul Ehrlich, *Human Natures: Genes, Cultures, and the Human Prospect,* Penguin, 2002, pp 39–40.

11. See for example, Sherman et al, *Recognition Systems.* In *Behavioural Ecology,* J. R. Krebs and N. B. Davies (eds), Blackwell Scientific 1994.

12. Bruce Springsteen, 'Highway Patrolman', *Nebraska,* Columbia 1981.

13. Discussed in chapter 14.

14. G M Alexander and M Hines, 'Sex differences in response to children's toys in non-human primates', *Evolution and Human Behaviour,* 23 (6), 2002, pp

GAVIN EVANS

467–479. See also, Cordelia Fine, *Delusions of Gender: The Real Science Behind Sex Differences*, Icon Books, London, 2010, pp 233–125.

15. Steven Pinker in 'The science of gender and science – Pinker vs Spelke: a debate', Harvard University Mind/Brain/Behavior Initiative, 16 May 2005, *Edge: The Third Culture, www.edge.org/3rd_culture/debate05/debate05_index.html*

16. J M Hassett, E R Siebert & K Wallen, 'Sex differences in rhesus monkey toy preference s parallel those of children,' *Hormones and Behaviour* 54(3) 2008, pp 359–364. See also Fine (2010), Ibid, p p 124–125.

17. Fine (2010), Ibid, p269, notes 26 and 27.

18. Frances Burton, 'Ethology and the development of sex and gender identity in non-human primates,' *Acta Biotheoretica* 26 (1) 1977, pp 1–18 & Fine 2010, Ibid, pp 126–129.

19. The 98.8 percent figure comes from measuring the base building blocks of the genes shared by chimps and humans. But when their entire genomes are compared the figure of 94 or 95 percent is used – 'What does it mean to be human', *Smithsonian Museum of Natural History – http://humanorigins.si.edu/evidence/genetics*

20. Frans de Waal, 'Bonobo Sex and Society', *Scientific American*, March 1995, pp 82–88.

21. Frans de Waal, 'Sex as an alternative to aggression in the bonobo', in P R Abrahamson and S D Pinkerton (eds), *Sexual Nature/Sexual Culture*, University of Chicago Press, 1995, p48.

22. Among gibbons it is even lower – in fact the males do not outweigh the females.

23. Ehrich, op cit, p 153.

24. Ibid, p 91.

25. Anne Fausto-Sterling, 'Beyond Difference: Feminism and Evolutionary Psychology', in *Alas Poor Darwin*, op cit, p 182.

26. Shirley Strum, *Almost Human: A Journey into the World of Baboons*, Random House, 1987.

27. Patricia Adair Gowaty, 'Field Studies of Parental Care in Birds: New Data Focus Questions on Variation Among Females', in CT Snowdon and JS Rosenblatt (eds), *Advances in the Study of Behaviour*, 24, 1995.

28. P Gagneux, D S Woodruff and C Boesch, 'Furtive mating in female chimpanzees,' *Nature* 387, 1997, pp 358–359.

29. The Cambridge University ethology professor, Patrick Bateson lists nine different meanings of the term, ranging from inherited behaviour shared by all members of the species to behavioural differences within a species caused by genetic difference. (Patrick Bateson, 'Taking the Stink out of Instinct', *Alas Poor Darwin*, op cit, p164).

30. Ibid, pp 166–167.

31. Ibid, p 167.

32. Brooke L Sargent and Janet Mann, 'From Social Learning to Culture: Intrapopulation Variation in Bottlenose Dolphins', in Kevin N Laland and Bennett G Galef, *The Question of Animal Culture,* Harvard UP, 2009, pp 152–173.

33. For example, ravens have been observed displaying a 'theory of mind' (a term used to describe the ability to see things through another's eyes and consider what they might be thinking). They were observed altering their behaviour when they thought they were being spied on by others, even those they couldn't see, using tricks when storing food, to prevent discovery from competitors. Under test conditions at the University of Houston most were able to act on information from their own experience, and combine it with novel information, to predict how the other ravens might act, and then to adapt their own behaviour accordingly. However, one of the ten ravens never mastered the technique, suggesting that like humans, not all ravens are alike. (Thomas Bugnyar, Stephan A Reber & Cameron Buckner, 'Ravens attribute visual access to unseen competitors', *Nature Communications* 7, February 2 2016).

34. A Whitten, J Goodall, W.C. McGrew, T Nishida, V Reynolds, Y Sugiyama, C.E.G Tutin, R.W. Wrangham and C. Boesch, 'Cultures in Chimpanzees', *Nature* 399, 1999, pp 682–685.

35. Catherine Hobaiter, Timothee Poisot, Klaus Zuberbuhler, William Hoppitt & Thibaud Gruber, 'Social Network Analysis Shows Direct Evidence for Social Transmission of Tool Use in Wild Chimpanzees,' *PLOS Biology*, September 30 2014.

36. Ibid.

37. 'Altruistic' chimps act for the benefit of each other', *New Scientist*, June 25, 2007.

38. Bateson, op cit, p 167.

39. Frans de Waal, quoted in 'Is 'Do Unto Others' written into our genes?' *New York Times*, September 18, 2007.

40. Felix Warneken, quoted in ' 'Altruistic' chimps act for the benefit of each other', *New Scientist*, June 25, 2007.

41. ' 'Altruistic' chimps act for the benefit of each other', op cit.

42. Researchers found that in some of the orphans there was a 'virtual black hole' where the orbitofrontal cortex should have been (the part of the brain enabling people manage their emotions and relate to each other, experience pleasure and appreciate beauty. (See Sue Gerhardt, *Why Love Matters: How Affection Shapes a Baby's Brain,* Routledge, 2010).

43. See for example the interview with Dr Ronald Federici (a psychologist who founded several US relief efforts for Romanian orphans): 'Dr Ronald Federici: Romanian Orphans Q&A', in *Developments in Therapy*, June 25, 1999.

## Chapter 5: Penis Envy and the Solar Phallus Man

1. The fisher people of the Blombos and Pinnacle Point caves on the west coast of South Africa were among the first to display the habits of modern humans, at least 100,000 years ago.
2. Marjorie Shostak, *Nisa: The Life and Words of a !King Woman*, Vintage Books, New York, p 13
3. Ibid, pp 10–25.
4. Archaeologists, palaeontologists, biological anthropologists and evolutionary biologists keep pushing the date back on when humans with modern intelligence (humans like us) emerged. See chapter 2 of my book *Black Brain, White Brain: Is intelligence skin deep?* Thistle and Jonathan Ball, 2015.
5. James B Pritchard (ed), *Ancient Near Eastern Texts Relation to the Old Testament*, Princeton University Press, 1950, p 412.
6. Hatshepsut was the fifth pharaoh of the 18th dynasty in the 1400s BC; Cleopatra came from a Greek dynasty, but spoke Egyptian, portrayed herself as the reincarnation of the Egyptian goddess, Isis, and adopted Egyptian customs.
7. Zenobia (240 to 275 AD) was queen of the Palmyran empire in Roman Syria. She ruled over Egypt until being conquered by the Roman Emperor Aurelian in 274 AD.
8. Carolyn Fluehr-Lobban, 'Nubian Queens in the Nile Valley and Afro-Asiatic Cultural History', Museum of Fine Arts, Boston, 1998.
9. Cartimandua was another female queen of Boudica's time. She rule the Brigantes tribe in northern Britain and is said to have collaborated with the Romans.
10. In Celtic Britain girls could be trained to fight with weapons, and it was not uncommon for women to bear arms, and to use them.
11. This applies to all of what are known as the Eastern religions as well. For example, many Buddhists believe that men are a higher form of life than women, and that if a woman lives a good life, she may be reincarnated as a man.
12. Genesis, 3, 16 (New English translation).
13. There is another version written a couple of hundred years later but also in the first two chapters of Genesis, in which men and women were created simultaneously. The two versions would seem to contradict each other.

14. Orthodox Jewish morning prayer.
15. Qu'ran, Sura 4:35.
16. New Testament, I Timothy 2:12.
17. Mohammad, 'Prophet' of Islam, in Sunan Abudawud, Book 11, Hadith 2135.
18. Potentially, but rarely. 'Proof' in science is rarer than we think. Usually it is a case of mounting evidence to support a theory.
19. Sigmund Freud, *Civilization, Society and Religion vol 12*, Penguin Freud Library, 1991, p. 131.
20. Sigmund Freud, *The Future of an Illusion*, Pacific Publishing Studio, 2010, p 31.
21. Sigmund Freud, 'Some Psychological Consequences of the Anatomical Distinction between the Sexes', paper delivered by Anna Freud at the Hamburg International Psycho-Analytical Congress, September 3, 1925, and published in the International Journal of Psychoanalysis V111, p 138.
22. Ibid.
23. Steven Jay Gould, *The Mismeasure of Man*, Penguin, London, 1996, p 143.
24. Quoted in Ibid, p143.
25. Nancy Chodorow, *The Reproduction of Mothering*, New Haven, Yale University Press, 1999, p 176.
26. Ibid, pp 78–80.
27. For a detailed discussion of the debates around empathy, the best summary I have read is chapter two of Cordelia Fine's excellent, *Delusions of Gender: The Real Science Behind Sex Differences*, Icon Books, London, 2012, pp 14–26.
28. Nancy Chodorow, *Feminism and Psychoanalytic Theory*, Yale University Press, 1991 p 76.
29. M W Clearfield & N M Nelson, 'Sex Differences in mothers' speech and play behaviour with 6, 9 and 14-month-old infants', *Sex Roles*, 54, pp 127–137. Cited in, C Fine, *Delusions of Gender: The Real Science Behind Sex Differences*, Icon, London, 2010, p 198.
30. W Donovan, N Taylor & L Leavitt, 'Maternal sensory sensitivity and response bias in detecting change in infant facial expressions: Maternal self-efficacy and infant gender labelling, *Infant Behaviour and Development* 30(3), pp 436–452. Cited in C Fine, Ibid.
31. The authors of the study noted that the association between father absence and teenage depression 'was stronger in girls than in boys and remained after adjusting for a range of socio-economic, maternal and familial confounders assessed prior to the father's departure'. And it concluded: 'Father absence in early childhood increases the risk of for adolescent depressive symptoms, particularly in girls.' Incidentally, they also found that girls whose father left during their first

five years were more likely to suffer depression than those whose fathers left during middle childhood (five to 10 years). I Culpin, JE Heron, R Araya, R Melotti and CJ Johnson, 'Father absence and depressive symptoms in adolescence: findings from a UK cohort', *Psychological Medicine*, May 14, p1.

32. Cited by Dr Peter Martin, vice-chair of the British Psychological Society's Division of Clinical Psychology, in 'Absent fathers and depressed adolescents', British Psychological Society, May 15 2013, *http://www.bps.org.uk/news/absent-fathers-and-depressed-adolescents*

33. This is discussed in my book *Black Brain, White Brain* (Jonathan Ball and Thistle, 2015). He believed African, Jewish and European mythical themes could be explained by inherited distinctions between these 'races' – justified by his view that characteristics acquired in the lifetime of members of one generation could be passed on biologically to the next and that we carry traces of our primitive past in our psyches. He saw adult Africans as comparable to European children, prompting his desire to study the 'archetypes' of European children and of 'primitive' African adults. [See F Dalal, 'The racism of Jung', *Race and Class* 29/3, 1988. Also Michael Ortiz Hill, *'CG Jung – In the Heart of Darkness'*] Jung visited Kenya and Uganda in 1925 for a 'scientific inquiry' into 'primitive psychology' and 'primordial darkness', though he admitted his real intent was to ask himself 'the rather embarrassing question: What is going to happen to Jung the psychologist in the wilds of Africa?'[Carl Jung, *Memories, Dreams, Reflections*, ed. A Jaffe, Collins, New York, 1973, p272.] While there he had a dream featuring the black barber he'd used in Tennessee 12 years earlier – where this man held a red-hot iron to style his hair. He woke in terror but later decided his dream was a warning from his unconscious that he was in danger of being swallowed by this primitive African world. 'At the time I was obviously all too close to 'going black'', he wrote. He warned Europeans against co-existing with Africans because they too could face the danger of going black. 'Even today the European ... cannot live with impunity among the Negroes in Africa; their psychology gets into him unnoticed and unconsciously he becomes a Negro.'[Carl Jung, *Collected Works 10: Civilisation in Transition*, Princeton University Press, 1970, p121] He added that the 'inferior man has a tremendous pull because he fascinates the inferior layers in the psyche'.[Ibid, p507]

34. Carl Jung, *The Archetypes and the Collective Unconscious*, Routledge and Kegan Paul, London, 1996, p43.

35. Richard Noll, *The Jung Cult: Origins of a Charismatic Movement*, Princeton University Press, 1995, pp 181–187.

36. J J Honegger, who committed suicide in 1911.

37. Ben Macintyre, 'Harvard scholar says Jung was fraud,' The Times, June 5 1995.

38. Jung's 'Woman in Europe' (1928) quoted in Dan McGowan, *What's Wrong with Jung*, Prometheus, London, 1994, p100.

39. Carl Jung, 'The significance of the father in the destiny of the individual' in A Samuals, *The Father: contemporary Jungian perspectives*, Free Association Books, London, 1985.

40. Devon Anthony Stevens, The Jung Page, *www.cgjungpage.org* , November 3 2006, pp 5–7.

41. Steven Pinker, *The Blank Slate: The Modern Denial of Human Nature*, Penguin, London, p 69.

42. Ibid.

43. This is discussed in more detail in chapter 7.

44. Leda Cosmides and John Tooby, 'Evolutionary Psychology: A Primer', Center for Evolutionary Psychology, University of California, Santa Barbara, January 13 1997, *http://www.cep.ucsb.edu/primer.html*.

## Chapter 6: Swiss Army Knife minds and balanced brains

1. Leda Cosmides and John Tooby, 'Evolutionary Psychology: A Primer', Center for Evolutionary Psychology, University of California, Santa Barbara, January 13 1997, *http://www.cep.ucsb.edu/primer.html*.

2. Leda Cosmides and John Tooby quoted in David Buss (ed), *The Handbook of Evolutionary Psychology*, John Wiley & Sons, New Jersey, 2005, p5.

3. Donald Symons, 'Adaptiveness and Adaptation' *Ethology and Sociobiology* 11, 1992, p 142.

4. Ibid, p139

5. John Tooby and Leda Cosmides, 'On the Universality of Human Nature and the Uniqueness of the Individual: The Role of Genetics and Adaptation,' *Journal of Personality* 58 1990, p 19.

6. Steven Pinker, *How the Mind Works*, Norton, 1997, p 21.

7. Leda Cosmides and John Tooby, 'The Modular Nature of Human Intelligence', in A B Scheibel and J W Schopf (eds), *The origin and Evolution of Human Intelligence*, Jones and Bartlett, Sudbury, Massachusetts, 1997, p 84.

8. For a fuller summary, see David J Buller, *Adapting Minds: Evolutionary Psychology and the Persistent Quest for Human Nature*, Bradford Books, The MIT Press, Cambridge, Massachusetts, 2006, pp 63–71.

9. Ibid, p 81.

10. This view of innate grammar has been criticised partly because its critics conceive of language acquisition in terms of the development of the brain in relation to its environment, rather than in terms of an evolutionary trigger launching a grammatical module. Brain imaging studies of children show that grammar is processed by both hemispheres of the brain until they are about six-years old, and only after that does the left hemisphere begin to specialise, discrediting the notion of a discreet, grammatical module. (Annette Karmiloff-Smith, 'Why Babies' Brains Are Not Swiss Army Knives, in Hilary and Steven Rose (eds), *Alas Poor Darwin: Arguments Against Evolutionary Psychology*, Vintage, London, 2001, p 152). It is also disputed because the rules are less universal than Chomsky et al assumed. One example comes from Daniel Everett's studies of the Piraha people in the Amazon, who do not seem to share key aspects of Chomsky's supposedly universal grammar. (Daniel Everett, *Don't Sleep, There are Snakes: Life and Language in the Amazon Jungle*, Profile Books, London, 2009).

11. Steven Rose, in 'The Two Steves: Pinker vs Rose – a Debate', part 2, questions and answers, Institute of Education, University of London, January 21 1998.

12. Leda Cosmides and John Tooby, 'The Psychological Foundations of Culture', in J H Barkow, L Cosmides and J Tooby (eds) *The Adapted Mind: Evolutionary Psychology and the Generation of Culture*, Oxford University Press, New York, 1992, p113.

13. David Buller, op cit, pp 69–70.

14. Ibid, p 71.

15. Robert Wright, *The Moral Animal: Why We Are the Way We Are: The New Science of Evolutionary Psychology*, Pantheon, New York, 1994, p 357.

16. Robert Wright, 'Feminists Meet Mr Darwin', *New Republic*, November 28 1994, pp 34–46.

17. John Tooby and Leda Cosmides, Foreword, in Simon Baron-Cohen, *Mindblindness: An Essay on Autism and Theory of Mind*, MIT Press, Cambridge, Massachusetts, 1995, p xiii.

18. Buller, op cit, p 130.

19. Jeffrey Elman, cited by Buller, ibid, pp 133–134.

20. Annette Karmilof-Smith, 'Why Babies' Brains Are Not Swiss Army Knives' in Hilary and Steven Rose (eds), *Alas Poor Darwin: Arguments Against Evolutionary Psychology*, Vintage, London, 2001, p 154.

21. Buller, op cit, p 150.

22. Jeffrey Elman's research cited in Buller, ibid, pp 150–151.

23. Buller, ibid, p151.

24. Simon Baron-Cohen, 'Don't blame it on the biological determinists,' Comment is free, *The Guardian*, May 4 2010.

25. Simon Baron-Cohen, *The Essential Difference: Men, Women and the Extreme Male Brain*, London, Allen Lane, 2003, p 184.

26. S Baron-Cohen, R Knickmeyer & M Belmonte, 'Sex differences in the brain: Implications for explaining autism,' *Science*, 310, 2005, table 1, p 821.

27. His tests can be found on his Autism Research Centre website: *http:// autismresearchcentre.com/arc_tests*

28. See Cordelia Fine, op cit, pp 41–53.

29. See Fine, ibid, p 16.

30. Simon Baron-Cohen, 2003, op cit, p 105.

31. J H Gilmore, W Lin, M Prastawa, C Looney, Y Vetsa, R Knickmeyer et al, 'Regional gray matter growth, sexual dimorphism and cerebral asymmetry in the neonatal brain,' *Journal of Neuroscience* 27(6), 2007, pp 1255–1260.

32. Fine, op cit, p 262.

33. D H Skuse, 'Is autism really a coherent syndrome in boys, or girls?', *British Journal of Psychology*, 100, 2009, p 33.

34. See R Jordan-Young, footnote 16, *Brain Storm: The Flaws in the Science of Sex Differences*, Harvard University Press, pp 329–330.

35. Autism Research Centre, op cit.

36. Simon Baron Cohen, op cit, p 64.

37. J Connellan, S Baron-Cohen, S Wheelwright, A Batki & J Ahluwalia, 'Sex differences in human neonatal social perception,' *Infant Behaviour & Development*, 23, 2000, pp 113–118.

38. L Sax, op cit, p 19.

39. Cordelia Fine, op cit, p 113.

40. See A and G Grossi, 'Picking Barbie's brain: Inherent sex differences in scientific ability', *Journal of Interdisciplinary Feminist Thought*, 2 (1), Article 5, 2007, p 9; L Elliot, op cit, pp 72–74 and C Fine, op cit, pp 114–116.

41. R T Leeb & F G Rejskind, 2004, 'Here's looking at you, kid! A longitudinal study of perceived gender differences in mutual gaze behaviour in young infants,' *Sex Roles*, 50 (1/2) pp 1–14.

42. L Elliot, *Pink Brain Blue Brain: How Small Differences Grow into Troublesome Gaps – and What We Can Do About It*, Oneworld, 2012, pp 73–74.

## Chapter 7: The colour-coded brain

1. Robin McKie, 'Girl Power', *The Observer Magazine*, June 20 1999.

2. Ibid.

3. Ibid.

4. Cordelia Fine, *Delusions of Gender: The Real Science Behind Sex Difference*, Icon Books, London, 2010, p xxiv.

5. Ibid, p 132.

6. For a fuller account of the 'science' of brain weighing, see Stephen Jay Gould, *The Mismeasure of Man*, Penguin, London, 1996, pp 120–149.

7. CE Russett, *Sexual science: The Victorian construction of womanhood*, Harvard University Press, Cambridge, MA, 1989, p 36.

8. George J Romanes quoted in C Fine, op cit, p 141.

9. C Fine, op cit, p 146.

10. Dr Charles L Dana, cited in Ibid, p131.

11. Rebecca M Jordan-Young, *Brainstorm: The Flaws in the Science of Sex Differences*, Harvard University Press, Cambridge, MA, 2011, p 51.

12. It has been reported that with 95 percent of right-handed men and 90 percent of right-handed women, language is located in the left hemisphere. But with left-handers estimates range from 61 to 72 percent. (See S Knecht, B Dräger, M Deppe, L Bobe, H Lohmann, A Flöel, E Ringelstein & H Henningsen. 'Handedness and hemispheric language dominance in healthy humans'. *Brain* 123 (12), 2000, pp 2512–2518).

13. See C Fine, op cit, p143–144.

14. C M Leonard, S Towler, L Halderman, R Otto, M Eckart & C Chiarello, 'Size matters: Cerebral volume influences sex difference in neuroanatomy', *Cerebral Cortex* 18(12), 2008,,p 2929

15. Dr Gina Rippon on 'Women's Hour', *BBC Radio 4*, April 21 2015.

16. G De Vries, 'Sex differences in adult and developing brains: compensation, compensation, compensation,' *Endocrinology* 145(3), 2004, p 1064.

17. Ibid, pp 1063–8. See also C Fine, op cit, p142–143.

18. Rippon, op cit.

19. *The Observer Magazine*, op cit.

20. Cited in Lise Eliot, *Pink Brain, Blue Brain*, Oneworld, 2012, p 10.

21. Ibid.

22. Anne Fausto-Sterling, *Sexing the Body*, Basic Books, New York, 2000, pp 127–135.

23. Eliot, op cit, p 10.

24. Mikkel Wallentin, 'Putative sex differences in verbal abilities and language cortex: A critical review,' *Brain and Language* 108(3), 2009, p 178.

25. Leonard Sax, *Why Gender Matters: What parents and teachers need to know about the emerging science of sex differences*, Broadway Books, New York, 2005.

26. C Fine, op cit, p 134.

27. Ibid, p 135.

28. Ibid, pp 133–136.

29. They used 521 females and 428 males, all aged between eight and 22 (Madhura Ingalhalikara, Alex Smitha, Drew Parkera, Theodore D. Satterthwaiteb, Mark A. Elliott, Kosha Ruparelb, Hakon Hakonarsond, Raquel E. Gurb, Ruben C. Gurb & Ragini Verma, 'Sex differences in the structural connectome of the human brain', *Proceedings of the National Academy of Sciences*, vol. 111 no. 2, January 2014).

30. Steve Connor, 'The hardwired difference between male and female brains could explain why men are 'better at map reading'', *The Independent*, December 2 2013.

31. BBC Radio 5 News, December 3 2013.

32. Ingalhalikara et al, p 1.

33. Ibid.

34. Ragini Verma quoted in Steve Connor, op cit.

35. Ragini Verma quoted in Ian Sample, 'Male and female brains wired differently, scans reveal,' *The Guardian* December 2 2013.

36. J. Antony Movshon quoted in Anna North, 'Sex and the brain: The trouble with 'hard-wiring,'' *Salon* December 5 2013.

37. Georgina Rippon quoted in Ibid.

38. Daphna Joel, Zohar Berman, Ido Tavor, Nadav Wexler, Olga Gager, Yaniv Stein, Nisan Shefi, Jared Pool, Sebastian Urchs, Daniel S Margulies, Franziskus Liem, Jurgen Hanggi, Lutz Jancke & Yaniv Assaf, 'Sex beyond genitalia: The human brain mosaic', *Proceedings of the National Academy of Sciences of the United States of America*, vol 112, no 50, pp 15468–15473.

39. Ibid.

40. Daphna Joel, quoted in Ian Sample, 'Men are from Mars, women are from Venus? New brain study says not', *The Guardian*, November 30 2015.

41. Ibid.

42. Daphne Joel quoted in Kate Wheeling, 'The brains of men and women aren't really that different, study finds', *Science* magazine, November 30 2015.

43. Timo Maentylae, quoted in Agence France-Presse, 'Men, not women, are better multitaskers', *Cosmos*, October 25 1012.

44. Keith Laws quoted in James Morgan, 'Women "better tat multitasking" than men, study finds,' *BBC News* October 24 2013.

45. For a summary of these critiques, see C Fine, ibid, pp 99–100 and 157–162; R Jordan-Young, op cit, p 50 and L Eliot, op cit, pp 73–79.

46. Louanne Brizendine, *The Female Brain*, Morgan Road Books, New York, 2006, p 91.

47. Ibid.

48. R Jordan-Young, op cit, p 50.

49. Ibid, p 298–299.

50. Ibid, pp 49–51.

51. L Elliot, op cit, pp 32–33.

52. The most famous case, involved David Reimer, who, as a result of a circumcision accident, was re-assigned to become a girl, but later reverted and eventually committed suicide at the age of 38. However, his case is not typical because he was only castrated at 22-months-old, by which age toddlers are well aware of their gender, and also because he had a twin brother.

53. Heinz Meyer-Bahlburg, 'Gender identify outcome in female-raised 46, XY persons with penile agenesis, cloacal exstrophy of the bladder, or penile ablation,' in *Archives of Sexual Behaviour* , 34, pp 423–438, cited in L Elliot, ibid, p 35.

54. Ibid, pp 36–38.

55. Jordan-Young, op cit, pp 211–213.

56. Fine, op cit, p 122.

57. Ibid, p 123.

58. See L Elliot, op cit, pp 38–42.

59. Eliot, op cit, p 269.

## Chapter 8: EP and women's IQs

1. *Black Brain, White Brain: Is intelligence skin deep?* Thistle and Jonathan Ball, 2015.

2. Richard Lynn and Paul Irwing, Sex differences on the progressive matrices: A meta-analysis, *Intelligence* 32, 2004, pp 481–498.

3. Paul Irwing and Richard Lynn, Sex differences in means and variability on the progressive matrices in university students: A meta-analysis. *British Journal of Psychology*, 96, 2005, pp 505–524.

4. Richard Lynn, 'Sorry men ARE more brainy than women (and more stupid too!). It's a simple scientific fact, says one of Britain's top dons', *Mail Online*, 8 May 2010.

5. Ibid.

6. Ibid.

7. Steve Blinkhorn, quoted in Robin McKie, 'Focus: Battle of the sexes – Who has the bigger brain?' *The Guardian,* November 6 2005.

8. Steve Blinkhorn, 'Gender Bender', *Nature*, Vol 438, 3rd November 2005, p 31.

9. Steve Blinkhorn in McKie, op cit.

10. Ibid.

11. Steve Blinkhorn, *Nature,* op cit, p 32.

12. Helena Cronin, 'Why do men dominate society' in James Randerson, 'Second thoughts on life, the universe and everything by the world's best brains', *The Guardian* January 1 2008.

13. Steven Pinker, 'Groups of people may differ genetically in their average talents and temperaments', in 'The *Edge* Annual Question – 2006', *Edge: The World Question Center*, 2006, *www.edge.org/q2006/q06_print.html#pinker*

14. Steven Pinker, 'The lessons of the Ashkenazim', *The New Republic Online*, 17 June 2006.

15. Steven Pinker, 'Genetic tests said I would be intelligent, swayed by novelty and bald. Two out of three ain't bad', *The Sunday Times*, February 1 2009.

16. Ibid.

17. The only claim in this regard, made two years before Pinker's gene test, came from the University of Chicago biologist Bruce Lahn who announced he'd identified two genes (microcephalin and ASPN) more common among non-Africans and that they affected brain size and were 'probably' associated with higher IQ. He speculated these gene variants were the product of breeding with Neanderthals. Other geneticists savaged his methodology and conclusions, finding that the gene variants had no impact on brain size and there was no evidence they affected intelligence. This damning verdict was backed up by five subsequent studies, including one from Lahn's own laboratory. Since then, the two co-authors of Lahn's original paper distanced themselves from their conclusions, while his university withdrew a patent application to use his work to develop a DNA-based intelligence test. Among those who had themselves tested for these alleles was Lahn himself, and he admitted that although the results were indecisive, 'it wasn't looking good'. (Chapter 8, Gavin Evans, *Black Brain, White Brain: Is Intelligence Skin Deep*, Jonathan Ball and Thistle, 2015).

18. But soon after resurfaced through being appointed by President Barack Obama as director of the US National Economic Council.

19. Steven Pinker in 'The science of gender and science – Pinker vs Spelke: a debate', Harvard University Mind/Brain/Behavior Initiative, 16 May 2005, *Edge: The Third Culture*, www.edge.org/3rd_culture/debate05/debate05_index.html

20. Ibid.

21. Elizabeth Spelke in Ibid.

22. Steven Pinker, 'The lessons of the Ashkenazim', op cit.

23. Girls averaged 100.64; boys averaged 100.48 for boys. Ian J Deary, Graham Thorpe, Valerie Wilson, John M Starr, Lawrence J Whalley, 'Population sex differences in IQ at age 11: the Scottish mental survey' *Intelligence*, 31 vol 6, November–December 2003, pp 537–538.

24. Ibid.

25. Susan Pinker, *The Sexual Paradox*, Atlantic Books, 2008, p 13.

26. Ibid, p 534.

27. A Feingold, 'Gender Differences in variability in intellectual abilities: cross-cultural perspective' in *Sex Roles*, 30 (1/2),1994, pp 81–92.

28. J S Hyde, S M Lindberg, M C Linn, A B Ellis & CC Williams, 'Gender similarities characterise math performance', *Science* 321, 2008, pp 494–495.

29. L Guiso, F Monte, P Sapienza & L Zingales, 'Culture, gender and math', *Science 320 (5880), 2008, pp 1164–1165.*

30. See Cordelia Fine, *Delusions of Gender: The Real Science Behind Sex Differences*, Icon Books, 2012, p 181.

31. Ibid, p 182.

32. Alred Binet quoted in Stephen Jay Gould, *The Mismeasure of Man*, Penguin, London, 1997, p 181.

33. Ibid.

34. Jim Flynn quoted in Marek Kohn, *The Race Gallery*, Jonathan Cape, London, 1995, p105.

35. James R Flynn, *What is Intelligence?*, Cambridge University Press, Cambridge, 2009, p36.

36. Interview with Howard Gardner in Dipin Damodharan of OneIndia News, 'The circuitry of multiple intelligence', *Education Insider*, 29 December 2012.

37. Adam Hampshire, Roger Highfield, Beth Parkin and Adrian Owen, 'Fractionating human intelligence', *Neuron*, 76 (6), 20 December 2012, pp1225–37.

38. Dr Roger Highfield, quoted in Steve Connor, 'IQ tests are 'fundamentally flawed' and using them alone to measure intelligence is a 'fallacy', study finds', *The Independent*, 21 December 2012.

39. IJ Deary, M Lawn and DJ Bartholomew, 'A conversation between Charles Spearman, Godfrey Thomson and Edward L Thorndike: the International Examinations Inquiry Meetings 1931–1938'; 'Correction to Deary, Lawn and Bartholomew (2008)', *History of Psychology*, 11 (3), 2008, p157.

40. CC Brigham, 'Intelligence tests of immigrant groups', *Psychological Review*, 37, 1930, p164.

41. Charles Spearman, quoted in Gould, op. cit., p298.

42. Cyril Burt, *The Backward Child*, D Appleton, New York, 1937, p110.

43. This is discussed in more detail in chapter 15 of my book, *Black Brain, White Brain: Is intelligence skin deep*, Thistle, 2015, pp 298–319.

44. Ibid.

45. Ibid.

46. Beverly Insel, Antonia Calafat, Xinhua Liu, Frederica Perera, Virginia Rush, Robin Whyatt, 'Persistent Associations between Maternal Prenatal Exposure to Phthalates on Child IQ at Age 7 Years', *Plos One*, December 10 2014.

47. Gavin Evans, *Black Brain, White Brain*, op cit.

48. Susan Farber, *Identical Twins Reared Apart*, Basic Books, New York, 1981.

49. Thomas J Bouchard Jr., David T Lykken, Matthew McGue, Nancy L Segal, and Auke Tellegen, 'Sources of human psychological differences: the Minnesota Study of Twins Reared Apart', *Science*, Vol. 250, 1990.

50. Nancy Segal quoted in Susan Dominus, 'The Mixed-Up Brothers of Bogota', *New York Times Magazine*, July 9 2015.

51. Paul Ehrlich, *Human Natures: Genes, Cultures and the Human Prospect*, Penguin, London, 2002, p 11.

52. Michel Duyme, Annick-Camille Dumaret and Stanislaw Tomkiewicz, 'How can we boost IQs of 'dull children'?: A late adoption study'. *Proceedings of the National Academy of Sciences* 96 (15): pp 8790–4, 1999.

53. Steven Pinker, op cit.

54. James R Flynn, *What is Intelligence?* Cambridge University Press, Cambridge, 2009

55. Jim Flynn, quoted in 'Women overtake men in IQ stakes for the first time since tests began', *Daily Record*, 6 July 2012.

## Chapter 9: Lady drivers and gentleman parkers

1. Steven Pinker in 'The science of gender and science – Pinker vs Spelke: a debate', Harvard University Mind/Brain/Behavior Initiative, 16 May 2005, *Edge: The Third Culture*, www.edge.org/3rd_culture/debate05/debate05_index.html

2. Ibid.

3. Ibid.

4. Ibid.

5. Ibid.

6. Ibid.

7. Elizabeth Spelke in Ibid.

8. Ibid.

9. Ibid.

10. Sarah-Jane Leslie, Andrei Cimpian, Meredth Meyer, Edward Freeland, 'Expectations of brilliance underlie gender distributions across academic disciplines," *Science*, 347 no 6219, 16 January 2015, p 262.

11. Ibid.

12. Ibid, pp 262–265.

13. Dr House was the hero of the American television comedy-drama series *House;* Hermione Granger was a heroine of the *Harry Potter* children's novels and films; Sherlock Holmes was the hero of the turn-of-the-century (19th-20th) crime novels by Arthur Conan-Doyle.

14. Andrei Cimpian quoted in Rachel Feltman, 'Gender gap: Women welcome in 'hard working' fields, but 'genius' fields are male dominated, study finds', *The Washington Post*, January 15 2015.

15. Andrei Cimpian quoted in Steve Connor, 'Women are less likely to become scientists because of a 'misconceived idea of brilliance', study finds', *The Independent*, January 15 2015.

16. Helen Mason, 'Go for it, girls, be confident and change the culture', *The Independent*, January 15 2015.

17. Cordelia Fine, *Delusions of Gender*, Icon Books, London, 2012, p27.

18. MJ Sharps, JL Price and JK Williams, 'Spatial cognition and gender: instructional and stimulus influences on mental image rotation performance', *Psychology of Women Quarterly*, 18 (3), 1994, pp413–25.

19. Cited in Cordelia Fine, op cit, p28.

20. Ibid.

21. A Moè, 'Are males always better than females at mental rotation? Exploring a gender belief explanation', *Learning and Individual Differences*, 19 (1), 2009, pp21–27.Cited in Cordelia Fine, ibid, p 28–29.

22. Fine, ibid, p 250.

23. Ibid, pp 27–28 & p 251.

24. C Goode, J Aronson and J Harder, 'Problems in the pipeline: stereotype threat and women's achievement in high-level math courses', *Journal of Applied Developmental Psychology*, 19 (1), 2008, p25. Cited in Fine, op cit, pp 30–31.

25. M Cadinu, A Maass, A Rosabianca and J Kiesner, 'Why do women underperform under stereoptype threat? Evidence for the role of negative thinking', *Psychological Science*, 16 (7), 2005, p 574.

26. Cordelia Fine, op cit, p 33.

27. See Ibid, pp27–33.

28. Claude Steele, 'Thin ice: stereotype threat and black college students', *Atlantic Monthly*, August 1999.

29. Janet Shibley Hyde, 'The Gender Similarities Hypothesis', *American Psychologist*, September 2005, pp 581–592.

30. Ibid.

31. Ibid, p 587.

32. Ibid, pp 587–588.

33. Ibid, p 590.

34. Nigel Short, 'Viva La Difference' *New in Chess*, 2015/2.

35. Nigel Short, quoted in *Sky News* April 20 2015.

36. Nigel Short writing in @nigelshortchess, *Twitter,* April 18 2015.

37. Nigel Short, quoted in Hannah Ellis-Petersen, 'Nigel Short says men 'hardwired' to be better chess players than women', *The Guardian*, April 20 2015.

38. Judit Polgar, on 'Women's Hour', *BBC Radio 4*, April 21 2015.

39. Judit Polgar quoted in Noah Rayman, 'Female Chess Legend: "We are Capable of the Same Fight as Any Other Man', *Time*, April 20 2015

40. Judit Polgar, @GMJuditPolgar, *Twitter* April 20 2015.

41. Robert Howard, 'Explaining male predominance in chess', *Chess News* June 19 2014.

42. Sue Maroroa quoted in Hannah Ellis-Petersen, op cit.

43. Sabrina Chevannes quoted in Ibid.

44. Rita Atkins quoted in Ibid.

45. Dr Gina Rippon on 'Women's Hour', *BBC Radio 4,* April 21 2015.

46. Sammons, P, Toth, K and Sylva, K,, Background to Success: Differences in A-level entries by ethnicity, neighbourhood and gender, *The Sutton Press*, London 2015.

47. JCQ data cited in George Arnett, 'A-level results: the full breakdown', *The Guardian*, August 14 2014.

48. Date from Higher Education Policy Institute, published in Sean Coughlan, 'Why do women get more university places?', BBC News, May 12 2016.

49. Data from David Matthews, 'Men in higher education: the numbers don't look good, guys', *Times Higher Education,* March 6 2014.

## Chapter 10: Men, women, words

1. Deborah Cameron quoted in Stephen Moss, 'Do women really talk more', *The Guardian,* November 27, 2006.

2. Louann Brizendine, *The Female Brain*, Morgan Road Books, New York, 2006.

3. Mark Liberman, 'Sex on the Brain', *The Boston Globe,* September 24 2006.

4. Ibid.

5. Ibid.

6. Mark Liberman quoted in *The Guardian,* op cit.

7. Mark Liberman, *The Boston Globe*, op cit.

8. Louann Brizendine quoted in *'The Guardian* op cit.

9. Janet Shibley Hyde, 'The Gender Similarities Hypothesis', *American Psychologist*, September 2005, pp 583–584.

10. J K Chambers, *Sociolinguistic Theory*, Blackwell, Oxford, 1995, p 136.

11. Janet Shibley Hyde & Marcia Linn, 'Gender Differences in Verbal Ability: A Meta-Analysis', *Psychological Bulletin*, 104, 1998, pp 53–69.

12. Deborah Cameron, *The Myth of Mars and Venus: Do men and women really speak different languages,* Oxford University Press, Oxford, 2007, p45.

13. Deborah James and Janice Drakish, 'Understanding Gender Differences in Amount of Talk,' in Deborah Tannen (ed), *Gender and Conversational Interaction,* Oxford University Press, New York, 1993, pp 281–212.

14. Deborah Cameron, *The Myth of Mars and Venus*, op cit, p 118.

15. Ibid, p 119.

16. M. Liberman, Sex-Linked Lexical Budgets, *http://itre.cis.upenn.edu/~myl/languagelog/archives/003420.html* , August 6 2006.

17. Men averaged 15,669 words per day; women 16,215. This slight difference, they said, 'does not meet conventional thresholds for statistical significance'. They added: 'Thus, the data fail to reveal a reliable sex difference in daily word use. Women and men both use on average about 16,000 words per day, with very large individual differences around this mean.' (M R Mehl, S Vazire, N Ramirez-Esparza, R B Slatcher and J W Pennebaker, 'Are women really more talkative than men?' *Science* July 6 2007, p 82).

18. Ibid.

19. Professor James Pennebaker quoted in *reality-check*, May 5 2007 – *https://www.reality-check.ca/threads/122575-Women-don-t-talk-more-than-men!*

20. Deborah Cameron quoted in *The Guardian*, op cit.

21. Deborah Cameron, *The Myth of Mars and Venus*, op cit pp 111–113.

22. Rhawn Joseph, 'The Evolution of Sex Differences in Language, Sexuality and Visual-Spatial Skills,' *Archives of Sexual Behavior* 29/1, 2000, *pp 35–66.*

23. Deborah Cameron, *The Myth of Mars and Venus,* op cit, p 120.

24. Ibid p 115.

25. Ibid, pp 7–8.

26. Ibid, p 12.

27. Thomas Hardy, *Far From the Madding Crowd*, Vintage Classics, 2015, p379.

28. See Don Kulick, 'Speaking as a Woman: Structure and Gender in Domestic Arguments in a New Guinea Village', *Cultural Anthropology* 8/4 1993, p 522. Cited in Deborah Cameron, *The Myth of Mars and Venus*, op cit, pp 32–33.

29. bid, p 34.

30. Elinor Ochs Keenan, 'Norm-Makers, Norm-Breakers: Uses of Speech by Men and Women in a Malagasy Community', in Richard Bauman and Joel Sherzer (eds), *Language, Gender and Sex in Comparative Perspective*, Cambridge University Press, Cambridge, 1987, p 119. Cited in Deborah Cameron, *The Myth of Mars and Venus*, op cit, pp 34–36.

31. Professor Sophie Scott, Woman's Hour, *BBC Radio 4*, May 13 2009.

## Chapter 11: EP and the predatory male

1. Janet Shibley Hyde, 'The Gender Similarities Hypothesis', *American Psychologist*, September 2005, p 586.

2. D Buss, D & D Schmitt, 'Evolutionary psychology and feminism', *Sex Roles*, 64(9–10), 2011, pp 768–787.

3. Monique Borgerhoff Mulder quoted in Natalie Angier, 'Skipping Spouse to Spouse Isn't Just a Man's Game,' *New York Times*, August 31 2009.

4. Sarah Blaffer Hrdy, quoted in Ibid.

5. Paul Ehrlich, *Human Natures: Genes, Cultures, and the Human Prospect*, Penguin, 2002, p 194.

6. Paul Ehrlich quoted in 'Paul Ehrlich challenges evolutionary psychology and the 'selfish gene' in his new book, Human Natures', *Stanford Report*, September 20, 2000.

7. See David Buss, 'The evolution of human mating', *Acta Psychologica Sinica*, 39, 2007, pp 502–512 and Buss, D., & D Schmitt, 'Evolutionary psychology and feminism' *Sex Roles*, 64, 2011, pp 768–787.

8. Adrienne Burgess, *Fatherhood Reclaimed: The Making of the Modern Father*, Vermilion, 1998, p 50.

9. Figures from 2003 study the UK Office for National Statistics, reported in 'More women marrying younger men', *BBC News*, 12 December 2003, and in Rosie Kinchen and Robin Henry, 'Playtime at the alter as girls bag their toy boys', *The Sunday Times*, August 5 2011.

10. Married Couple Family Groups, By Presence Of Own Children Under 18, And Age, Earnings, Education, And Race And Hispanic Origin Of Both Spouses",

*U.S. Census Bureau, Current Population Survey, 2013 Annual Social and Economic Supplement. 2013.*

11. Family Formation: Age at First Marriage', *Australia Social Trends 1997*, Australian Bureau of Statistics, June 19 1997.

12. Martin Kolk, 'Age differences between couples in Sweden,' *http://paa2012. princeton.edu/papers/122548 , 2012.*

13. United Nations Department of Economic and Social Affairs, 'World Marriage Patterns 2000' – http://www.un.org/esa/population/publications/worldmarriage/worldmarriagepatterns2000.pdf

14. Statistical release P0307: Marriages and Divorces 20112,' *Statistics South Africa*, December 10 2012.

15. Data from StatsSA, cited in Laura Grant, '10 Things about Marriange in South Africa', *Mail & Guardian* May 19 2015.

16. Study by Sven Drefahl of the Max Planck Institute for Demographic Research, published in *Demography*, cited in Ian Sample, 'Marrying a younger man increases a woman's mortality rate,' *The Guardian*, May 12 2010.

17. George Eliot, *Adam Bede*, Wordsworth Classics, 1997, p 130.

18. Kimya Dawson, 'I like giants' from her album 'Remember that I love you', *K Records* 2006.

19. EO Wilson quoted in Charles Jencks 'EP, Phone Home', in Hilary Rose & Steven Rose (eds), *Alas Poor Darwin: Arguments Against Evolutionary Psychology*, Vintage, London, 2000.

20. Roger Bingham quoted in Sharon Begley, 'Can We Blame our Bad Behavior on Stone-Age genes?' *Newsweek*, June 20 2009.

21. Ibid.

22. Elizabeth Cashdan, 'Waist-to Hip Ratio across Cultures: Trade-offs between androgen and estrogen traits', *University of Chicago Press – Journals*, vol 49, no 6, p 1104.

23. See for example Ehrlich, 2002, op cit, p 181.

24. Randy Thornhill & Craig T Palmer, *A Natural History of Rape: Biological Bases of Sexual Coercion*, The MIT Press, 2000, pp. 126, 133–135, 138–139.

25. Michael Kimmel, *An Unnatural History of Rape* In Travis, Cheryl Brown. *Evolution, Gender, and Rape*. MIT Press, 2003, pp. 221–233.

26. Kim Hill quoted in Sharon Begley, op cit.

27. Survey of 511 women and 487 men, headed by Dr Rachel Jewkes for the Medical Research Foundation, 2010. Results reported in Nastaya Tay, 'South Africa's Rape Study: More Than 1 in 3 Men Admit to Rape, *The World Post*, May 25, 2011.

28. A 2008 Medical Research Foundation survey, also headed by Dr Rachel Jewkes found that 28 percent of men in both the Eastern Cape and KwaZulu-Natal provinces admitted they had raped a woman or a girl. Ibid.

29. Elizabeth Ardafio-Schandorf, *Violence against women: the Ghanaian case,* United Nations Division for the Advancement of Women, 2005, p 9. The survey involved a sample of 3,047 people, 66 percent women and 34 percent men.

30. The United National Office on Drugs and Crime Global Study on Homicide table for murder rates per 100,000 inhabitants for 2012.

31. 'Rape Rate: Countries Compared', *NationMaster, http://www.nationmaster.com/country-info/stats/Crime/Rape-rate*

32. Martin Daly and Margo Wilson, 'Evolutionary Social Psychology and Family Homicide,' *American Association for the Advancement of Science,* 1988, p 521.

33. Ibid.

34. Ibid, p 523.

35. Figures cited in Sharon Begley, op cit.

36. Figures cited in Denis Campbell, 'More than 40% of domestic violence victims are male, report reveals', *The Guardian* January 7 2010.

37. Quoted in Ibid.

38. Office for National Statistics, Chapter 2, 'Homicide', February 13 2014.

## Chapter 12: Botox, Brazilians and boob jobs

1. Donald Symons, 'Beauty Is in the Adaptions of the Beholder: The Evolutionary Psychology of Human Female Sexual Attractiveness,' in Paul R Abramson & Steven Pinkerton (eds) 'Sexual Nature Sexual Culture' *University of Chicago Press,* 1995, pp 80–118.

2. George Eliot, *Adam Beed*, Wordsworth Classics, 2003, p 192.

3. Leo Tolstoy, *War and Peace,* Vintage, 2009, p 8.

4. American Osteopathic Association, 'The Real Harm of High Heels', *www.osteopathic.org*

5. Karmen Wai, Philip Douglas Thompson, Thomas Edmund Kimer, 'Fashion victim: rhabdomyolysis and bilateral peroneal and tibial neuropathies as a result of squatting in "skinny jeans"', *Journal of Neurology, Neurosurgery & Psychiatry*, June 23, 2015.

6. Ibid.

7. Naomi Wolf, 'The Beauty Myth', Vintage, 1991,p 17.

8. Simone de Beauvoir, *The Second Sex*, Vintage Classics, New Ed Edition, 1997, book 1, part 2, chapter 1.

9. Natasha Walter, *the new feminism*, Virago, 2011, p 86.

10. Ibid, p 105.

11. Natasha Walter, *Living Dolls: The Return of Sexism*, Virago, 2010, p 119.

12. Ibid, p 125.

13. Jan Moir, 'Give up the war paint? Don't be a powder puff Hillary!' *The Daily* Mail, May 10 2012.

14. Naomi Wolf, op cit, p 273.

15. Interview with Jane Couch, November 22 1996.

16. Iain Gately, 'Niger's dandy Gerewol festival', *The Times,* July 4 2004.

17. Naomi Wolf, op cit, p 12

18. Ibid, pp 12–13.

19. Donald Symons, op cit.

20. Afua Hirsch, 'Up Front', *OS Magazine* May 19 2013.

21. 'Revenue of the cosmetic industry in the United States from 2002 to 2014 (in billion US dollars), *statista: The Statistics Portal, http://www.statista.com/statistics/243742/revenue-of-the-cosmetic-industry-in-the-us/*

22. The figures thrown about in the media differ widely. For example, one study found that British women aged 45 to 54 spent an average of £2,238 per year on make-up and other forms of beautification, compared to £1,759 per year for teenagers. (*Escentual.com* data cited in Rosie Millard, 'The real lesson of Helen Mirren', *The Independent* April 16 2015). These amounts, however, seem like an exaggeration. A survey of 2,000 British women by Superdrug found that the average woman spent a little over £18,000 on face products in a lifetime or £279.41 a year. (Laura Mitchel, 'The Price of beauty: average woman spends £18,000 on face products in a lifetime,' *Express http://www.express.co.uk/life-style/style/433831/The-price-of-beauty-Average-woman-spends-18-000-on-face-products-in-a-lifetime*) If we add in hair, nails, Botox, cosmetic surgery, waxing and so-on, the average would be raised considerably, but nowhere near the £2,000 mark.

23. Figures cited in Women's Hour, *BBC Radio 4*, November 16 2015.

24. At least those are the figures cited by the Cambridge scholar Professor Mary Beard in 'Glad to be Grey', *BBC Radio 4*, March 3 2016.

25. British Association of Aesthetic Plastic Surgeons data quoted in 'Cosmetic surgery ops on the rise', *BBC News*, February 8 2016.

26. British Association of Aesthetic Plastic Surgeons data quoted in Rachel Moss, 'Cosmetic Surgery on the Rise, With 51,000 Brits Undergoing Procedures Last Year, *Huffington Post,* February 2 2016.

## Chapter 13: Super mums and not-so-new dads

1. Interview, Brian Hick, November 12 1998.
2. Office for National Statistics UK survey on working hours cited by Maurice Chittenden, 'Women scent victory in the chore wars ...', *The Sunday Times* July 31 2011.
3. Statistics extrapolated from the UK Time Use Survey, published by Oxford University's Centre for Time Use, cited in ibid.
4. Ibid.
5. Ibid.
6. Data from the European Commission's Gender Pay Gap survey for 2012 – http://ec.europa.eu/justice/gender-equality/gender-pay-gap/situation-europe/index_en.htm
7. Office for National Statistics UK data cited in Mona Chalabi, 'Single fathers: UK statistics', *The Guardian*, June 13 2013.
8. Data from Aviva, cited in Mark King, 'Stay-at-home dads on the up: one in seven fathers are main childcarers', *The Guardian,* October 25 2011.
9. Office for National Statistics Lifestyle Survey, cited in Mark King, ibid.
10. Interview, Jonathan Gershuny, June 25 1997.
11. Data from Oxford University and Economic and Social Research Council, cited in Roger Waite, 'Fond fathers nurture a family revival', *The Sunday Times* March 22 2009.
12. Office for National Statistics data cited by Chalabi, op cit.
13. Data from Mark King, op cit.
14. Data cited in Kim Parker and Wendy Wang, 'Modern Parenthood: Roles of Moms and Dads Converge as They Balance Work and Family', *Pew Research Center*, March 14 2013. See also Oriel Sullivan, 'Changing differences in the division of domestic labor; the case of education,' *Sociology Working Paper February 2011*, University of Oxford, p 7.
15. Data cited by Gretchen Livingston, 'The Rise of Single Fathers', *Pew Research Center,* July 2 2013.
16. Data drawn from Maddy Dychtwald, 'Influence: How Women's Soaring Economic Power Will Transform Our World for the Better', *Hachette Books*, 2010. See also Dychtwald quoted in John Harlow, 'Women poised to overtake men on pay', *The Sunday Times* June 20 2010.
17. Data from Andrew Beveridge of Queens College, New York, cited in Harlow, ibid.
18. Data from the survey conducted by the insurer LV=, reported in Steve Hawkes, 'Women now the main breadwinner in 41pc of homes', *The Telegraph*, July 18 2013.

19. Data from 'Secondary Analysis of the Gender Pay Gap: Changes in the gender pay gap over time', *Department for Culture, Media & Sport*, March 2014.

20. Office for National Statistics figures quoted in Kate Mansey & Daniel Bates, ' 'Men get broody as women chase jobs,' *The Sunday Times* February 13 2011.

21. Figures cited in Bryan Strong & Theodore Cohen, *The Marriage and Family Experience: Intimate Relationships in a Changing Society*, 12th edition, Watsworth Cengage Learning, 2013, p 358.

22. Andrew Beveridge in Harlow, op cit.

23. 'As marriage and parenthood drift apart, public is concerned about social impact: generation gap in values, behaviour,' Pew Research Center, July 1 2007.

24. Maddy Dychtwald, op cit.

25. Helen Fisher quoted in Mansey & Bates, op cit.

26. Statistical Bulletin: Families and Households 2013, *Office for National Statistics*, October 31 2013.

27. Data from the Office for National Statistics, reported in Steven Swinford, 'Most children will be born out of wedlock by 2016', *The Daily Telegraph* July 10 2013.

28. 'Unmarried Childbearing', *Centers for Disease Control and Prevention* report, January 22 2015.

29. Pew Research Centre analysis of American Community Survey (ACS) and Decennial Census data, published in Gretchen Livingston, 'Less than half of US kids today live in a "traditional" family', *Pew Research Center,* December 22 2014. *https://www.childwelfare.gov/pubPDFs/putative.pdf*

30. See 'The Rights of Unmarried Fathers', *State Statures*, January 2014

31. See for example, Gavin Evans, 'A father's place is in the home', *New Statesman* May 15 1998; Gavin Evans, 'Paternity Suits'. *Frank* June 1998 and Gavin Evans, 'Mum won't let me see you again, Dad', *The Independent* July28 1996.

32. See Gov.UK, 'Shared Parental Leave and Pay', April 2015 and Kevin Peachy, 'How the UK's new rules on parental leave work', *BBC News*, April 5 2015.

33. Research among 200 UK employers conducted by the firm My Family Care, reported in Hilary Osborne, 'Tiny proportion of new fathers are opting for shared parental leave,' *The Guardian*, April 5 2016.

34. Quoted in 'More or Less', *BBC Radio 4*, April 8 2015.

35. See 'Gender Equality in Sweden', *https://sweden.se/society/gender-equality-in-sweden/*

36. Swedish Institute of Labour Market Policy Evaluation study, March 2010, cited in Katrin Bennhold, 'In Swede, Men Can Have It All', *The New York Times* June 9 2010.

37. Melanie Phillips, *The Sex-Change State* (memorandum), Social Market Foundation, 1997 and Melanie Phillips, *The Sex-Change Society*, Social Market Foundation, 1999.

38. University of Yale study, cited in Cherry Norton, 'Fathers raise brighter kids' *Sunday Times* May 17 1998.

39. Study headed by Daniel Nettle from the Centre for Behaviour and Evolution at the Institute of Neuroscience at Newcastle University, published in the journal, *Evolution and Human Behaviour*, and cited in 'Fatherly contact and child intelligence', *NHS Choices*, October 1 2008.

40. Daniel Nettle quoted in 'Time with dad is time well spent', *New Scientist* December 8 2008.

41. Daniel Nettle quoted in Urmee Khan, 'Children who spend time with their fathers have a higher IQ', *The Telegraph* September 30 2008.

42. Adrienne Burgess, *Fatherhood Reclaimed: The Making of the Modern Father*, Vermilion, 1998.

43. Thomas More's diary of 1517 quoted in ibid, p 37.

44. Ibid, p 47–48.

45. George Eliot, *Silas Marner*, Everyman Library, 1976, p 145.

46. Ibid, pp 51–55.

47. Ibid, pp 153–4.

48. Burgess, op cit, p 57.

49. Barry Hewlett, *Intimate Fathers: the nature and content of Aka Pygmy paternal infant care*, University of Michigan Press, Ann Arbor, 1991.

50. Ibid, chapter 2.

51. Ibid. See also Burgess, op cit, pp 87–90.

52. Barry Hewlett quoted in Joanna Moorhead, 'Are the men of the African Aka tribe the best fathers in the world?' *The Guardian* June 15, 2005.

53. Hewlett, 1991, op cit, p 34.

54. Ibid pp 33–34.

55. Ibid p 31.

56. Ibid, p 34.

57. Pralip Kumar Narzary & Shilpi Mishra Sharma, 'Daughter Preference and Contraceptive-use in Matrilineal Tribal Societies in Meghalaya, India', *Journal of Health, Population and Nutrition,* June 31 2013. *http://www.ncbi.nlm.nih.gov/pmc/articles/PMC3702350/*

58. Narzary & Sharma, op cit.

59. Ibid.

60. See Julien Bouissou, 'It's a woman's world', *Le Monde* (republished in *The Guardian Weekly,* January 21 2011.

61. Ibid.

## Chapter 14. Maternal instinct, cousin love and the Cinderella effect.

1. Susan Pinker, *The Sexual Paradox: Men, Women and the Real Gender Gap*, Atlantic Books, 2008.
2. Ibid.
3. Ibid.
4. Ibid.
5. Ibid.
6. See Cordelia Fine, *Delusions of Gender: The Real Science Behind Sex Differences*, Icon Book, 2012, pp 148–149.
7. Ibid, p 149.
8. Ibid, p 150.
9. Discussed in chapter 6.
10. See, for example, Lise Eliot, *Pink Brain, Blue Brain: How Small Differences Grow into Troublesome Gaps and What We Can Do About it*, Oneworld, 2010, p 73.
11. Emily Bazelon, 'Hormones, Genes and the Corner Office', Sunday Book Review, *The New York Times* March 9 2008.
12. Susan Pinker, op cit.
13. Anna Fels, 'Women's Work', *The Washington Post* April 13 2008.
14. Lise Eliot, op cit, p 320.
15. A B W Fries, T E Ziegler, JR Kurian, et al, 'Early experience in humans is associated with changes in neuropeptides critical for regulating social behaviour', *Proceedings of the National Academy of Sciences USA*, 102,2005, pp 27237–40.
16. Ibid.
17. Ruth Feldman, Ilanit Gordon, Inna Schneiderman,Omri Weisman & Orna Zagoory-Sharon, 'National variations in maternal and paternal care are associated with systematic changes in oxytocin following parent-infant contact', *Psychoneuroendocrinology* 35 (8), September 2010, pp 1133–1141.
18. Eliot, op cit,, p 269.
19. Lee Gettler, quoted in 'This is your brain on fatherhood: Dads experience hormonal changes too, research shows', *NBC News*, June15 2013.
20. William Leith, 'At last, I think I know why so many women over 40 are experiencing a 'man shortage', *The Guardian*, January 21 2009.
21. Out of an initial sample of 195. The 56 students chose were those who had all four categories of cousin.
22. Joonghwan Jeon & David M Buss, 'Altruism towards cousins', *Proceedings of the Royal Society B*, 374 (1614) http://rspb.royalsocietypublishing.org/content/274/1614/1181.

23. Ibid.

24. Ibid.

25. Roger Highfield, 'Why we are closer to cousins from our mother's side', *The Telegraph* February 28 2007.

26. Alok Jha, 'Maternal cousins more likely to find favour, says study' *The Guardian* February 28 2007.

27. Joongwhan, op cit.

28. Alan Cumming, *Not My Father's Son: A Memoir*, Dey Street Books, 2014.

29. Martin Daly & Margo Wilson, 'Descriminative Parental Solicitude and the Relevance of Evolutionary Models to the Analysis of Motivational Systems' in M S Gazzaniga (ed) *The Cognitive Neurosciences*, MIT Press, 1995, p 1274.

30. David J Buller, *Adapting Minds: Evolutionary Psychology and the Persistent Quest for Human Nature*, MIT Press, 2006, p 350.

31. M Daly & M Wilson, 'Child abuse and other risks of not living with both parents" ' *Ethology and Sociobiology* 6 (4), 1985, p 197.

32. Martin Daly and Margot Wilson, *The Truth about Cinderella: a Darwinian View of Parental Love*, Yale University Press 1999, pp 37–38.

33. Martin Daly & Margot Wilson, *Homicide*, Aldine de Gruyter,1988, p 75.

34. Martin Daly and Margot Wilson, 'Child Abuse and Other Risks of Not Living with Both Parents, *Ethology and Sociobiology* 6, 1985, pp 201–202.

35. Martin Daly & Margot Wilson 1999, op cit, pp 32–33.

36. Ibid, p 32.

37. Ibid, p 30.

38. Steven Pinker in 'The Two Steves – Pinker vs. Rose – A Debate,' *Edge: The Third Culture,* March 25 1998.

39. Steven Pinker, *The Blank State: The Modern Denial of Human Nature*, Viking, 2002, p 164.

40. David Buss, *Evolutionary Psychology: The New Science of the Mind,* Allyn and Bacon, 1999, pp 202–203.

41. Catherine M Malkin, Michael E Lamb, 'Child Maltreatment: A Test of Sociobiological Theory, *Journal of Comparative Family Studies* 25, 1994 p 129.

42. See Buller, op cit, pp 363–364.

43. Hans Temrin, Susanne Buchmayer & Magnus Enquist, 'Stepparents and Infanticide: New Data Contradict Evolutionary Predictions,' *Proceedings of the Royal Society of London B, 263, 2000,* p 945.

44. Martin Daly & Margo Wilson, 'An Assessment of Some Proposed Exceptions to the Phenomenon of Nepotistic Discrimination against Stepchildren, *Annales Zoological Fennici* 38, 2001, pp 287–296.

45. Richard J Gelles & John W Harrop, 'The Risk of Abusive Violence among Children with Non-genetic Caretakers', *Family Relations* 40, pp 78–83.

46. Martin Daly & Margot Wilson, 'A Reply to Gelles: Stepchildren *Are* Disproportionately Abused, and Diverse Forms of Violence *Can* Share Causal Factors,' *Human Nature 2*, 1991, pp 419–426.

47. See Buller, op cit, pp 387–388.

48. Hilary Rose, 'Colonising the Social Sciences?', in Hilary Rose & Steven Rose (eds), *Alas Poor Darwin: Arguments Against Evolutionary Psychology*, Vintage, 2001, p 121.

49. bid, p 122.

50. Ibid.

51. Ibid, p 123.

52. Buller, op cit, p 372.

53. Hilda Parker & Seymour Parkers, 'Father-Daughter Sexual Abuse: An Emerging Perspective', *American Journal of Orthopsychiatry* 56, p 533.

54. Ibid, pp 531–549 and Buller, op cit p 373.

55. Buller, ibid, p 375.

56. Ibid, pp 401–409.

57. Tessa Crume, Carolyn DeGuiseppi, Tim Byers, Andrew P Sirotnak & Carol J Garrett, 'Underascertainment of Child Maltreatment Families by Death Certificates, 1990–1998', *Pediatrics* 110(2): e18, 2002, p 4 and Buller, op cit, p 408.

58. Buller, ibid, p 397–399.

59. Ibid, p 400.

60. Ibid, p 394

61. Ibid 376–378.

62. Ibid, p 379.

63. Ibid, p 380.

64. Ibid, p 381–2.

65. Ibid, p 401.

66. Friedrich Schiller, *The Robbers*, The Floating Press, 2010.

67. Buller, op cit, p 413.

68. See ibid, pp 414–416.

69. Ibid, p 417.

70. Ibid, p 412.

# BIBLIOGRAPHY

Abrahamson, P R and S D Pinkerton (eds), *Sexual Nature/Sexual Culture*, University of Chicago Press, Chicago, 1995

Alexander, G M and M Hines, 'Sex differences in response to children's toys in non-human primates', *Evolution and Human Behaviour*, 23 (6), 2002, pp 467–479

Alonso, WJ & C Schuck-Paim 'Sex-ratio conflicts, kin selection, and the evolution of altruism' *PNAS* 99 (10), pp 6843–6847

American Osteopathic Association, 'The Real Harm of High Heels', *www.osteo-pathic.org*

Angier, Natalie, 'Skipping Spouse to Spouse Isn't Just a Man's Game,' *New York Times*, August 31 2009

Ardafio-Schandorf, Elizabeth, *Violence against women: the Ghanaian case,* United Nations Division for the Advancement of Women, 2005

Arnett, George, 'A-level results: the full breakdown', *The Guardian*, August 14 2014

Ardry Robert, *The Territorial Imperative: A Personal Inquiry Into the Animals Origins of Property and Nations*, Collins, London, 1967

Augustin, 'Sally, Shopping Brings Out Our Inner Hunter/Gatherer,' *Psychology Today,* December 24 2010.

Bailey, Laura, 'Genes account for male, female shopping styles,' *The University Record Online*, University of Michigan, December 7 2009

Baron-Cohen, Simon, *Mindblindness: An Essay on Autism and Theory of Mind*, MIT Press, Cambridge, Massachusetts, 1995

Baron-Cohen, Simon, *The Essential Difference: Men, Women and the Extreme Male Brain*, London, Allen Lane, 2003

Baron-Cohen, Simon, R Knickmeyer & M Belmonte, 'Sex differences in the brain: Implications for explaining autism,' *Science*, 310, 2005

Baron-Cohen, Simon, 'Don't blame it on the biological determinists,' Comment is free, *The Guardian*, May 4 2010

315

Bateson, Patrick, 'Taking the Stink out of Instinct', *Alas Poor Darwin: Arguments Against Evolutionary Psychology*, Vintage, London, 2001

Niel Barnard, *Secret Revolution: Memoirs of a Spy Boss'*, Tafelberg, 2015

Barrow, Nora (ed), *The Autobiography of Charles Darwin, 1809–1882, with Original Omissions Restored*, Harcourt, Brace, 1958

Bazelon, Emily, 'Hormones, Genes and the Corner Office', Sunday Book Review, *The New York Times* March 9 2008

Beard, Mary, 'Glad to be Grey', *BBC Radio 4*, March 3 2016.

Begley, Sharon, 'Can We Blame our Bad Behavior on Stone-Age genes?' *Newsweek*, June 20 2009

Bennhold, Katrin, 'In Swede, Men Can Have It All', *The New York Times* June 9 2010

Blackmore, Susan, *The Meme Machine*, Oxford University Press, 1999

Blair, C, "How similar are fluid cognition and general intelligence? A developmental neuroscience perspective on fluid cognition as an aspect of human cognitive ability," *Behavioral and Brain Sciences* 29, pp 109–160

Blinkhorn, Steve, 'Gender Bender', *Nature*, Vol 438, 3rd November 2005, p 31

Bocklandt, S; S Horvath, E Vilain, D.H. Hameer, "Extreme skewing of X chromosome inactivation in mothers of homosexual men", *Human Genetics* 118 (6), February 2006, pp 691–694

Bouchard, Thomas J Jr.; David T. Lykken, Matthew McGue, Nancy L. Segal, and Auke Tellegen, "Sources of Human Psychological Differences: The Minnesota Study of Twins Reared Apart," *Science*, Vol. 250, 1990

Bouissou, Julien, 'It's a woman's world', *Le Monde* (republished in *The Guardian Weekly*, January 21 2011

Brigham, C C, *A study of American intelligence*, Princeton University Press, Princeton, New Jersey, 1923

Brigham, C C, "Intelligence tests of immigrant groups", *Psychological Review* 37, 1930

Brizendine, Louanne, *The Female Brain*, Morgan Road Books, New York, 2006

Bugnyar, Thomas, Stephan A Reber & Cameron Buckner, 'Ravens attribute visual access to unseen competitors', *Nature Communications* 7, February 2 2016

Buller, David J, *Adapting Minds*, Bradford Books, MIT Press, Cambridge, Massachusetts, 2006

Bunn, Geoff, Episode 10, "A History of the Brain", *BBC Radio 4*, November 18 2011

Adrienne Burgess, *Fatherhood Reclaimed: The Making of the Modern Father*, Vermilion, 1998, p 50

Burt, Cyril, *The Backward Child*, D Appleton, New York, 1937

Burt, Cyril, "Factor analysis and its neurological basis", *British Journal of Statistical Psychology* 14 1961

Burt, Cyril, "Ability and income", *British Journal of Educational Psychology* 13, 1943

Burton, Francis, 'Ethology and the development of sex and gender identity in non-human primates,' *Acta Biotheoretica* 26 (1), 1977, pp 1–18

Buss, David, *Evolutionary Psychology: The New Science of the Mind,* Allyn and Bacon, 1999

Buss, David, (ed), *The Handbook of Evolutionary Psychology*, John Wiley & Sons, New Jersey, 2005

Buss, David, 'The evolution of human mating', *Acta Psychologica Sinica*, 39, 2007, pp 502–512

Buss, David & D Schmitt, 'Evolutionary psychology and feminism', *Sex Roles*, 64(9–10), 2011, pp 768–787

Cadinu, M; A Maass, A Rosabianca & J Kiesner, "Why do women underperform under stereoptype threat? Evidence for the role of negative thinking", *Psychological Science* 16(7), 2005

Campbell, F A and C T Ramey, "Effects of early intervention on intellectual and academic achievement: A follow-up study of children from low-income familes," Child Development 65, 1994, pp 684–698

Cameron, Deborah, *The Myth of Mars and Venus: Do men and women really speak different languages,* Oxford University Press, Oxford, 2007

Campbell, Denis, 'More than 40% of domestic violence victims are male, report reveals', *The Guardian* January 7 2010

Carruthers, Malcolm, *The Testosterone Revolution*, Thorsons, 2001

Cashdan, Elizabeth, 'Waist-to Hip Ratio across Cultures: Trade-offs between androgen and estrogen traits', *University of Chicago Press – Journals,* vol 49, no 6, p 1104

Castelli, L, V De Dea & D Nesdale, "Learning social attitudes: Children's sensitivity to non-verbal behaviours of adult models during interracial interactions", *Personality and Social Psychology Bulletin*, 34(11)

Castelli, L, C Zogmaiser & S Tomelleri, "The transmission of racial attitudes within the family", *Developmental Psychology* 45(2), pp 586–591

Chambers, J K, *Sociolinguistic Theory*, Blackwell, Oxford, 1995, p 136

Chittenden, Maurice, 'Women scent victory in the chore wars ...', *The Sunday Times* July 31 2011

Chodorow, Nancy, *The Reproduction of Mothering*, New Haven, Yale University Press, 1999

# GAVIN EVANS

Chodorow, Nancy, *Feminism and Psychoanalytic Theory*, Yale University Press, 1991

Clearfield, M W & N M Nelson, 'Sex Differences in mothers' speech and play behaviour with 6, 9 and 14-month-old infants', *Sex Roles*, 54, pp 127–137

Cohen, Tamara, 'Surprise! Men and women really ARE different: Sexes share just 10 per cent of their personality traits. Psychologists reach verdict after probing 10,000 people', *Daily Mail*, January 4 2012

Collins, Nick, 'Men and women have distinct personalities', Daily Telegraph, January 4 2012

Connellan, J; S Baron-Cohen, S Wheelwright, A Batki & J Ahluwalia, 'Sex differences in human neonatal social perception,' *Infant Behaviour & Development*, 23, 2000, pp 113–118

Connolly, Kevin and Margaret Martlew (eds), 'altruism, *Psychologically Speaking: A Book of Quotations,* BPS Books, 1999

Connor, Steve, "IQ tests are 'fundamentally flawed' and using them alone to measure intelligence is a 'fallacy', study finds," *The Independent* 21 December 2012

Connor, Steve, "Fear can be inherited via father's sperm, says study," *The Independent*, December 2 2013

Connor, Steve, 'The hardwired difference between male and female brains could explain why men are 'better at map reading", *The Independent*, December 2 2013

Connor, Steve, 'Men up to five times more likely to commit sex crimes than the average male if they have brother or father convicted of a sex offence,' *The Independent,* April 8 2015

Connor, Steve, 'Women are less likely to become scientists because of a 'misconceived idea of brilliance', study finds', *The Independent*, January 15 2015

Cooney, CA, AA Dave and GL Wolff, "Maternal Methyl Supplements in Mice Affect Epigenetic Variation and DNA Methylation of Offspring" in *Journal of Nutrition* 132 (8 Suppl), 2002,: 2393S–2400S

Cosmides, Leda and John Tooby, 'Evolutionary Psychology: A Primer', Center for Evolutionary Psychology, University of California, Santa Barbara, January 13 1997, *http://www.cep.ucsb.edu/primer.html*

Cosmides, Leda and John Tooby, 'The Modular Nature of Human Intelligence', in A B Scheibel and J W Schopf (eds), *The origin and Evolution of Human Intelligence*, Jones and Bartlett, Sudbury, Massachusetts, 1997

Cosmides, Leda and John Tooby quoted in David Buss (ed), *The Handbook of Evolutionary Psychology*, John Wiley & Sons, New Jersey, 2005

Cronin, Helena, 'Why do men dominate society' in James Randerson, 'Second thoughts on life, the universe and everything by the world's best brains', *The Guardian* January 1 2008

Crume, Tessa, Carolyn DeGuiseppi, Tim Byers, Andrew P Sirotnak & Carol J Garrett, 'Underascertainment of Child Maltreatment Families by Death Certificates, 1990–1998', *Pediatrics* 110(2): e18, 2002

Culpin, I, JE Heron, R Araya, R Melotti and CJ Johnson, 'Father absence and depressive symptoms in adolescence: findings from a UK cohort', *Psychological Medicine*, May 14 2013

Cumming, Alan, *Not My Father's Son: A Memoir*, Dey Street Books, 2014

Dabbs, J, D De la Rue and PM Williams, 'Testosterone and occupational choice: Actors, ministers and other men', *Journal of Personality and Social Psychology* 1990; 59, 1261–5

Dalal, F, "The Racism of Jung", *Race and Class* 29/3, 1988

Daley, T C; S E Whaley, MD Sigman, M P Espinosa & C Neumann, "IQ on the rise: The Flynn effect in rural Kenyan children." *Psychological Science* 24, 2003

Daly, Martin & Margo Wilson, 'Child abuse and other risks of not living with both parents'' *Ethology and Sociobiology* 6 (4), 1985

Daly, Martin and Margot Wilson, 'Child Abuse and Other Risks of Not Living with Both Parents, *Ethology and Sociobiology* 6, 1985, pp 201–202

Daly, Martin and Margo Wilson, 'Evolutionary Social Psychology and Family Homicide,' *American Association for the Advancement of Science,* 1988

Daly, Martin & Margot Wilson, *Homicide*, Aldine de Gruyter, 1988

Daly, Martin & Margot Wilson, 'A Reply to Gelles: Stepchildren *Are* Disproportionately Abused, and Diverse Forms of Violence *Can* Share Causal Factors,' *Human Nature* 2, 1991, pp 419–426

Daly, Martin & Margo Wilson, 'Descriminative Parental Solicitude and the Relevance of Evolutionary Models to the Analysis of Motivational Systems' in M S Gazzaniga (ed) *The Cognitive Neurosciences*, MIT Press, 1995

Daly, Martin and Margot Wilson, *The Truth about Cinderella: a Darwinian View of Parental Love*, Yale University Press 1999

Daly, Martin & Margo Wilson, 'An Assessment of Some Proposed Exceptions to the Phenomenon of Nepotistic Discrimination against Stepchildren, *Annales Zoological Fennici* 38, 2001

Damodharan, Dipin, Interview with Howard Gardner, "The circuitry of multiple intelligence", , *Education Insider*, December 29 2012

Darwin, Charles, *On the Origin of Species,* Murray, London, 1859

Darwin, Charles, *The Descent of Man and Selection in Relation to Sex*, 1st editon, John Murray, 1874

Darwin, Charles, *The Descent of Man and Selection in Relation to Sex*, 2nd edition, John Murray, 1874

Darwin, Erasmus, *Zoonomia; or the Laws of Organic Life*, (4th American ed.), Edward Earle, Philadelphia

Dawkins, Richard, *The Selfish Gene*, Oxford University Press, 1976

Dawkins, Richard, *The Selfish Gene*, Oxford University Press, 1989

Dawkins, Richard, *The Selfish Gene* (30th anniversary edition), Oxford University Press, 2006

Dawkins, Richard, "It's All in the Genes", *Sunday Times*, March 12 2006

Dawkins, Richard, *The Ancestors Tale: A Pilgrimage to the Dawn of Evolution*, Mariner Books, 2005

Dawkins, Richard, *The God Delusion*, Bantam Press, 2006, pp 218–220

Dawkins, Richard, interviewed for the BBC "Belief" programme in April 2004, republished October 22 2009 *http://www.bbc.co.uk/religion/religions/atheism/people/dawkins.shtml*

Dawkins, Richard, "Growing Up in Ethology", chapter 9 of Drikamer, L & D Dewsxbury, *Leaders of Animal Behaviour – The Second Generation*, Cambridge University Press, Cambridge, 2009

Richard Dawkins interviewed on YouTube, on 'gay genes, April 2010, *http://www.youtube.com/watch?v=MHDCAllQgS0*

Dawkins, Richard, interviewed on "Midweek", BBC Radio 4, December 11, 2013

Dawson, Kimya, 'I like giants' from her album 'Remember that I love you', *K Records* 2006

Deary, Ian J, Graham Thorpe, Valerie Wilson, John M Starr, Lawrence J Whalley, 'Population sex differences in IQ at age 11: the Scottish mental survey' *Intelligence*, 31 vol 6, November–December 2003, pp 537–538

Deary, I J; M Lawn & D J Bartholomew. "A conversation between Charles Spearman, Godfrey Thomson, and Edward L. Thorndike: The International Examinations Inquiry Meetings 1931–1938": Correction to Deary, Lawn, and Bartholomew (2008)". *History of Psychology* 11 (3), 2008

De Beauvoir, Simone, *The Second Sex*, Vintage Classics, New Ed Edition, 1997

Dennett, Daniel D, *Darwin's Dangerous Idea: Evolution and the Meanings of Life*, Simon & Schuster, 1995

De Waal, Frans, 'Bonobo Sex and Society', *Scientific American*, March 1995, pp 82–88

De Waal, Frans, 'Sex as an alternative to aggression in the bonobo', in P R Abrahamson and S D Pinkerton (eds), *Sexual Nature/Sexual Culture*, University of Chicago Press, Chicago, 1995

Donovan, W N Taylor & L Leavitt, 'Maternal sensory sensitivity and response bias in detecting change in infant facial expressions: Maternal self-efficacy and infant gender labelling, *Infant Behaviour and Development* 30(3), pp 436–452

Douglas, Ed, "Darwin's Natural Heir", *The Guardian*, February 17 2001

Dodds, David, "The Social Life of Genes", *Pacific Standard*, September 3 2013

Dominus, Susan, 'The Mixed-Up Brothers of Bogota', *New York Times Magazine*, July 9 2015

Dusek, Val, Sociology Sanitized: The Evolutionary Psychology and Genetic Selectionism Debates', *Science as Culture*

Duyme, Michel, Annick-Camille Dumaret and Stanislaw Tomkiewicz, 'How can we boost IQs of 'dull children'?: A late adoption study'. *Proceedings of the National Academy of Sciences* 96 (15): pp 8790–4, 1999

Dychtwald, Maddy, 'Influence: How Women's Soaring Economic Power Will Transform Our World for the Better', *Hachette Books*, 2010

Dye, Lee, 'Why Women Love to Shop', *abc NEWS*, December 9 2009

Ehrlich, Paul, *Human Natures: Genes, Cultures and the Human Prospect* Shearwater Books/Island Press, 2002

Eliot, George, *Silas Marner*, Everyman Library, 1976

Eliot, George, *Adam Bede,* Wordsworth Classics, 1997

Eliot, Lise, *Pink Brain Blue Brain: How Small Differences Grow into Troublesome Gaps – and What We Can Do About It*, Oneworld, 2012

Niles Eldredge, *Time Frames*, Simon & Schuster, 1985

Ellis-Petersen, Hannah, 'Nigel Short says men 'hardwired' to be better chess players than women', *The Guardian*, April 20 2015

European Commission, European Commission's Gender Pay Gap survey for 2012 – http://ec.europa.eu/justice/gender-equality/gender-pay-gap/situation-europe/index_en.htm

Evans, Gavin, 'Mum won't let me see you again, Dad', *The Independent* July28 1996

Evans, Gavin, 'A father's place is in the home', *New Statesman* May 15 1998

Evans, Gavin, 'Paternity Suits'. *Frank* June 1998

Evans, Gavin, *Black Brain, White Brain: Is intelligence skin deep?* Thistle, London & Jonathan Ball, Cape Town, 2015

Everett, Daniel L, *Don't Sleep, There Are Snakes: Life and Language in the Amazonian Jungle*, Pantheon, 2008

Farber, Susan, *Identical Twins Reared Apart*, Basic Books, New York, 1981

Fausto-Sterling, Anne, *Sexing the Body*, Basic Books, New York, 2000

Fausto-Sterling, Anne, 'Beyond Difference: Feminism and Evolutionary Psychology', in *Alas Poor Darwin: Arguments Against Evolutionary Psychology,* Vintage, London, 2001

Feingold, A, 'Gender Differences in variability in intellectual abilities: cross-cultural perspective' in *Sex Roles*, 30 (1/2), 1994, pp 81–92

GAVIN EVANS

Fels, Anna, 'Women's Work', *The Washington Post* April 13 2008

Fluehr-Lobban, Caroline, 'Nubian Queens in the Nile Valley and Afro-Asiatic Cultural History', Museum of Fine Arts, Boston, 1998

Ron Federici, "Dr Ronald Federici: Romanian Orphans Q&A", in *Developments in Therapy*, June 25, 1999 – *http://developmentsintherapy.wordpress.com/2010/04/17/dr-ronald-federici-romanian-orphans-qa*

Feldman, Ruth, Ilanit Gordon, Inna Schneiderman,Omri Weisman & Orna Zagoory-Sharon, 'National variations in maternal and paternal care are associated with systematic changes in oxytocin following parent-infant contact', *Psychoneuroendocrinology* 35 (8), September 2010, pp 1133–1141

Feltman, Rachel, 'Gender gap: Women welcome in 'hard working' fields, but 'genius' fields are male dominated, study finds', *The Washington Post*, January 15 2015

Fernandez, Alvaro, "Can Intelligence Be Trained? Martin Buschkuehl shows how" *SharpBrains*, May 13 1998, http://sharpbrains.com/blog/2008/05/13/can-intelligence-be-trained-martin-buschkuehl-shows-how/

Fine, Cordelia, *Delusions of Gender*, Icon Books, London, 2012

Flintoff, John-Paul and Jonathan Leake, "How to make your child more intelligent," *The Sunday Times*, May 17 2009

James R Flynn, *What is Intelligence*, Cambridge University Press, Cambridge, 2009

Freud, Sigmund, *Civilization, Society and Religion, vol 12,* Penguin Freud Library, 1991.

Freud, Sigmund, *The Future of an Illusion*, Pacific Publishing Studio, 2010

Freud, Sigmund, 'Some Psychological Consequences of the Anatomical Distinction between the Sexes', paper delivered by Anna Freud at the Hamburg International Psycho-Analytical Congress, September 3, 1925, and published in the International Journal of Psychoanalysis V111, p 138

Fries, A B W; T E Ziegler, JR Kurian, et al, 'Early experience in humans is associated with changes in neuropeptides critical for regulating social behaviour', *Proceedings of the National Academy of Sciences USA,* 102,2005, pp 27237–40

Gaeggi,Susanne; Martin Buschkuehl, John Jonides & Water J Perrid, "Improving fluid intelligence with training on working memory," *Proceedings of the National Academy of Sciences of the United States of America*, March 18 2008

Gagneux, P; D S Woodruff and C Boesch, 'Furtive mating in female chimpanzees,' *Nature* 387, 1997, pp 358–359

Galton, Francis, *Hereditary Genius: An Inquiry into its Laws and Consequences*, London, Macmillan, 1892

Garner, Richard, "Working-class white boys do worst in class", *The Independent*, September 3 2013

Gately, Iain, 'Niger's dandy Gerewol festival', *The Times*, July 4 2004

Gazzaniga, M S (ed) *The Cognitive Neurosciences*, MIT Press, 1995

Gelles, Richard J & John W Harrop, 'The Risk of Abusive Violence among Children with Non-genetic Caretakers', *Family Relations* 40, pp 78–83

Gerhardt, Sue, *Why Love Matters: How Affection Shapes a Baby's Brain*, Routledge, 2010

Ghose, Tia, "Light Drinking While Pregnant Could Lower Baby's IQ", *livescience*, November 14 2012

Gilmore, J H; W Lin, M Prastawa, C Looney, Y Vetsa, R Knickmeyer et al, 'Regional gray matter growth, sexual dimorphism and cerebral asymmetry in the neonatal brain,' *Journal of Neuroscience* 27(6), 2007, pp 1255–1260

Gleick, James, *Isaac Newton*, Fourth Estate, London, 2003

Goldacre, Ben, 'Out of the Blue', *The Guardian*, August 25 2007

Goldschmidt, L; G A Richardson, J Wilford & N L Day, "Prenatal marijuana exposure and intelligence test performance at age 6", University of Pittsburgh Medical Centre, PA, USA, *Journal of American Academic Child and Adolescent Psychiatry* 47 (3), March 2008, pp 254–263

Goode, C; J Aronson & J Harder, "Problems in the pipeline: Stereotype threat and women's achievement in high-level math courses," *Journal of Applied Developmental Psychology*, 19(1), 2008

Gould, Stephen Jay and Richard Lewontin, "The Spandrels of San Marco and the Panglossian paradigm: a critique of the adaptationist programme," *Proceedings of the Royal Society of London*, Series B, Vol 205, No 1161 1979, pp 581–589

Gould, Stephen Jay, *The Mismeasure of Man*, Penguin, London, 1997

Gould, Stephen Jay, "Darwinian Fundamentalism," *The New York Review of Books*, June 12 1997

Gould, Stephen Jay, "More Things in Heaven and Earth", in H Rose & S Rose, *Alas Poor Darwin*, Vintage, London, 2001

Gould, Stephen Jay and Steven Rose (eds), *The Richness of Life: The Essential Stephen Jay Gould*, WW Norton & Co, 2007

Gould, Stephen Jay, "Evolutionary Psychology: An Exchange", *The New York Review of Books*, vol 44, no 15, October 1997, *www.nybooks.com/articles/1070* , pp 3–4

Gowaty, Patricia Adair, 'Field Studies of Parental Care in Birds: New Data Focus Questions on Variation Among Females', in CT Snowdon and JS Rosenblatt (eds), *Advances in the Study of Behaviour*, 24, 1995

Gray, John, *Men Are From Mars, Women Are From Venus*, HarperCollins, New York, 1992

Grossi, A and G Grossi, 'Picking Barbie's brain: Inherent sex differences in scientific ability', *Journal of Interdisciplinary Feminist Thought*, 2 (1), Article 5, 2007, p 9;

L Elliot, op cit, pp 72–74Groves, Jason, "Working class white boys still at the bottom of learning table, despite millions spent by Labour," *Daily Mail*, 1 January 2011

Guiso, L; F Monte, P Sapienza & L Zingales, 'Culture, gender and math', *Science 320 (5880), 2008, pp 1164–1165*

Hall, Stephen S, "Darwin's Rottweiler", *Discover*, September 9, 2005

Hamilton, W D, 'The Genetical Evolution of Social Behaviour'. *Journal of Theoretical Biology* 7 (1), 1964, pp 1–16

Hamilton, W D, 'A review of *Dysgenics: Genetic Deterioration in Modern Populations*', *Annals of Human Genetics,* 64 (4), 2000, pp363–74

Hampshire, Adam, Highfield, R, Parkin, B & Owen, A, "Fractionating Human Intelligence", *Neuron* 76 (6), December 20 2012, pp 1225–1237

Hanon, A, 'What else can you expect from a caveman?' *Toronto Sun* December 13 2009

Hardy, Thomas, *Far From the Madding Crowd*, Vintage Classics, 2015

Harlow, John, 'Women poised to overtake men on pay', *The Sunday Times* June 20 2010

Hassett, J M; E R Siebert & K Wallen, 'Sex differences in rhesus monkey toy preference s parallel those of children,' *Hormones and Behaviour* 54(3) 2008, pp 359–364. See also Fine (2010), Ibid, p p 124–125

Hawkes, Steve, Women now the main breadwinner in 41pc of homes', *The Telegraph*, July 18 2013

Hearnshaw, Leslie, *Cyril Burt: Psychologist*, Hodder and Stoughton, London, 1979

Heijmans, B T, Elmar W Tobi, Aryeh D Stein, Hein Putter, Gerard J Blauw, Ezra S Susser, P Eliine Slagboom & L H Lumey, "Persistent epigenetic differences associated with prenatal exposure to famine in humans", *Proceedings of the National Academy of Sciences of America*, 105 (44), 2008

Hewlett, Barry, *Intimate Fathers: the nature and content of Aka Pygmy paternal infant care,* University of Michigan Press, Ann Arbor, 1991

Highfield, Roger, 'Why we are closer to cousins from our mother's side', *The Telegraph* February 28 2007

Hirsch, Afua, 'Up Front', *OS Magazine* May 19 2013

Hobaiter, Catherine, Timothee Poisot, Klaus Zuberbuhler, William Hoppitt & Thibaud Gruber, 'Social Network Analysis Shows Direct Evidence for Social Transmission of Tool Use in Wild Chimpanzees,' *PLOS Biology*, September 30 2014

Hyde, J S; S M Lindberg, M C Linn, A B Ellis & CC Williams, 'Gender similarities characterise math performance', *Science* 321, 2008, pp 494–495

Ingalhalikara, Madhura; Alex Smitha,Drew Parkera, Theodore D. Satterthwaiteb, Mark A. Elliott, Kosha Ruparelb, Hakon Hakonarsond, Raquel E. Gurb, Ruben C. Gurb & Ragini Verma, 'Sex differences in the structural connectome of the human brain', *Proceedings of the National Academy of Sciences*, vol. 111 no. 2, January 2014

Howard, Robert, 'Explaining male predominance in chess', *Chess News* June 19 2014

Hurley, Dan, "Can you make yourself smarter?" *New York Times Magazine*, April 18 2012

IANS, 'Genes dictate shopping styles,' *The Hindu*, December 4 2009

Insel, Beverly, Antonia Calafat, Xinhua Liu, Frederica Perera, Virginia Rush, Robin Whyatt, 'Persistent Associations between Maternal Prenatal Exposure to Phthalates on Child IQ at Age 7 Years', *Plos One*, December 10 2014

Irwing, Paul and Richard Lynn, Sex differences in means and variability on the progressive matrices in university students: A meta-analysis. *British Journal of Psychology*, 96, 2005, pp 505–524

Jha, Alok, 'Maternal cousins more likely to find favour, says study' *The Guardian* February 28 2007.

Jencks, Charles, 'EP, Phone Home', in Hilary and Steven Rose (eds), *Alas Poor Darwin: Arguments Against Evolutionary Psychology*, Vintage, 2001

Jeon, Joonghwan & David M Buss, 'Altruism towards cousins', *Proceedings of the Royal Society B*, 374 (1614

Joel, Daphna, Zohar Berman, Ido Tavor, Nadav Wexler, Olga Gager, Yaniv Stein, Nisan Shefi, Jared Pool, Sebastian Urchs, Daniel S Margulies, Franziskus Liem, Jurgen Hanggi, Lutz Jancke & Yaniv Assaf, 'Sex beyond genitalia: The human brain mosaic', *Proceedings of the National Academy of Sciences of the United States of America*, vol 112, no 50, pp 15468–15473

Johnson, John A, Joseph Carroll, Jonathan Gottschall and Daniel Kruger, 'Hierarchy in the Library: Egalitarian Dynamics in Victorian Novels, *Evolutionary Psychology*, vol, no 4, 2008, pp715–738

Johnson, Steven B, *Everything bad is good for you: How today's popular culture is actually making us smarter*, Rimerhead Books, New York, 2005

Jordan-Young, Rebecca, *Brain Storm: The Flaws in the Science of Sex Differences*, Harvard University Press

Joseph, Rhawn, 'The Evolution of Sex Differences in Language, Sexuality and Visual-Spatial Skills,' *Archives of Sexual Behavior 29/1, 2000, pp 35–66*

Jung, Carl, *Memories, Dreams, Reflections*, ed A Jaffe, Collins, New York, 1973

Jung, Carl, *Collected Works 10: Civilisation in Transition*, Princeton University Press, 1970

Jung, Carl, *The Archetypes and the Collective Unconscious*, Routledge and Kegan Paul, London, 1996

Jung, Carl, 'The significance of the father in the destiny of the individual' in A Samuals, *The Father: contemporary Jungian perspectives*, Free Association Books, London, 1985

Khan, Urmee, 'Children who spend time with their fathers have a higher IQ', *The Telegraph* September 30 2008

Kalow, Werner & Harold Kalant from the Department of Pharmacology at the University of Toronto on selection at species level – "Evolutionary Psychology: An Exchange", *The New York Review of Books*, vol 44, no 15, October 1997, *www.nybooks.com/articles/1070* , pp 3–4

Karmilof-Smith, Annette, 'Why Babies' Brains Are Not Swiss Army Knives' in Hilary and Steven Rose (eds), *Alas Poor Darwin: Arguments Against Evolutionary Psychology*, Vintage, London, 2001

Keenan, Elinor Ochs, 'Norm-Makers, Norm-Breakers: Uses of Speech by Men and Women in a Malagasy Community', in Richard Bauman and Joel Sherzer (eds), *Language, Gender and Sex in Comparative Perspective*, Cambridge University Press, Cambridge, 1987, p 119

Kevles, D J, "Testing the army's intelligence: psychologists and the military in World War 1", *Journal of American History* 55, 1968, pp 565–581

Kimmel, Michael, *An Unnatural History of Rape* In Travis, Cheryl Brown. *Evolution, Gender, and Rape.* MIT Press, 2003, pp. 221–233

Kimura, Mootoo, *The neutral theory of molecular evolution*, Cambridge University Press, Cambridge, 1968

Kinchen, Rosie and Robin Henry, 'Playtime at the alter as girls bag their toy boys', *The Sunday Times,* August 5 2011

King, Mark, 'Stay-at-home dads on the up: one in seven fathers are main childcarers', *The Guardian,* October 25 2011

Knapton, Sarah, 'Sex offending is written in DNA of some men, Oxford University finds', *Daily Telegraph*, April 9 2015

Knecht, S; B Dräger, M Deppe, L Bobe, H Lohmann, A Flöel, E Ringelstein & H Henningsen. 'Handedness and hemispheric language dominance in healthy humans'. *Brain* 123 (12), 2000, pp 2512–2518

Kohn, Marek, *The Race Gallery*, Jonathan Cape, London, 1995, p105

Kolk, Martin, 'Age differences between couples in Sweden,' *http://paa2012.princeton. edu/papers/122548, 2012*

Krebs, J and NDavies (eds), *Behavioural Ecology*, Blackwell Scientific 1994

Kruger, D & Byker, D, 'Evolved Foraging Psychology Underlies Sex Differences in Shopping Experiences and Behaviours.' *Journal of Social, Evolutionary, and Cultural Psychology*, 13 (4) December 2009

Kulick, Don, 'Speaking as a Woman: Structure and Gender in Domestic Arguments in a New Guinea Village', *Cultural Anthropology* 8/4 1993, p 522

Långström, Nikas, Q Rahman, E Carlström, P Lichtenstein. "Genetic and environmental effects on same-sex sexual behavior: a population study of twins in Sweden". *Arch Sex Behav* 39 (1) February 2010, pp 75–80

Långström, Nikas, Kelly M Babchisin, Seen Fazel & Paul Frisell, 'Sexual offending runs in families: A 37-year nationwide study' , *International Journal of Epidemiology*, April 9 2015

Leeb. R T & F G Rejskind, 2004, 'Here's looking at you, kid! A longitudinal study of perceived gender differences in mutual gaze behaviour in young infants,' *Sex Roles*, 50 (1/2) pp 1–14

Leith, Willian, 'At last, I think I know why so many women over 40 are experiencing a 'man shortage', *The Guardian*, January 21 2009

Leonard, C M; S Towler, L Halderman, R Otto, M Eckart & C Chiarello, 'Size matters: Cerebral volume influences sex difference in neuroanatomy', *Cerebral Cortex* 18(12), 2008, p 2929

Leslie, Sarah-Jane, Andrei Cimpian, Meredth Meyer, Edward Freeland, 'Expectations of brilliance underlie gender distributions across academic disciplines," *Science*, 347 no 6219, 16 January 2015, p 262

Liberman, Mark, Sex-Linked Lexical Budgets, *http://itre.cis.upenn.edu/~myl/languagelog/archives/003420.html* , August 6 2006

Liberman, Mark, 'Sex on the Brain', *The Boston Globe,* September 24 2006

Livingston, Gretchen, 'The Rise of Single Fathers', *Pew Research Center,* July 2 2013

Livingston, Gretchen, 'Less than half of US kids today live in a "traditional" family', *Pew Research Center,* December 22 2014

Lorenz, Konrad, *On Aggression*, Methuen, London, 1966

Lynn, Richard and Paul Irwing, Sex differences on the progressive matrices: A meta-analysis, *Intelligence* 32, 2004, pp 481–498

Lynn, Richard and Satoshi Kanazawa, "A Longitudinal Study of Sex Differences in Intelligence at ages 7, 11 and 16 Years," *Personality and Individual Differences*, 53, 2012, pp 90–93

Lynn, Richard, "Sorry men ARE more brainy than women (and more stupid too!) It's a simple scientific fact, says one of Britain's top dons", *Mail Online*, May 8 2010

Macintyre, Ben, 'Harvard scholar says Jung was fraud,' The Times, June 5 1995

# GAVIN EVANS

Matthews, David, 'Men in higher education: the numbers don't look good, guys', *Times Higher Education,* March 6 2014

McKie, Robin, 'Girl Power', *The Observer Magazine,* June 20 1999

Maguire, E A; D G Gadian, I S Johnsrude, C D Good, J Ashburner, RSJ Frackowiak & C D Frith, "Navigation-related structural change in the hippocampi of taxi drivers," *Proceedings of the National Academy of Sciences* 97, 2000, pp 4398–4403

Malkin, Catherine M, Michael E Lamb, 'Child Maltreatment: A Test of Sociobiological Theory, *Journal of Comparative Family Studies 25,* 1994

Mansey, Kate & Daniel Bates, ' 'Men get broody as women chase jobs,' *The Sunday Times* February 13 2011

Mason, Helen, 'Go for it, girls, be confident and change the culture', *The Independent,* January 15 2015

Mehl, M R; S Vazire, N Ramirez-Esparza, R B Slatcher and J W Pennebaker, 'Are women really more talkative than men?' *Science* July 6 2007, p 82

Meyer-Bahlburg, Heinz, 'Gender identify outcome in female-raised 46, XY persons with penile agenesis, cloacal exstrophy of the bladder, or penile ablation,' in *Archives of Sexual Behaviour* , 34, pp 423–438

Midgley Mary, "Why Memes", in H Rose & S Rose, *Alas Poor Darwin*, Vintage, London, 2001

Mitchel, Laura, 'The Price of beauty: average woman spends £18,000 on face products in a lifetime,' *Express http://www.express.co.uk/life-style/style/433831/The-price-of-beauty-Average-woman-spends-18-000-on-face-products-in-a-lifetime*

Moe, A, "Are males always better than females at mental rotation? Exploring a gender belief explanation," *Learning and Individual Differences* 19(1), 2009, pp 21–27

Moir, Anne and David Jessel's, *Brain Sex: The Real Difference between Men and Women,* Delta Books, New York, 1991

Moir, Anne and Bill Moir's, *Why Men Don't Iron: The Fascinating and Unalterable Differences between Men and Women*, Citadel, New York, 1999

Moir, Jan, 'Give up the war paint? Don't be a powder puff Hillary!' *The Daily* Mail, May 10 2012

Morgan, James, 'Women "better tat multitasking" than men, study finds,' *BBC News* October 24 2013

Moorhead, Joanna, 'Are the men of the African Aka tribe the best fathers in the world?' *The Guardian* June 15, 2005

Morris Desmond, *The Naked Ape*, Vintage Books, London, 2005

Morris, Desmond, *The Human Zoo,* Vintage, 1994

Morris, Desmond, *The Naked Ape*, McGraw-Hill, 1967

Morris, Desmond, *The Naked Woman*, Macmillan, 2007

Morris, Desmond, *The Naked Ape*, Vintage Books, London, 2005

Moss, Rachel, 'Cosmetic Surgery on the Rise, With 51,000 Brits Undergoing Procedures Last Year, *Huffington Post*, February 2 2016

Moss, Stephen, 'Do women really talk more', *The Guardian*, November 27, 2006 'Do women really talk more', *The Guardian*, November 27, 2006

Narzary, Pralip Kumar & Shilpi Mishra Sharma, 'Daughter Preference and Contraceptive-use in Matrilineal Tribal Societies in Meghalaya, India', *Journal of Health, Population and Nutrition*, June 31 2013

Neisser, U, "Rising Scores on Intelligence Tests", *American Scientist* 85, 1997, p 440–447

Noll, Richard, *The Jung Cult: Origins of a Charismatic Movement*, Princeton University Press, 1995, pp 181–187

Norton, Cherry, 'Fathers raise brighter kids' *Sunday Times* May 17 1998

Norton, Cherry, "Smacking 'hits a child's IQ," *The Sunday Times*, August 2 1998

Nowak, Martin, Corina Tarnita & E O Wilson (2010). 'The evolution of eusociality' *Nature* 466, pp 1057–1062

Office for National Statistics Statistical Bulletin: Families and Households 2013, *Office for National Statistics*, October 31 2013

Osborne, Hilary, 'Tiny proportion of new fathers are opting for shared parental leave,' *The Guardian*, April 5 2016

Parker, Hilda & Seymour Parkers, 'Father-Daughter Sexual Abuse: An Emerging Perspective', *American Journal of Orthopsychiatry* 56

Parker, Kim and Wendy Wang, 'Modern Parenthood: Roles of Moms and Dads Converge as They Balance Work and Family', *Pew Research Center*, March 14 2013

Partlow, Joshua, 'People flee as warring street gangs drive up murder rate', *Washington Post* report published in *The Independent*, January 7 2016

Peachy, Kevin, 'How the UK's new rules on parental leave work', *BBC News*, April 5 2015

Phillips, Melanie, *The Sex-Change State* (memorandum), Social Market Foundation, 1997

Phillips, Melanie, *The Sex-Change Society*, Social Market Foundation, 1999.

Pinker, Susan, *The Sexual Paradox*, Atlantic Books, 2008

Pinker, Steven; Werner Kalow, Harold Kalant & reply by Stephen Jay Gould, "Evolutionary Psychology: An Exchange," *The New York Review of Books*, October 9 1997

Pinker, Steven and Steve Rose, "The Two Steves – Pinker vs Rose – A Debate", Institute of Education, University of London, January 21 1998, published online by *EDGE Third Culture*, March 25 1998 – *http://www.edge.org/3rd_culture/pinker_rose/pinker_rose_p1.html*

Pinker, Steven, *How the Mind Works*, W.W.Norton & Company, 1999

Pinker, Steven, *The Blank State: The Modern Denial of Human Nature*, Viking, 2002

Pinker, Steven, in "The Science of Gender and Science. Pinker vs Spelke: A Debate," Harvard University Mind/Brain/Behavior Initiative, May 16 2005, *Edge The Third Culture*, http://www.edge.org/3rd_culture/debate05/debate05_index.html

Pinker, Steven, "The Lessons of the Ashkenazim," *The New Republic Online*, June 17 2006

Pinker, Steven, "Groups of people may differ genetically in their average talents and temperaments," in "The *Edge* Annual Question – 2006," *Edge The World Question Centre*, 2006, http://www.edge.org/q2006/q06_print.html#pinker

Pinker, Steven, 'Genetic tests said I would be intelligent, swayed by novelty and bald. Two out of three ain't bad', *The Sunday Times*, February 1 2009

Plomin, Robert and Oliver S P Davis, "The future of genetics in psychology and psychiatry: mircroarrays, genome-side association, and non-coding RNA", in *The Journal of Child Psychology and Psychiatry*, vol 50, issue 1–2, 2009, pp 63–71

Pritchard, James (ed), *Ancient Near Eastern Texts Relation to the Old Testament*, Princeton University Press, 1950, p 412

Quinn, P C, J Hahr, A Kuhn, A M Slater & O Pascalis, "Representation of the gender of human faces by infants: A preference for female", *Perception* 31(9), pp 1109–1121

Ramey, S L and C T Ramey, "Early experience and early intervention for children 'at risk' for developmental delay and mental retardation," *Mental Retardation and Developmental Disabilities Research Reviews* 5, 1999, pp 1–10

Rayman, Noah, 'Female Chess Legend: "We are Capable of the Same Fight as Any Other Man', *Time*, April 20 2015

Rauscher, Frances and Gordon L Shaw, "Listening to Mozart enhances spatial-temporal reasoning: towards a neurophysiological basis". *Neuroscience Letters* 185, 1995, pp 44–47

Richardson, Karen, "Smoking, Low Income and Health Inequalities: Thematic Discussion Document", report for *Health Development Agency*, May 2001

Ridley, Matt, *The Rational Optimist: How Prosperity Evolves*, HarperCollins, 2010

Rose, Hilary and Steven Rose, *Alas Poor Darwin: Arguments Against Evolutionary Psychology, Vintage,* London, 2001

Rose, Hilary 'Colonising the Social Sciences?', in Hilary Rose & Steven Rose (eds), *Alas Poor Darwin: Arguments Against Evolutionary Psychology*, Vintage, 2001

Rose, Steven "Commentary: heritability estimates--long past their sell-by date", *International Journal of Epidemiology* 35 (3), June 2006

Russett, C E, *Sexual science: The Victorian construction of womanhood*, Harvard University Press, Cambridge, MA, 1989

Sammons, P, Toth, K and Sylva, K, Background to Success: Differences in A-level entries by ethnicity, neighbourhood and gender, *The Sutton Press*, London 2015

Sample, Ian, 'Marrying a younger man increases a woman's mortality rate,' *The Guardian*, May 12 2010

Sample, Ian, 'Male and female brains wired differently, scans reveal,' *The Guardian* December 2 2013

Samuals, A, *The Father: contemporary Jungian perspectives*, Free Association Books, London, 1985

Sargent, Brooke L and Janet Mann, 'From Social Learning to Culture: Intrapopulation Variation in Bottlenose Dolphins', in Kevin N Laland and Bennett G Galef, *The Question of Animal Culture*, Harvard UP, 2009, pp 152–173

Sax, Leonard, *Why Gender Matters: What parents and teachers need to know about the emerging science of sex differences*, Broadway Books, New York, 2005

Schellenberg, E Glenn; "Music Lessons Enhance IQ". *Psychological Science* 15 (8), 2004, pp 511– 514

Schellenberg, E Glenn, "Music Lessons, Emotional Intelligence, and IQ". *Music Perception: An Interdisciplinary Journal* 29 (2), 2011, pp 185–194

Scheibel, A B and J W Schopf (eds), *The origin and Evolution of Human Intelligence*, Jones and Bartlett, Sudbury, Massachusetts, 1997

Schwartz, G; R Kim, A Kolundzija, G Rieger, A Sanders, "Biodemographic and physical correlates of sexual orientation in men", in *Archives of sexual behaviour* 39 (1), 2010, pp 93–109

Sharps, M J; J L Price & J K Williams, "Spatial cognition and gender: Instructional and stimulus influences on mental image rotation performance," *Psychology of Women Quarterly*, 18 (3),1994, pp 413–425

Sherwin, B B, 'A comparative analysis of the role of androgens in human male and female behaviour: Behavioural specificity, critical thresholds, and sensitivity, *Psychology* 16(4), 1988, 416–425

Shibley Hyde, Janet & Marcia Linn, 'Gender Differences in Verbal Ability: A Meta-Analysis', *Psychological Bulletin*, 104, 1998, pp 53–69

Shibley Hyde, Janet, 'The Gender Similarities Hypothesis', *American Psychologist*, September 2005, pp 583–584

Schiller, Friedrich, *The Robbers*, The Floating Press, 2010

Short, Nigel, 'Viva La Difference' *New in Chess*, 2015/2

GAVIN EVANS

Shostak, Marjorie, *Nisa: The Life and Words of a Kung Woman*, New York, Vintage Books, 1983

Siddique, Haroon, 'Algorithm predicts sexual orientation of men with up to 70% accuracy, say researchers' *The Guardian*, October 8 2015

Skuse, D H, 'Is autism really a coherent syndrome in boys, or girls?', *British Journal of Psychology*, 100, 2009

Snowdon, C T and JS Rosenblatt (eds), *Advances in the Study of Behaviour*, 24, 1995

Spelke, Elizabeth in "The Science of Gender and Science. Pinker vs Spelke: A Debate," Harvard University Mind/Brain/Behavior Initiative, May 16 2005, *Edge The Third Culture*, http://www.edge.org/3rd_culture/debate05/debate05_index.html

Springsteen, Bruce, 'Highway Patrolman', *Nebraska*, Columbia 1981

Steele, Claude, "Thin Ice: Stereotype Threat and Black College Students", *Atlantic Monthly*, August 1999

Stevens, Devon Anthony, The Jung Page, *www.cgjungpage.org* , November 3 2006

Strong, Bryan & Theodore Cohen, *The Marriage and Family Experience: Intimate Relationships in a Changing Society*, 12th edition, Watsworth Cengage Learning, 2013

Strum, Shirley, *Almost Human: A Journey into the World of Baboons*, Random House, 1987

Sullivan, Oriel, 'Changing differences in the division of domestic labor; the case of education,' *Sociology Working Paper February 2011*, University of Oxford

Swinford, Steven, 'Most children will be born out of wedlock by 2016', *The Daily Telegraph* July 10 2013

Symons, Donald, 'Adaptiveness and Adaptation' *Ethology and Sociobiology* 11, 1992

Symons, Donald, 'Beauty Is in the Adaptions of the Beholder: The Evolutionary Psychology of Human Female Sexual Attractiveness,' in Paul R Abramson & Steven Pinkerton (eds) 'Sexual Nature Sexual Culture' *University of Chicago Press*, 1995, pp 80–118

Tannen, Deborah, *You Just Don't Understand: Men and Women in Conversation*, Morrow, New York, 1999

Tay, Nastaya, 'South Africa's Rape Study: More Than 1 in 3 Men Admit to Rape, *The World Post*, May 25, 2011

Temrin, Hans, Susanne Buchmayer & Magnus Enquist, 'Stepparents and Infanticide: New Data Contradict Evolutionary Predictions,' *Proceedings of the Royal Society of London B, 263, 2000*

Thornhill, Randy & Craig T Palmer, *A Natural History of Rape: Biological Bases of Sexual Coercion*, The MIT Press, 2000

Tolstoy, Leo, *Resurrection*, Nekhludoff's Third Interview with Maslova in Prison, Penguin Classics, 2009

Tolstoy, Leo, *War and Peace*, Vintage, 2009, p 8

Tooby, John and Leda Cosmides, 'On the Universality of Human Nature and the Uniqueness of the Individual: The Role of Genetics and Adaptation,' *Journal of Personality* 58 1990

United Nations Department of Economic and Social Affairs, 'World Marriage Patterns 2000' – http://www.un.org/esa/population/publications/worldmarriage/worldmarriagepatterns2000.pdf

Wade, Nicholas, "Gay Men Are Found to Have Different Scent of Attraction", *New York Times*, May 9 2005

Wai, Karmen, Philip Douglas Thompson, Thomas Edmund Kimer, 'Fashion victim: rhabdomyolysis and bilateral peroneal and tibial neuropathies as a result of squatting in "skinny jeans"', *Journal of Neurology, Neurosurgery & Psychiatry*, June 23, 2015

Waite, Roger, 'Fond fathers nurture a family revival', *The Sunday Times* March 22 2009

Wallace, Alfred Russel, 'On the Tendency of Varieties to Depart Indefinitely From the Original', paper delivered to the Linnean Society of London, July 1 1858

Wallace, Alfred Russel, 'Human Selection', *Fortnightly* Review, Volume 48, September 1890

Wallace, Alfred Russel, *Social Environment and Moral Progress*, London, Cassell, 1913

Wallace, Alfred Russel, *The Malay Achipelago*, New York, Dover, 1962

Walter, Natasha, *Living Dolls: The Return of Sexism*, Virago, 2010

Walter, Natasha, *the new feminism*, Virago, 2011

Mikkel Wallentin, 'Putative sex differences in verbal abilities and language cortex: A critical review,' *Brain and Language* 108(3), 2009

Wheeling, Kate, 'The brains of men and women aren't really that different, study finds', *Science* magazine, November 30 2015

Whitten, A; J Goodall, W.C. McGrew, T Nishida, V Reynolds, Y Sugiyama, C.E.G Tutin, R.W. Wrangham and C. Boesch, 'Cultures in Chimpanzees', *Nature* 399, 1999, pp 682–685

Wilson, E O, *Sociobiology: The New Synthesis*, Harvard University Press, 1975

Wilson, E O, *On Human Nature*, Harvard University Press, 1979

Wilson, E O, *Genes, Mind and Culture: The co-evolutionary process*, Harvard University Press, 1981

Wilson, E O, *Consilience: the Unity of Knowledge*, Alfred Knopf, New York, 1998

Wilson, D S and E O Wilson, "Survival of the Selfless", *New Scientist,* November 3, 2007, pp 42–46

Wolf, Naomi, 'The Beauty Myth', Vintage, 1991

Wright, Robert, 'Feminists Meet Mr Darwin', *New Republic*, November 28 1994, pp 34–46

Wright, Robert, *The Moral Animal: Why We Are the Way We Are: The New Science of Evolutionary Psychology*, Pantheon, New York, 1994, p 357

Emile Zola, *Germinal*, Penguin Books, 2004